Educating for Balance and Resilience

Educating for Balance and Resilience

Developmental Movement, Drawing, and Painting in Waldorf Education

Jeff Tunkey

Bell Pond Books › 2020

Published by Bell Pond Books
an imprint of SteinerBooks
402 Union Street #58, Hudson, New York 12534
www.steinerbooks.org

Copyright 2020 by Jeff Tunkey. All rights reserved. No part of this publication may be reproduced, stored in a retrieval system, or transmitted, in any form or by any means, electronic, mechanical, photocopying, recording, or otherwise, without the prior written permission of the publisher.

Print: 978-1-952166-00-6
eBook: 978-1-952166-01-3

Printed in the United States of America

Contents

Acknowledgements vi
Foreword vii
Guiding Thoughts x

1: Lenses on Teacher Development

Introduction	1
Practical and Ethical Considerations	4
The Hierarchy of Learning Readiness	7
Working with the Twelve Senses	8
… Or Is It Sixteen Senses?	13
Faith, Love and Hope in the Classroom	15
Cowboy Wisdom	30

2: Foundations for Student Capacities and Readiness

On Inner Development	33
16 Keys to Student Needs	39
Boys and Girls in Movement	49
Parallels in Academic and Athletic Development	56
Summary	58

3: Exercises and Activities for Strengthening the Whole Class

Introduction	59

Foundations for Developmental Movement

Jumping Rope	60
Copper Rod Exercises	63
Crawlasthenics and Zoorobics	67
Balance, Ball and Beanbag Activities	75
Clay Activities	79
Foot Circles	80

Foundations for Writing and Reading

Strengthening the Pencil Grip	81
Painting Handwriting	83
Shaded Drawing	85

Foundations for Arithmetic

The Connections Between Math and Movement	87
Strengthening Arithmetic Foundations	89
Numeracy Activities and Screening Tables	92
Review Exercise Worksheet	96

4: The Values of Organized Play

Introduction	97
The Use of Games	98
Movement Standards for Third Grade	104
Movement Program Organization	105
A Taxonomy of Games, and a Sampler	108
Games and Movement Resources	118

5: Building a Schoolwide Culture

Sharing the Work	120
A Model for Inservices and Classroom Blocks	120
The Fourfold Process for Success	125

6: Building Bridges with Parents

Parent-Teacher Meetings	131
Education for Balance and Resilience	133

Appendix & Resources

Observation, Documentation and Support	136
A Paper Trail Protocol	142
An Educational Support Team Model	149

Afterword 153
Bibliographic Notes 155
Index of Exercises 157

Acknowledgements

In my childhood, I had inklings that I was meant to be a teacher when I grew up. However, this (growing up, that is) had to wait until my young 40s—and an inspired nudge from my wife Susan—to begin to become a reality. A long-time Waldorf class teacher, she helped me take step one, and then provided inspiration, very objective advice, and a steady and encouraging sounding board every day.

Other noteworthy influences whom I want to thank for copious inspiration and guidance along the way include Mary Jo Oresti, Jaimen McMillan, Maureen Curran, and Ralph Brooks.

I would like to also thank Kathy Donchak of SteinerBooks for her patient guidance throughout the creative process. And Jennifer Snyder, a Waldorf public school teacher who has provided objective, clear-cut support and feedback all along the way.

The many Waldorf teachers I've had the privilege of meeting through my workshops and lectures have given me invaluable opportunities for on-the-job research and professional development. And finally, of course, my best teachers have been the children I've taught at Aurora Waldorf School here in Western New York.

Foreword

There is growing recognition in wide educational circles that helping children to build the skills they need to thrive in adult life, including communication, persistence in the face of challenge, adaptability, teamwork, good manners, self-control, responsibility, and punctuality, is as important as delivering content linked to achievements on benchmark tests. Healthy classroom environments and schools forge these lifetime habits of resilience—"grit"—by consistently working to foster caring relationships, maintain high expectations for all students, and provide meaningful opportunities for students to participate and contribute.

For Waldorf educators, this is not just a thought. A unifying goal for every Waldorf School—big or small, anywhere in the world—is to provide a progression of challenging academic content for which the students in a given class are (or are just about to be) emotionally and physiologically ready. Waldorf teachers know that all true learning requires inner composure and mobility, and that what can be seen and developed through outer movement is vital for mental health and acuity throughout life. Physical activity not only fuels the brain with oxygen and decreases stress; but also, every movement creates and strengthens connections within the brain and in the nerve pathways throughout the body.

The importance of developmental movement is clearly validated by modern science as a pathway to physiologic and emotional development, and may be as important as academic presentation, especially in the early grades. Activities that build up such basics as postural control, spatial orientation, movement coordination, and body geography are not just classroom extras. All children (probably now more than ever before) need a rich diet of the kind of developmental movement, drawing and painting exercises that have been indicated by Rudolf Steiner, Audrey McAllen, Karl König, Olive Whicher, and others.

I hope that both the theory and practice in this book will help educators to understand how to apply these methods for strengthening academic capacities of students through a whole-school approach to developmental movement, drawing and painting activities, as well as enrich their capacity for student observation. Although almost all of these tools have for decades been within the domains of Extra Lesson practitioners and Waldorf movement teachers, I believe they are meant to be staples for all students, in all classes, every day.

I have four areas of bridge-building in mind:

A bridge from the past to the present and future. At the beginning of the Waldorf School movement in the early part of the twentieth century, the first Waldorf teachers were already immersed in the spiritual approach to humanity that founder Rudolf Steiner had named anthroposophy. This group shared a practical understanding of the meaning of many anthroposophic terms and concepts that might now seem, at first impression, to be antiquated, eccentric or unfamiliar. Thus, words and phrasing that were commonly familiar and understood back then — even to most of the general audiences for his hundreds of public lectures—can today be roadblocks when discussing the Waldorf approach to education in the culture of our modern world. So, I hope to help build a bridge between "Steiner Words" you will encounter in this book — words like "astral" and "etheric" and phrases like "twelve senses"—and parallel mainstream words and scientific/educational insights. I'll offer some current synonyms or terminology whenever possible, while steadfastly reflecting the utmost respect for the roots of the Waldorf approach to education and its anthroposophic source material.

To truly be an educator means maintaining a career-long study of the developing human being. In a Waldorf setting, teachers must also carefully consider Rudolf Steiner's ideas about educating in his many lectures and books, and then use this groundwork as a starting point whenever (and wherever) it makes sense in today's context. I have found that striving to build myself bridges to today's mainstream educational terminology and concepts about education can be the source of fresh insights that are helpful every day — for planning, lesson approaches, student observation, and self-reflection.

Doctor Steiner time and again repeated two cautions. First, he had no quarrel with science. He gave the analogy that science is like a floodlight in a cave, whereas his spiritual-scientific insights could provide a flashlight to look additionally into the more hidden corners. And second, he would not want anyone to use his indications dogmatically. He wanted his listeners and readers to continue to research for themselves and come to their own conclusions. There is much in this book that attempts to do just that; I will offer many ideas and graphic illustrations based on my attempts to study, find connections, and put the vast heritage of pedagogical insights into practice. In the pages that follow I have tried to make both a comprehensive compilation of material, clearly cited, from Steiner and others, and a synthesis from my own research and daily striving to do right by the children in front of me and the designation "Waldorf Teacher."

A bridge from the present to the past. A generation or two ago, the Waldorf movement, at least in North America, was still small enough that those beginning their paths as Waldorf educators usually had the benefit of learning, in person, from experienced teachers who themselves were only one or two generations distant from Rudolf Steiner and his immediate colleagues or their mentees. They were able to immerse themselves in learning for an extended period of time, and the teacher trainings were able to delve deeply into topics like the Curative Education Course, constitutional types, and the pedagogical law. But those master teachers who were close to the beginnings have passed from the scene, and today's economic factors have meant that fewer beginning teachers can have the luxury of being able to devote time and resources to an extended training. Of necessity, many now take a more learning-while-doing path, supported by mentors and briefer program intensives. There are many pluses to this process of becoming a Waldorf teacher, and the bridge-building goal of Section 1 is to offer an accessible, thought-provoking overview of background concepts, and a guide to books that can help with filling in some vital foundations.

A bridge between teaching realms. Experienced Waldorf Class teachers, even those who have studied the deeper aspects of Waldorf pedagogy, may have the impression that the activities presented in this book belong exclusively to the domains of Movement and Extra Lesson teachers. But, in fact, a lot of these activities used to be part of general school programs, even before there were Waldorf schools. In any event, all children need the kind of developmental activities offered here. In many schools I've visited, the Extra Lesson teacher's role is primarily or entirely that of a specialist working with students who need support. But I think the training and experience that Extra Lesson teachers have is often "a lamp hidden under a bushel," and I hope here to offer inspiration and support for expanded appreciation and collaboration between Movement and Extra Lesson teachers and their Class teacher colleagues; that this book may help them blaze a path to helping their schools develop and run a whole-class developmental approach, adding this wider role to their vital work with the individual students with challenges. I'm also hoping my fellow Movement teachers will find that this book enhances their understanding of the physiological/developmental "whys" of their work; that it will give them deeper insight into what they are already doing and a stronger, more accessible vocabulary for expressing to their school colleagues and their parent communities the implications of the right kinds of movement at each developmental stage.

A bridge between teachers and parents. Gaining new lenses on the connections between foundational Waldorf concepts/terminology and mainstream ways at looking at the same educational considerations will strengthen the ability to relate to and work with parents of your students. Section 6 provides thoughts on how to draw on the Pedagogical Law to meet parents where they are and transform difficulties into fruitful dialog. And a comprehensive paper trail system for observation and support plans, like the one offered in the Appendix, can be the key to shared understandings and teamwork.

In short, my aim is for this book to serve as a ready source for developmental additions to the daily classroom repertoire and as a work/study guide to core concepts and background readings for teachers in all realms. Some key topics in Sections 1 and 2 are:

- What is developmental movement?
- Brain pathways — math, reading, executive function, resilience.
- Learning challenges and mainstream labels.
- Hope, Love and Faith: how can we better understand and more consistently harness the power of those three words?
- Comparative movement needs and learning styles of boys and girls.

Modern research demonstrates that the activities and exercises presented in Sections 3 and 4 are vital ingredients in learning readiness:

- Activities and exercises for developmental movement.
- Foundations for reading, writing, and numeracy.
- Values of organized play.

A maxim of Extra Lesson teaching is: "the assessment is the therapy." A steady, whole-class inclusion of the activities and exercises in these sections will strengthen every student in the class (not just those in the bottom third or so) and at the same time will provide the teacher with a new vista of student observation modalities and experiences.

Section 5 provides pointers to the step-by-step building of a class-wide and school-wide culture of all-student support.

Thus, in total, I hope to offer a road map of the transforming principles and practices that have strengthened those few Waldorf students who have received individual help into a program benefiting all students. This can encompass:

- Developmental additions to Main Lesson times
- Activities at the beginning of Extra Main classes
- Guides for creating entire Extra Main class periods filled with capacity building
- Games and exercises that will make your "physical education" program a true partner in academic progress
- Ways for teachers to share the work of taking up these new possibilities

I think that the exercise of open-mindedly meeting Waldorf's foundational concepts and then looking for connections in modern research can strengthen one's ability to teach and communicate in the right way. This is exactly "what the Doctor ordered." So, please also approach this book in the same vein: as a new research project. Weigh for yourself what I have to say in the theoretical parts, put them into practice, and come to your own conclusions. I'll be very glad if this book opens up for you some new inspirations and collaborations in service to a whole class of students, and even a whole school.

Guiding Thoughts

" Our rightful place as educators is to be removers of hindrances.

Hence we must see to it that we do not make the children into copies of ourselves, that we do not seek forcibly and tyrannically to perpetuate what was in ourselves in those who in the natural course of things develop beyond us. Each child in every age brings something new into the world from divine regions, and it is our task as educators to remove bodily and psychical obstacles out of its way; to remove hindrances so that his spirit may enter in full freedom into life. These then must be regarded as the three golden rules of the art of education, rules which must imbue the teacher's whole attitude and all the impulse of his work. The golden rules which must be embraced by the teacher's whole being, not held as theory, are: reverent gratitude to the world in the person of the child which we contemplate every day, for the child presents a problem set us by divine worlds. Thankfulness to the universe. Love for what we have to do with the child. Respect for the freedom of the child — a freedom we must not endanger; for it is to this freedom we educate the child, that he may stand in freedom in the world at our side.
... If we realize the full import of this we shall say to ourselves: the main task of the teacher or educator is to bring up the body to be as healthy as it possibly can be; this means, to use every spiritual measure to ensure that in later life a man's body shall give the least possible hindrance to the will of his spirit. If we make this our purpose in school we can develop the powers which lead to an education for freedom. "

— Rudolf Steiner, *The Spiritual Ground of Education*, Lecture 4[1]

1 Lenses on Teacher Development

Introduction

I consider myself very fortunate to have begun my explorations of anthroposophy and Waldorf education in the late 1980s, shortly after I turned 40. At that time, there were still teachers and lecturers in North America whom I would classify as being in the "second circle from the sun." That is, not part of the generation who were colleagues and associates of Rudolf Steiner, but among those who came along during the immediate period thereafter, i.e., beginning in the 1930s or 40s, and who had met some of the founding circle, or who had even been younger colleagues of those involved during Steiner's career. Leading lights I was blessed to hear talks by, or even meet a little, included Henry and Christy Barnes, Werner Glas, William Ward, Ann Pratt, and a few others now lost to (my) memory. Then, my early years of teaching at Aurora Waldorf School (AWS) near Buffalo, NY, would not have been possible without contact with and help from many in the "third circle from the sun" — master teachers still leading the schools movement in the 90s. One of these, with a pithy ten-word question, set me running on the path to what I hope has been a serious attempt at Waldorf teaching.

The question

This highlight moment occurred during my Spacial Dynamics® training with Jaimen McMillan. One evening in a discussion circle, Jaimen posed to the group the following rhetorical question: "By what right do you call yourself a Waldorf Teacher?" The meaning, for me at least, was bracingly clear: Consider very carefully the responsibility of thinking oneself and representing oneself to be a Waldorf teacher.

Let's follow that along. What would Rudolf Steiner say — or do — if he were to walk into my classroom today? Cringe, grimace and have me hauled off to the Goetheanum, there to be dealt with by a squad of punitive eurythmists? How can I possibly know if I'm actually "doing Waldorf" a century after its founder passed from the scene, and in such a changed world? During his relatively brief life, Dr. Steiner gave some six thousand lectures, not all of which have been translated into English. His philosophy of the human being, his indications for education, were presented from many perspectives in hundreds of different lectures now collected in scores of different books that comprise the teachers' canon. And then, important pedagogical gems are also found here and there in the nooks and crannies of hundreds of other lectures on seemingly nonpedagogical topics. I do feel like I'm walking the winding yellow brick road seeking courage and a brain. By what right, I ask, may I call myself a Waldorf Teacher?

Teacher trainings

As I began my teaching career, striving to create a cohesive program blending insights from gym program movement and remedial/student support, I decided to make myself a checklist of topics to keep studying and working to apply. I filled one book cabinet, and then a few more. Completing each book lead me to add to, not shorten, my to-read list.

After about 10 years of studying, attending workshops, and receiving a lot of mentoring, I noticed that sometimes the newer class teachers joining AWS from Waldorf teacher training institutes seemed less well versed in these foundational themes than those who had taken certificate courses in the past. This might be because—as the Waldorf movement evolves and passes from one generation to the next and the "circles from the sun" get wider—the orbit that teachers need to travel in order to gain understanding increases by a factor of pi or more. Perhaps some of Rudolf Steiner's core concepts are a little less likely to be passed through oral traditions, and more likely to be fractured by pressures on curriculum and tested results. Does this ring true to you?

In any event, I began getting requests to provide faculty meeting study guides at AWS, and workshops at other Waldorf schools. For AWS, I formed a monthly book study course, dubbed "A Scaffold for Waldorf Teaching." Each month for a year, participants completed a reading assignment; then we'd gather for five or six hours on a Saturday to discuss the topic and explore it through movement, speech, and artistic activities. I led three cycles of this course, and almost all of the teachers then at AWS attended it at least once. The syllabus and reading list for this course is provided in Section 4. The balance of the chapters in this section will take up many of these foundations, and also provide some ways to find connections between these gifts from spiritual science and the findings of modern science.

Conclusion

In a lecture titled "Facing Karma,"[2] Rudolf Steiner suggested we should never lapse into a sort of basking in personal pleasure when success comes our way (as for instance when a teaching day goes blissfully well) but rather should remember to be thankful for the gifts of wisdom that passed through us. And, when things go less well and we feel discouraged, that we can find help outside of ourselves, through the One who walks along with us on our earthly journey.

All of the study items listed are not only interesting in the abstract; they are invaluable lenses for daily lesson planning, student observation, and self-evaluation. When a lesson or school day goes well, one can find ingredients of success in these staples of anthroposophy; when things go otherwise, invariably help for redeeming the next day can also be found by reflection on the list. Did I include laughter and tears? What was the quality of breathing in the room? Was there a student or students in shutdown mode? How was my posture?

A century after Rudolf Steiner began the Waldorf school movement, none of us can know for sure if our pedagogy and approaches would be what he might have intended. However, the world clearly needs Waldorf schools, so I believe we can all continue to provisionally claim to be Waldorf teachers so long as we keep striving to read and listen, and to discipline ourselves to place our self-evaluations in the light of the framework provided from the past.

Thus, in order to stand in front of students, parents and colleagues as a Waldorf educator, one must be willing to travel on a never-finished journey of research and self-understanding. Hold to the motto that every step forward with pedagogy requires two steps forward with personal development.

A scaffold for Waldorf teaching

A. Steiner's description of the human being

   Threefold human; thinking, feeling and willing
   Faith, love and hope
   Four temperaments
   Six constitutional types
   Twelve senses
   Karma
   Supersensible bodies
   Steiner's presentation of temptation and psychology
   The spatial human and the upper and lower triangles
   Good and evil; the human being as the product of balance; left and right brain
   Currents of the earth; chakras
   Structural physical body and constitutional physical body

B. Steiner's pedagogical indications – general

   Rhythm and breathing: the teacher's primary task
   Imitation and authority
   Teaching from the whole to the part
   Historical evolution of consciousness in societies
   Evolution of consciousness from birth to old age; picture thinking; intellectualizing; media
   Preparation and lesson planning
   Pedagogical law
   Meditation
   Goethean observation
   Laterality; The human being and the currents of the Earth

C. Developmental aspects and other sources

   Dealing with parents: the gifts of fear, shame and anger
   Multiple intelligences
   Six developmental keys according to *Take Time*
   Development according to Dutch Waldorf schools
   The polarities of hysteria and epilepsy; kleptomania
   Birth order
   The organs as mirror of the cosmos

To wonder at beauty,
Stand guard over truth,
Look up to the noble,
Resolve on the good;
This leads us truly
To purpose in living,
To right in our doing,
To peace in our feeling,
To light in our thinking.
And teaches us trust
In the workings of God
In all that there is
In the widths of the world,
In the depths of the soul.

— "At the Ringing of the Bells," verse given by Rudolf Steiner for the opening of the Stuttgart Waldorf School, September 1919. In *Truth-Wrought-Words*, Anthroposophic Press, 1979

Practical and Ethical Considerations

The purpose of this chapter is to describe—and advocate for—a comprehensive spectrum of whole-class developmental strengthening; to outline approaches that can be added to movement program and individual support services your school may already offer.

In seating a student behind a desk, we as teachers and parents are anticipating that the child is physiologically and emotionally ready, or soon will become ready, for the academic progressions about to be presented. But realistically, every child will likely be at least somewhat challenged with some aspect of the academic environment: for myriads of individual reasons, each child every day will need a little help to thrive. Perhaps it might be a challenge to sit in balance, or to listen quietly, or to muster the fine motor skills for writing, etc. Thus, we must remember that through the gifts of developmental movement, drawing, and painting inspired by anthroposophy, every child can be more fully observed, and helped to reach his or her full potential.

The basis for a school-wide, all-students approach to learning foundations

To begin, let us look at two practical aspects of Waldorf education that by their nature will lead us to focus on related ethical considerations. By keeping these interrelated issues in focus, we can gain additional resolve for our Michaelic educational journey.

First, Waldorf academic paths are in some ways "slower" or in any event less test-driven than is common today. For writing and reading, we take the stance that parents can be patient, and not fret, if their child hasn't begun book reading in grade one, or two, or even three. For arithmetic, we are trying to be working, initially, to have the student "at home in the house of numbers" before emphasizing skill-and-drill computational learning.

Therefore, I believe, Waldorf schools have a heightened responsibility to observe carefully each child's developmental foundations and capacities. Yes, it is right to provide daily learning challenges, while still leaving early-grades students free to awaken to the intellect at a pace harmonious to each individual. However, it would obviously not be ethically upright for a school or teacher to wait until third grade (or later) 'for the light to go on', only then to find out that a student actually lacks the foundations; nor for a school to wait until there is a crisis brought by a parent or parents to begin filling in the developmental and assessment blanks. This book is about having a robust toolbox of student observation and support methods that can help teachers with this vital responsibility.

Threading the needle of class constellations

A second set of practical considerations often facing Waldorf educators is one that can tend to lead parents and schools to meet each other at an intersection of weaknesses. This issue underscores the need for the types of approaches provided by this book.

Parents who begin investigating a switch to Waldorf when their child is in grade two or above are often seeking an answer to a question that in some regard they wish to avoid bringing all the way to the surface. Their child is struggling or even suffering in a current school, and they are seeking relief—but not (for instance) the bright light of a learning-disability label. And, very often, Waldorf schools struggle with enrollment and financial needs that leave them open to accepting an overbroad range of student and family profiles. The ethical consideration is multifaceted. Questions that can arise include: "If we accept this child, can we serve and educate him as well as or better than any of the alternatives? Have we objectively and realistically weighed the child's needs and our pedagogical abilities, or do we feel pressure to 'give it a try' and hope for the best? And, will accepting this student make it less possible for other students to learn?"

After many years of wrestling with this second practical/ethical issue, my school arrived at an approach that helps us keep it real. When there is an application for a new student in any grade, the process includes consideration of four qualitative questions:

1. Does the student have the will to work?
2. Does the student have the academic ability to progress with the curriculum?
3. Do the parents support the pedagogical values of Waldorf education?
4. Is the student likely to be a positive social addition to the class constellation?

Our rule of thumb is that positive answers to at least three of these questions will be needed in order for the student to thrive and for us to carry out our professional responsibility. These same four points of relationship evaluation may come up again at any time during a student's career at our school. Before addressing how these can be observed over time, here is an outline of our Educational Support Program.

School-wide, all-students

Observing children through Main Lesson, movement classes, inservices, recess, and subject classes can provide tremendous insight into the needs of students. It is through these classes and other modalities that the faculty can bring forth questions and recommend assessments for individual services based on the development of the child.

Aurora Waldorf School (founded in 1991) was very fortunate that in its formative years several of its teachers were able to immerse themselves in studying Extra Lesson with Mary Jo Oresti, Rachel Ross, and other leaders of the Waldorf remedial movement; and Spacial Dynamics with Jaimen McMillan and Maureen Curran. Thanks to the wealth of pedagogical insights these trainings provided and to the enthusiastic support of the AWS faculty up to the present, a unique program was created and has continued to be strengthened. My hope is that, in presenting the model we have followed, readers will find elements they can add or enhance at their schools.

A guiding principle that we gleaned from these trainings is: "All students need support!" That is, the movement, drawing and painting exercises found in *The Extra Lesson*[3] and other anthroposophic sources are not meant only for one-on-one use by struggling students who are provided individual help outside the classroom; rather, all students can benefit from doing them. For instance, many of the activities serve to align us with the currents of the Earth, and contain a harmonizing, focusing element…and who doesn't need that from time to time!

At AWS, resource allocations and personnel have shifted somewhat over the years, but the broad outlines have remained the same. The ingredients of our integrated 'full spectrum' program in the grades are:

1. Recess outdoors every day.
2. At least two games/gym classes a week, plus one tumbling/gymnastics class. (Middle school students have gym every day, for a total of 6 periods per week.)
3. An additional class called "Enrichment" in grades 1, 2 and 3; this provides whole-class time for Extra Lesson and developmental movement activities.

4. Two eurythmy classes per week.
5. Classroom inservices: Extra Lesson teachers work with class teachers to model and mentor a core of whole-class remedial exercises, helping them add these to their repertoire of Main Lesson activities.
6. Protocol for a progression of student assessments, including:
   - First grade readiness
   - Periodic in-class numeracy and reading screenings by the EST during grades 1 to 4
   - Second grade assessment (blend of "First Lesson" and "Dutch model" [4])
   - Standardized reading and math screenings in third and fourth grade.
7. Individual student services provided:
   - Therapeutic eurythmy
   - Extra Lesson
   - Remedial reading
   - Remedial math
   - Assisted study hall
   - Referral for third-party services

Pullouts: minuses or pluses?

Individual or small-group services may take place on a weekly, biweekly, or daily basis depending on the needs of the child. Students are pulled out for sessions during all parts of the day: from the book-work portion of Main Lesson, an Extra Main, or a subject class (pullouts from movement and eurythmy classes are avoided). Schedule planning seeks to find the least-interruptive schedule based on each student's need. Naturally, no class or subject teacher would wish for any student to miss even one period, to have less of their subject—let alone to be away over an extended schedule. Nonetheless, teachers at AWS have come to accept over the years that students who need individual support are, in a manner of speaking, not actually "getting" their class, i.e., are not able to fully benefit until more concentrated help is given. And by focusing the majority of our remedial resources on the earlier grades, the need for pullouts has proven to be reduced by the time a student reaches the older, more academically-concentrated upper grades.

Learning is movement, movement is learning

As noted before, a movement program that's solidly based on the developmental needs of children can have many school-wide benefits, including reduced need for remedial services, and reduced teacher burnout because classes are more ready for daily academics. At AWS, we have proven to ourselves that an extended program of play and movement strengthens the developmental foundations needed for success in the grades and beyond, and is complementary to the remedial program.

Two keys to the thinking behind this approach might be as follows. First, Rudolf Steiner indicated that our task as educators is to "teach the children to breathe." Perhaps for our modern times this might be better translated as "help the children learn to self-regulate." (See Section 4 for more on this topic.) Secondly, Waldorf schools are supposed to provide—month after month and year after year—a progression of academic content for which the students are emotionally and physiologically ready, and which at the same time helps them take the next step.

Movement lessons can certainly make a contribution in both respects. Through age-appropriate movement, the developing human can gain basics like postural control, spatial orientation, movement coordination, the ability to change sight perception instantaneously between three dimensional and two dimensional space, good body geography, and confirmed dominance. Thus, we must remember that through movement every child can be helped in some way to reach his or potential.

Again, our experience at AWS has shown that students are able to move ahead more solidly when they are all provided with appropriate daily movement and artistic activities; this is made possible by an embrace by class teachers of whole-class Extra Lesson and related exercises. Classes as a whole, and even individual students in the top academic tier, have through this dedicated effort shown strengthened foundations for literacy, numeracy and deskwork capacities.

The Hierarchy of Learning Readiness

What kind of help is needed?

Every new school year draws the student into what might be thought of as a "new civilization," and it bears repeating that every child will meet some individual barriers during the move to this new level of awareness of the world. Therefore, students will be best served by a curriculum that breathes in and out, flows between difficult new tasks on the one hand, and familiar, relaxing and supportive activities on the other. With this flow between analysis and synthesis, most pupils will be able to adjust to the new order of things, and they will progress.

However, some will require additional individual support before our hopes for them can become achievable. Very often, in one way or another, the child is the one who lets the adults know that more help is needed. (As teachers we may struggle to keep in mind that a "discipline problem" might well be just such a signal.) Whatever the signs that more help is needed, our role as adults is to thoughtfully and carefully decide what kind of individual attention is needed. Both common sense and careful contemplation tell us that there is a hierarchy of needs and support within which we must work.

The realm of the physician

Is there a medical/physical problem or a constitutional imbalance? No amount of individual attention from a teacher can fully help a child who has, for example, an undiagnosed vision or hearing problem, or an unknown food allergy that is driving her off the deep end. Research has shown a connection between iron deficiency and math challenges. Problems of this nature are the domain of the physician. Additionally, a child may have an excess of one temperament or another (i.e., the overly sanguine child who loses focus, or the highly phlegmatic child who can write only one page while the others are writing five, etc.). Teachers can work pedagogically with temperaments to a degree, but a pronounced constitutional problem is also in the domain of the physician, perhaps working in concert with a therapeutic eurythmist and/or a homeopathist.

The realm of the soul

Is the problem in the realm of the psyche? Is there a family crisis, or a struggle with parenting, or an educational psychological problem? The teacher can provide a calm and loving classroom but needs in this realm will also demand outside professional help, and in some cases a specialized classroom or an Individual Educational Plan.

The realm of childhood development

Is the problem developmental? Many aspects of learning readiness—for instance spatial orientation, movement coordination, and the ability to change sight perception between three-dimensional and two-dimensional space—are the results of the child's body/environment movement exploration during the first seven years. A developmental assessment or a Sensory Integration assessment can identify such things as retention of early reflexes or ambidexterity, lack of good body image, hypersensitivity or hyposensitivity, lack of spatial orientation, inability to make mental pictures of sense impressions, and dyslexic symptoms. Without solid developmental faculties, a child will struggle with any curriculum, Waldorf or otherwise. Needs in areas like these can be addressed through a team effort by the child's teachers plus individual attention for Extra Lesson or Occupational Therapy/Sensory Integration.

The realm of teaching and tutoring

Is there a need for extra skill-building and skill repetition? Needs in this realm can also be addressed as a team effort, with additional individual attention in reading or math classes, plus tutoring.

Models for observation and reflection

In considering the needs or challenges of a child, it is important to try to form the clearest idea of which hierarchy or hierarchies might need to be addressed. These are:

Medical/constitutional — the realm of the physician, as well as the therapeutic eurythmist and/or homeopathist guided by the physician.

Examples:
- Allergies or chemical imbalance
- Birth difficulties
- Injuries or illness
- Constitutional types
- Excess of temperament
- Heredity

Soul/psyche — the realm of the parent, priest or psychologist.

Examples:
- Home life
- Biography
- Diagnosis of learning disabilities. IQ testing, mainstream labels with deeper connections
- Birth order

Developmental/pedagogical — the realm of the teacher.

Examples:
- Movement stages
- Twelve senses
- Six constitutional types
- Four temperaments
- Stretching and lifting
- Developmental keys: timing and rhythm; direction and goal; spatial orientation; sequencing; fine motor control and speech; midline barriers; imitation and anticipation; reflexes; radius and ulna; eye movement
- Family background of learning difficulties
- Learning style
- Home background for vocabulary, numeracy, will forces, etc.
- Breathing; laughter and tears
- Learning disability adaptations
- Laterality and dyslexia (*Laterality—i.e., the combination of eye, hand, foot, ear and brain dominant sides—and dyslexia have both a soul aspect and a developmental-pedagogical aspect.*

Working with the Twelve Senses

That humans have twelve senses, as presented in a variety of ways by Steiner a century ago, is often one of the first anthroposophic viewpoints that parents or others new to Waldorf will hear about. And if you're like many people for whom this was an informational starting point, you may have had a quizzical reaction when you heard someone state that humans have twelve senses, not just the six or seven commonly delineated by scientific textbooks (i.e., touch, sight, hearing, self-movement, taste, smell and balance). So, announcing that there are, as a fact, definitely a dozen senses might sound kind of "Waldorfy" at first blush.

But perhaps on this topic, as with many others, Steiner was ahead of his time, and modern science is just starting to catch up. For example, included in Steiner's model is what he termed a 'Life Sense,' the presence of an actual physical organ for sensing one's internal state of health and vitality. Off the beaten path? Or… pathfinding?

Well, a century later, the August 2018 issue of *Scientific American* magazine featured a lengthy and well-documented cover story titled "The Seventh Sense."[5] In that article, neuroscientist Jonathan Kipnis presented research that shines new light on the relationship between the nervous and immune systems: new findings that these two systems are not, as anatomy textbooks depict, isolated from each other. Rather, Kipnis stated: "Mounting evidence indicates that the brain and the immune system interact routinely, both in sickness and in health." The immune system may "qualify as a kind of surveillance organ that detects microorganisms in the body…and informs the brain about them, much as our eyes relay visual information and our ears transmit auditory signals." It will be fascinating to see how this new research is followed up in the future.

In any event, taking up Steiner's construct as a practical lens on the human organization can inspire fresh insights into the task of nurturing healthy childhood development and academic readiness. Those who want to explore the topic can find a wealth of reading, including books by Karl König,[6] Albert Soesman,[7] Gilbert Childs[8] and others. The following outline, given only for the purpose of keeping the main points in front of us, is a brief review of the twelve senses model that has been compiled from this rich background of sources.

The basics

Rudolf Steiner defined the human physical body as an archetypal form that is the sum of all the senses working together.[9] Through our structural physical body, we can perceive three-dimensional space, gain uprightness, stand and walk, and carry our ego through life on the earth.

The twelve senses can be grouped into three tiers. The first group of four is commonly called the lower, foundational, physical or inner senses. It is through these four that the infant begins to find the way into the physical body and life on earth.

Touch Sense is the inner sense of "where I end and the outer world begins." Its development starts with the birth event itself. Touching any outer object changes one's inner state.

Life Sense is the sense of one's own health and inner condition. Examples: the heightened perception of one's inner state during running and then cooling down; feeling the nutritional difference between lightly steamed fresh vegetables and microwaved frozen vegetables. The mainstream term "homeostasis" refers to somewhat similar aspects of sensing.

Self-Movement Sense refers to the inner sense of one's own movements, both fine and gross motor; proprioception is the equivalent mainstream term. This sense begins even before birth.

Balance Sense also begins before birth as the mother moves around, reclines, etc.; and then develops further as the infant rolls around, crawls and learns to walk.

Next, four middle senses are delineated. Also known as soul senses, they are at the boundary between the inner and outer world.

Smell and Taste senses are just as delineated in common parlance.

Sight Sense, in this paradigm, refers to the aspects of vision in which color, visual warmth, changes of scenery are perceived; sensing via the eyes also has a self-movement aspect, as our finest muscles move the eyes to focus and to process shapes.

Warmth Sense, distinct from touch, takes place at a wide margin between inner and outer (example: placing a very cold hand under lukewarm water). Dr. König points to the primacy of this sense in maintaining our balance between our inner and outer worlds.[10]

The four higher senses, also known as spiritual senses, connect us to the world of ideas and human interactions.

Hearing Sense — one of the twelve senses in common parlance.

Sense of Language or Word, encompasses all that it is to sense and "be in" a language: hearing/perceiving the language, speaking and reading, etc. Language represents an amazing human achievement and is all the more astounding in that it develops in the first few years of life.

Concept or Thought Sense is the ability to perceive thoughts.

Ego Sense is the ability to sense another person's ego or presence (not the development of one's own ego). Example: sensing when another person has entered a room (perhaps a teacher with good classroom presence). It affects the ability to wait for a parent or teacher to explain an activity, and to work in a group.

Connecting to students

How can this theoretical model help us as teachers (and parents)? How can it be put into practice? I believe, in two ways: it offers an alternative — and effective — vantage point on modern labels for learning disabilities and is an important approach to self-evaluation of lessons and classroom management.

For each of four lower senses, which appear in the first days and grow throughout childhood, there is a companion higher sense that appears later in development, representing a transformation or flowering of the lower sense. Another way of saying "the lower senses develop the higher senses."

Quite a few learning difficulties — challenges including inabilities to pay attention or stay with the class, struggling to form or remember thoughts, hindrances with language or listening skills — appear to relate to one or more of the four higher sense categories, and to call for tutoring or other direct intervention. But one can instead look at these challenges at the level of language, thought or human attention as possible needs for help in the development of corresponding lower senses, and then approach things from a different starting point rather than only working on the labeled problem/manifestation in the higher faculty.

Expressed in a positive way, this suggests that any activity that helps one of the four lower senses will also be vital to the development of its companion higher sense. Conversely, it could be counterproductive or even harmful to attack a learning obstacle head-on, without first assessing, and if needed addressing, the companion lower sense. Because almost every child has at least a little difficulty here and there, developmental games and activities can be given to any child, or to an entire class, with the knowledge that a few children deeply need them as hygienic experiences, and almost all will benefit. Thus, in thinking about a lesson or a school day, it can be of great benefit to review how one worked with the lower senses as avenues to connecting with higher-level learning.

Nurturing and development of Smell, Taste, Sight and Warmth senses is also fundamental to academic progress. Steiner once noted that human learning has a certain canine-like sniffing/tracking quality; we hunt for new ideas; try to dig out the truth.

Connections from lower to higher

The first lower-higher pole runs from the Touch sense to the Ego sense. This relationship is the reason it's so helpful to shake each student's hand, to remember to make direct eye contact, and when possible to touch a distracted student on the shoulder or arm rather than using (or raising) one's voice. It's worth wondering whether the epidemic of Attention Deficit Hyperactivity Disorder is to some degree driven by a deficit of bodily-kinesthetic pedagogical approaches in the modern school environment.

The Life sense is connected to the Thought or Concept sense: by and large people are more able to learn new things when well rested and feeling positive. Of the four lower senses, Life is perhaps the one where we as teachers are most in need of teamwork with parents: our teaching task of imparting new information can be made so much easier by a rhythmic and healthy home life. Quite frankly, we can build bridges to student learning only from our side of the river, i.e., when the student can arrive at school physiologically ready to meet the new school day. Every young child needs to be surrounded by adults who in word and deed convey the message "You look strong/healthy/well rested (etc.) today" or, when ill, "You are strong, you'll be well soon."

Self-movement and Language have a connection that can readily be observed through similarities between a child's speech and gross-motor movement patterns, as well as what can be seen of the fine-motor control for the jaw, tongue, etc., recruited for speech.

The organs for Balance and Hearing are co-located in the inner ear. Children who spin themselves around the classroom or who fall off their chairs are helping teachers remember to include movement breaks with an element of vestibular stimulation.

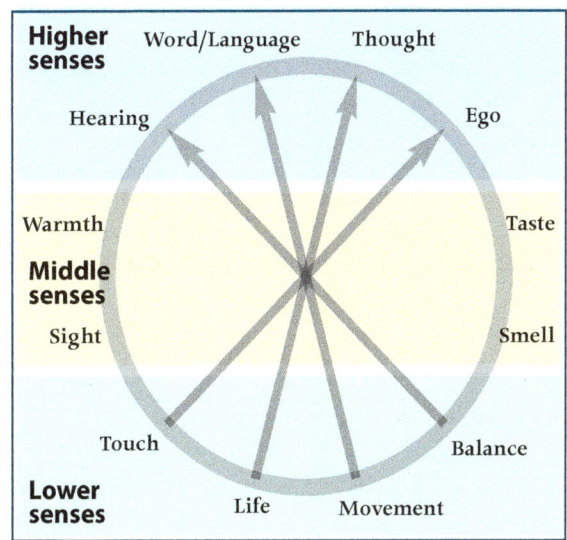

The lower senses and postural control

One aspect of a child's development calling for careful observation and helping attention can be summed up as the postural control system—how the network of bones, muscles and nerves can make it possible to sit at a desk, stand poised with the head upright, etc. The four lower senses can be a symphony that enable the student to breathe in and out, to shift between analysis and synthesis, between joyful movement and harmonious focus. Thus, strengthening the four lower senses is one of many reasons we as teachers must attend to our own posture: "be the change you wish to see!" There's a lot more to explore on this topic.

The common sense

These ideas about the twelve senses and the interesting connections between them, although superficially beyond the boundaries of mainline beliefs, are in fact supported by scores of common idioms—everyday expressions that point to a wider acceptance of these deeper truths. For the lower/higher poles, examples include: "I don't follow you," "a (verbal) pat on the back," "it (the

Connections between the Lower and Higher Senses – and How to Help

Touch & Ego	Life & Thought	Movement & Language	Balance & Hearing
Developing touch strengthens the ability to connect to other human beings	Developing health, and joyful appreciation for nature strengthens thinking ability	Developing proprioception strengthens langage – speaking, writing and reading	Developing balance helps to develop listening skills, postural control, arithmetic readiness
Qualities: Trust & Acceptance: In the physical and spiritual worlds In adults' and one's own judgments Acceptance of boundaries	Qualities: Joy & Wonder A sense of the whole Patience; acceptance of what is not fair, of differences Self-reflectiveness	Qualities: Dignity & Grace Industry and uprightness Connectedness to body and earth Synthesis – parts in relationship to the whole	Qualities: Resilience & Freedom Ability to move between tension and release, concentration and relaxation; to quiet oneself for listening
Hindrances: Early wakefulness Overprotected Shock or trauma Sedentary lifestyle Harsh discipline	Hindrances: Lack of boundaries, being treated like an adult Media; limited real play Nature deprivation Poor diet	Hindrances: Sedentary lifestyle Poor diet - obesity Lack of healthy models for imitation Youth competitive sports	Hindrances: Adults who are stuck in one way of being, or who are glib, sarcastic, exhausted or short-tempered
Help needed if: Hysteria, insecurity, mistrust, cynicism Over-connection with the earthly Defensiveness, withdrawal, little consideration for the needs of others; defiant and oppositional	Help needed if: Quick to correct and label others; low self esteem Fear, guilt; impatient, greedy; feeling victimized Disappointment in everything Obsessive or compulsive behavior	Help needed if: Inferiority, hopelessness Fixed concepts; rigidity of thoughts, feelings or actions Failure to pick up nonverbal or social cues Math or speech difficulty Disorganized movement Lost in space or time	Help needed if: Gravitational insecurity Motion sickness or dislike of spinning movements Fear of heights Hyper-vigilant Impulsive; blurting out Cannot take turns Poor short-term memory
Games that can help: Drawing on backs; Hand clapping games; London Bridge with rocking; Simon Says; Wrestling/ roughhouse games; and all throwing and catching, especially with a partner	Games that can help: Quiet activity - free play, nature walks, water color painting. Most of the work of helping to develop a healthy life sense must take place at home. Rhythm in daily, weekly, monthly and annual life is the key.	Games that can help: Tumbling Crawling games Jumping rope String games (cats cradle) Blindfold games Ball bouncing games - jacks, 7-up, etc.	Games that can help: Recreational gymnastics, and ANY activity that rotates the inner ear in space (e.g., rolling down a hill) or depends on balance (e.g., blindfold games) will provide a terrific benefit.

words of the speaker) made me dizzy/gave me a headache," etc. There are also common phrases pointing to how the middle senses relate to learning, including: "that [idea] doesn't pass the smell test/was in bad taste" "I see what you mean," "Let me chew on (or digest) that for a while," etc. So, "keep your eyes open" for other expressions that can "shed some light" on the twelve points of the spectrum of human senses.

Meetings at the level of the higher senses

Regarding the four higher senses, Soesman points out an interesting fact about their interrelationship. That is, in order to truly meet another person (Ego sense) one needs to somewhat suspend analyzing the thoughts being verbalized; in order to gain a full understanding of the thoughts (Concept sense) being verbalized, one needs to resist the urge to start parsing the words and phrases; and in order to truly listen to the words coming one's way, a great variety of sounds in the aural surroundings need to be filtered out.

That this is so can perhaps explain one of the great mysteries of life, which is that the early years of a romance or marriage will often be the most fraught with heated exchanges. How can it be that the person we love so deeply is the one with whom we will (hopefully only rarely) have the most intense spats? Here again, a common-sense application of the twelve senses model can shed some light. These episodes also have their typical phrases of escalation, including: "you never listen to me (failure at the level of the Hearing sense), "that's not what I said (Language)," "I didn't mean that (Thought)," and, ultimately, "you don't really love me!" And then (hopefully!) comes walking it all back: i.e., step one—apologies, tearful hugs, maybe flowers; step two—recognitions of each other's viewpoints; step three—return to pleasant speaking and listening. See how that works?

...Or is it Sixteen Senses?

For several years, I puzzled with a little question about the concept of strengthening the four lower senses as an avenue to strengthening higher-sense academic capacities. That is, the four higher senses seem to relate mostly, or most strongly, to the Language Arts curriculum: listening, speaking, comprehension of language, and interpersonal communication. Placed in comparison with Harvard professor Howard Gardner's modern theory of nine multiple intelligences, the higher senses as given in Steiner's model seemed to be mostly or only about just two of the intelligences in the Gardner model—the Language and Interpersonal intelligences—and to have very little to say about, for instance, the Math/Logical and Spatial intelligences. They only related to two of the three Rs: Reading and 'Riting, but not 'Rithmetic! This interested me at a practical level because the incidence of student challenges in arithmetic/math can be as frequent as those in reading acquisition and, if anything, more difficult to identify in the early stages.

Howard Gardner redefined intelligence to include the following nine facets of human capacity. The list below (with an example of genius for each) suggests some fields in which particular intelligences will be useful.

Language (poet, playwright, lawyer): *Maya Angelou*
Math/Logical (mathematician, engineer, philosopher): *Euclid*
Musical (musician, composer): *Aretha Franklin*
Spatial: *Albert Einstein*
Kinesthetic: *Michael Jordan*
Naturalist: *Marie Curie*
Interpersonal: *Martin Luther King*
Intrapersonal: *Henry Thoreau*
Existential: *Johann von Goethe*

The lower senses as foundations for arithmetic and higher mathematics

I was quite excited when I happened upon a typescript of talks on arithmetic that Karl König had given to Camphill teachers.[11] König drew on information that Rudolf Steiner had given in *The Boundaries of Natural Science*.[12] König noted:

> And then Rudolf Steiner goes one step further. He asks the question: Where do these powers of mathematics come from? And he has a clear-cut answer. He says that they arise out of the three lower senses. They arise from the sense of life, from the sense of movement, and from the sense of equilibrium; so that, so to speak, these living forces of mathematics—these living abilities of counting and reckoning—they work in the sensory organs of life, of movement, of equilibrium. And after these three senses are partially built up, these forces become available within the human mind. But these are not—and may I make this clear to you—these are not etheric powers. They are powers of the soul. We might also say these are the powers of the astral body. You see Rudolf Steiner describes very extensively, in the lectures to teachers, how etheric powers form our organs, form our tissues, form parts of our body, and as soon as they arise, after the second dentition, they become powers of thought.
>
> The astral body enters the sense of life, and in the sense of life it learns to experience a difference—the difference between the feeling of well-being and unwell-being. The child… has the experience of feeling all right, and then experiences the difference when it is hungry, thirsty, suffers pain, discomfort, and so on…. And then in the sense of movement the astral body learns to find out the ratio and relation of the limbs and parts of the body towards the stretching—all that is continuous, million-fold experience is an experience of learning the proportion here on earth. And in meeting the sense of balance the astral body learns a manifoldness which is hard to describe—a manifoldness which is not a simple experience of the negotiation between gravity and levity, between the darkness of earth and the light above.

König summarizes the above as:

SENSE OF LIFE = Difference
SENSE OF MOVEMENT = Ratio
SENSE OF BALANCE = Logarithm

Thirteen Senses? Fifteen?

Reading the above was, for me, an "Aha!" experience—my (perhaps slightly obsessive) desire for diagrammatic completeness with respect to the links between the twelve senses and the nine intelligences had been answered. Please read the booklet and draw your own conclusions, but clearly to me Steiner and König are both indicating the existence of a numeracy sense, or perhaps even that Difference, Ratio and Logarithm are three (separate) higher senses, transformations of three lower senses, and matching in the realm of numeracy the lower-higher schema of Language, Thought and Ego sense.

One more thing…

As will be noted later, in the numeracy foundations portion of Section 2, current research underscores the importance of two primary skills in arithmetic: subitizing, and counting. (Subitizing is the ability to perceive and accurately report small quantities of objects, without counting each item. The learning goal would be to reach automaticity with the dot patterns on dice or dominoes.) Until children are secure with these two steps in the progression of numeracy acquisition, they are not ready to move on to even the most rudimentary aspects of the computational work in the Waldorf first-grade arithmetic curriculum.

Dr. König's lectures didn't reference a link between a lower sense and a higher sense for counting/subitizing. But I believe it is safe to add the connection sketched into the diagram on the right:

Children can be helped to enter the house of numbers through the first doorway of the Touch sense. This underlines the importance of working with all sorts of manipulatives in early childhood and grade one classrooms.

Faith, Love and Hope in the Classroom

The following is a written version of a lecture I've had the privilege to present to teacher groups during the past few years. The presentation relies on an audience that is, at least for the most part, familiar with the fundamental ideas behind Steiner's pedagogical indications, particularly his description of the fourfold structure of the human being, his wonderful advice about the "Pedagogical Law," and his conceptualization of the senses. For readers who have not yet had the opportunity to begin a study of these three areas of anthroposophical research — but who are perhaps wanting to forge ahead and learn about what can be done to bring Faith, Love and Hope into the classroom — I would recommend reading, at the earliest opportunity, Karl König's accessible and invaluable book, *The Human Soul*.[13] During my talk, I would build up on the chalkboard the chart found on page 19, corresponding to our progression with the subject. I'll note which row is being referred to as we move along.

Lecture introduction

I certainly don't claim to add to the wealth of knowledge given to us by such leading researchers as Rudolf Steiner, Karl König, and Walter Holtzapfel; rather, I will try to offer, for you to evaluate, a

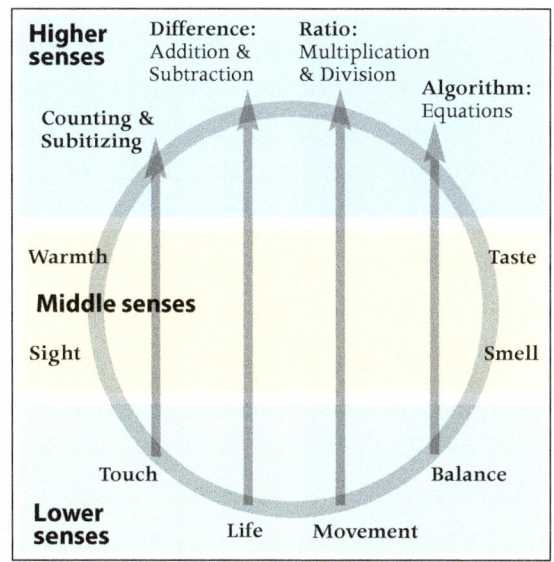

certain diagrammatic way of looking at and interweaving this background material…or, call it a lens that I hope will add to your appreciation of their ideas, and to your capacity to draw on these insights in working with children.

I'm going to try to weave together three of Rudolf Steiner's fundamental themes, groundwork areas that can be of such great help to us as teachers or, really, in any dealings with other people in any walk of life. Firstly, the human as a fourfold being, comprising: the physical body; the etheric body or habit body or body of life forces; the astral body or body of motion and emotion; and the ego body. Secondly, Steiner's Pedagogical Law, a maxim that can and should guide us as teachers or adults in working with this fourfold architecture. And thirdly, Steiner's classification of the twelve human senses.

Then, I would like to add two hidden gems to our studies — two seemingly non-pedagogical lectures by Steiner. By this, I mean to say that these lectures are not in the traditional canon for teacher trainings or faculty meeting studies, as are books like *Study of Man/Foundations of Human Experience* and *Balance in Teaching*.[14] Yet, they add wonderful depth to our understanding of the fourfold human structure. These two lectures have helped me immensely in my striving to be a better teacher. They have helped me plan a better lesson rhythm, and they have helped me hunt down my mistakes when a lesson hasn't gone nearly as well is I had imagined.

My wish is that I might be able to give you some new perspectives on these topics, that I can point you to some new connections between them and, most of all, that you will be inspired to continue your own reading and research.

A happy day at school

To set the stage, let us happily envision for a moment a Main Lesson that all class teachers dream about and would be quite pleased to approximate. Please place yourself in this story for a time today. The room is warm and sunny; nicely painted and decorated. Plants and flowers adorn a corner; the faint aroma of baking bread can be detected from the kindergarten down the hall. By about 9:05 a.m. the class will have had a cheerful and lively session of morning circle warm-up activities, and are now quietly and expectantly sitting at their desks. They are all poised and attentive as the teacher stands in front and begins to lead them on a journey to a new land; depending on the class, this might be a tale with a queen, or a tutorial on quadratic equations. They follow this new path blazed by the teacher for quite some time, and the minutes fly by. Then they get out their main lesson books and take up their individual work; their teacher walks around the room observing, providing help here and there. The next day, each student will be able to cheerfully and eagerly contribute something to the recall and review of this lesson.

As we shall see, this idealized description can be said to follow a very definite, fourfold pattern —a pattern that applies regardless of the class or the topic. It applies to an Extra Lesson with an individual student, and even to a gym class. This four-part process is based on the treasure of pedagogical path-finding we have received from Rudolf Steiner.

The important call for self-examination and inspired teaching has echoed in my mind throughout the decades since that evening Spacial Dynamics discussion: "By what right do you call yourself a Waldorf teacher?" I suggest that we all need to remember that when Dr. Steiner's life was near its end, he nominated a very small number of those who could speak for him and anthroposophy; I for one am so far distant in time and knowledge from that circle that probably the most I can say is that, well, I'm trying to become a Waldorf teacher, or, at least, a predominantly nice person who studies the lectures of Steiner and other leading lights, strives to apply this received wisdom, and who teaches in a Steiner-inspired Waldorf School.

The fourfold structure of the human being

Let's review the basics of what we know, from Steiner's thousands of lectures and writings, about his description of the fourfold human being at the current point in its evolution. According to his audience and topic, he offered a variety of labels for the fourfold parts of the human being. A very inspiring introduction to this structure is available in chapter II of Walter Holtzapfel's book *Children with a Difference*.[15]

It is worth bearing in mind that Rudolf Steiner was, among many other things, an architect; so let us carry at least a little of the visual/spatial sensibility of the architect into our study today, and see if we can sketch out a schematic as we go along.

We know that our physical body is what we have in common with all things in the material world; all things that can be measured, counted and weighed, including minerals, plants and animals. In addition to this visible, outermost body, Steiner points us to three others. He describes a supersensible body that he often called the etheric body: the body of life forces and growth that we have in common with plants and animals. When you observe a family from behind (say a mother, a father and a few children), you can perhaps see why Steiner also labeled the etheric body the "habit body." He indicated that our etheric body has a relationship to our picturing-thinking process. And we know from Steiner's foundational Waldorf lectures in *Balance in Teaching* and other books that the physical and etheric bodies develop downward from above; this fact is verified by simple observation of the head/limb proportions during the first three years of life on Earth. (Table p. 19, Row 1)

We experience joys, wishes and sorrows; we blush or turn pale; we make an infinite variety of facial expressions; and, unlike the plants, we move about freely. These are all related to what Steiner sometimes terms our astral body, that which we have in common with the animals. (And of course from time to time human behavior can become piggish or slothful or catty.) Steiner describes the astral body as the body of motion and emotion, and that it moves in the opposite direction from the direction of any movements made by the physical body.

And the fourth body is the innermost kernel of our being, our "I" or ego body. Holtzapfel describes this as: "We here encounter what is truly human within man, the spiritual centre of his being to which everything else relates and which provides him with inner steadfastness and confidence, which we designate with the word 'I.'"

We also know from *Balance in Teaching* that development of the astral and ego bodies together proceeds upward from the outside. (Row 3)

The senses

In the previous discussion about the twelve senses, I began a diagrammatic exploration of connections and teaching approaches. If you haven't yet had the opportunity to develop a good working familiarity with this area of Rudolf Steiner's research, I would recommend reading König's *The Human Soul* as well as his *Conferences and Seminars on Arithmetic*.[16] These and many other sources draw connections between the foundational senses of Touch, Life, Movement and Balance with the upper senses of Hearing, Speech/Language, Thought, and Ego. König's book on arithmetic adds a consideration of the relationship between Life, Movement and Balance with readiness for progress in math. (Row 2)

The Pedagogical Law

In the lecture series on curative education, Steiner provides a fundamental precept for all that we do, not only as teachers but really in any human interaction.[17] He sets this out as follows:

> Any one member of the being of man is influenced by the next higher member (from whatever quarter it approaches) and only under such influence can that member develop satisfactorily. Thus, whatever is to be effective for the development of the physical body must be living in the etheric body—in an etheric body. Whatever is to be effective for the development of an etheric body must be living in an astral body. Whatever is to be effective for the development of an astral body must be living in an ego; and an ego can be influenced only by what is living in a spirit-self, but there we should be entering the field of esoteric instruction. … The teacher's etheric body (and this should follow quite naturally as a result of his training) must be able to influence the

physical body of the child, and the teacher's astral body the etheric body of the child. The ego of the teacher must be able to influence the astral body of the child.... And I will show you how...the teacher's spirit-self— of which he himself is not yet in the least conscious— influences the child's ego.

Walter Holtzapfel paints this helpful picture:

> The heat from the sun cannot directly change the shape of a stone, but it is able to warm the air, thereby stimulating the circulation of the water, which rises into the air and falls again as rain to feed a brook. The flowing water finally shapes the stone into a pebble.[18]

Two "hidden" gems for teachers

Now we come to two series of Steiner lectures that I believe contain hidden treasures, in the sense that they are usually not included in the canon of lectures covered or even mentioned during teacher trainings, nor studied during faculty meetings.

In various venues near the end of 1911, Steiner delivered a two-lecture presentation entitled "Faith, Love and Hope: The Third Revelation."[19] And on January 14, 1917—shortly before the end of the First World War—he gave a series of thirty-three lectures on the historical background of that human calamity (and perhaps every other) from an esoteric perspective. One might say that this lengthy series, now published in two volumes as *The Karma of Untruthfulness*,[20] contains one of Steiner's most important lectures for anyone, especially those striving to succeed as a Waldorf teacher.

Faith, Love and Hope

Those of you who have read these 1911 lectures will recall that they have to do with the progression of the evolution of the Christ impulse from the Sinai revelation in which Moses received the Ten Commandments, to the revelation at the time of the Mystery of Golgotha, and to what is coming toward humanity in the current stage. In his online introduction to these 1911 lectures, Bobby Matherne[21] notes that an important aspect is "what the words 'faith, love, and hope' mean to humankind for the next 5,000 years." "These words," Matherne continues, "following St. Paul's letter to the Corinthians, are usually placed in this order: faith, hope, and love. Steiner makes an excellent case for the proper order of these words, considering the destiny of humankind, to be: faith, love, and hope." The theme of faith, love and hope also appears in a beautiful way in Steiner's second of four Mystery Dramas.[22]

The first 1911 lecture, which I feel privileged to talk about today, is subtitled "The Third Revelation." Here are some excerpts from the middle of this lecture.

> Today we will begin by first saying a few words about man's inner being. You know that if we start from the actual centre of his being, from his ego, we come next to the sheath to which we give the more or less abstract name of astral body. Further out we find the so-called etheric body, and still further outside, the physical body.

Steiner noted that many modern people and those in the scientific community now believe that:

> ...the ages of faith are long past; they were fit for humankind in the stage of childhood but people have now progressed to knowledge. Today they must have knowledge of everything and should no longer merely believe.

Somewhat later, Steiner rebutted this modern attitude:

> It is not for a person to decide whether to lay aside faith or not; faith is a question of life-giving

A Graphical Presentation of the Pedagogical Law

	Reference	Physical Body	Etheric Body	Astral Body	Ego Body
1	Reference	Minerals, Plants, Animals & Humans; Outermost	Plants, Animals & Humans Picture Thinking	Animals & Humans Movement - Emotion- Thinking	Humans Willing – Innermost
2	12 Senses; the 4 lower senses	Touch Sense Connected to the Ego Sense (other's). *Counting*	Life Sense Connected to the Thought Sense. *Addition/subtraction*	Movement Sense Connected to the Language Sense. *Multiplying/dividing*	Balance Sense Connected to the Hearing Sense. *Equations*
3	Holtzapfel *Children with a Difference*, Chapter II	Growth development from above, downwards; "the capacity for self-determined will-movement starts from the head and works downwards." At the top (dome) are rounded, immovable bones, and brain cells that never regenerate.		Child's development is controlled from above and yet directed upwards; gaining uprightness. Below, the antithesis – (pillars) linear/angular bones, and the capacity for constant motion and regrowth.	
4	Steiner lecture of Dec. 2, 1911	**Hope Body** Minerals, Plants, Animals & Humans; Outermost	**Love Body** Plants, Animals & Humans Picture Thinking	**Faith Body** Animals & Humans Movement - Feeling - Emotion	**Ego Body** Ego/self is sheathed in faith, love and hope
5	König, *Human Soul*	Shame	Anger	Fear	Care, anxiety
		Student's Physical Body	**Student's Etheric Body**	**Student's Astral Body**	**Student's Ego Body**
6	*Children with a Difference*, Chapter II	**Teacher's Etheric Body** Humor, the humor of life. Opposite- saturnine heaviness. Laughter and tears in every lesson. Summary: Humor – and humour	**Teacher's Astral Body** Interest in the mystery of the human organism. Compassion. Intense sympathetic experience of the child – this is why Child Study is effective – often, even when we're perplexed, the child is strengthened. Summary: Knowledge of man.	**Teacher's Ego** "The fire of enthusiasm lends strength to the ego of the teacher to work upon the astral body of the child." Enthusiasm for the truth – in head, feelings and will. Self-education. Summary: Enthusiasm for the truth.	**Teacher's Spirit-Self** (... an aspect we don't yet possess) The 'language genii' – the word. Visible speech of eurythmy, the gestures which accompany speech. Moral stories. Summary: Cultivation of the Word.
7	*Karma of Untruthfulness*, Lecture 19 3 forms of soul sickness	If etheric not properly anchored in the cerebral system/head, subject to the influence of Ahriman, causing envy, jealousy, disordered thought, being asleep to reality, spreading out into the environment, creating one's own world	If astral not properly anchored in the spinal cord/middle, subject to the influence of Lucifer – and some Ahriman - , causing manic/depressed behavior, lack of cohesive thought, withdrawal, hypochondria	We experience our Ego in the head, as waves washing up on the shore, but it needs to be anchored in the ganglia radiating from the area of the solar plexus. If not, subject to spite, cunning, lying, egoism, madness, inability to cope	.
8	Parents provide…	Nourishment and physical protection	Keep a sense of humor; constancy	Boundaries and guidance	Moral support; prayer
9	**Summary**	Who we are is what is important, not what we say! Who we are affects those around us much more strongly than the lessons we deliver and the speeches we make! **Humor/hope**	Objective, empathetic relationship. "I'll care what you know when I know that you care." **Interest/love**	Example – meeting "the undisciplined and perhaps challenging quirks and needs of adolescence out of the realm of the ego. This is no small feat!" Warmth. **Enthusiasm/faith**	Steiner's subsidiary and other exercises **Language/idealism**

forces in the soul. The important point is not whether we believe or not, but that the forces expressed in the word 'faith' are necessary to the soul. For the soul incapable of faith [will] become withered, dried-up as the desert.

He subsequently stated that:

If we do not possess forces such as are expressed in the word 'faith', something in us goes to waste; we wither as do the leaves in autumn.… By losing the forces of faith they would be incapacitated for finding their way about in life; their very existence would be undermined by fear, care, and anxiety. To put it briefly, it is through the forces of faith alone that we can receive the life which should well up to invigorate the soul. This is because, imperceptible at first for ordinary consciousness, there lies in the hidden depths of our being something in which our true ego is embedded. This something, which immediately makes itself felt if we fail to bring it fresh life, is the human sheath where the forces of faith are active. We may term it the faith-soul, or — as I prefer — the faith-body. It has hitherto been given the more abstract name of astral body. The most important forces of the astral body are those of faith, so the term astral body and the term faith-body are equally justified.

We can add a new row to our diagram (Row 4) and can add the word 'Faith' in the column for the astral body. The etheric body follows:

A second force that is also to be found in the hidden depths of a man's being is the force expressed by the word 'love'. Love is not only something linking men together; it is also needed by them as individuals. When a man is incapable of developing the force of love he, too, becomes dried-up and withered in his inner being. We have merely to picture to ourselves someone who is actually so great an egoist that he is unable to love. Even where the case is less extreme, it is sad to see people who find it difficult to love, who pass through an incarnation without the living warmth that love alone can generate — love for, at any rate, something on earth. Such persons are a distressing sight, as in their dull, prosaic way, they go through the world. For love is a living force that stimulates something deep in our being, keeping it awake and alive — an even deeper force than faith. And just as we are cradled in a body of faith, which from another aspect can be called the astral body, so are we cradled also in a body of love, or, as in Spiritual Science we called it, the etheric body, the body of life-forces.

Steiner went on to state that it is impossible for any person to completely empty his being of the force of love; that one who is highly egotistical will still, for example, at least love money.

This shriveling of the forces of love can also be called a shriveling of the forces belonging to the etheric body; for the etheric body is the same as the body of love. Thus at the very centre of a man's being we have his essential kernel, the ego, surrounded by its sheaths; first the body of faith, and then round it the body of love.

And finally he described a health-giving force for the physical body.

If we go further, we come to another set of forces we all need in life, and if we do not, or cannot, have them at all — well, that is very distinctly to be seen in a man's external nature. For the forces we need emphatically as life-giving forces are those of hope, of confidence in the future. As far as the physical world is concerned, people cannot take a single step in life without hope. They certainly make strange excuses, sometimes, if they are unwilling to acknowledge that human beings need to know something of what happens between death and rebirth. They say: "Why do we need to know that, when we don't know what will happen to us here from one day to another? So why are we supposed to know what takes place between death and a new birth?" But do we actually know nothing about the following day? We may have no knowledge of what is important for the details of our super-sensible life, or, to speak more bluntly, whether or not we shall be physically alive. We do, however, know one thing — that if we are physically alive the next day there will be morning, midday, evening, just as there are today. If to-day as a carpenter I have made a table, it will still be there tomorrow; if I am a shoemaker, someone will be able to put on to-morrow what I have made to-day; and if I have sown seeds I know that next year they will come up. We know about the future just as much as we need to know. Life would be impossible in the physical world were not future events to be preceded by hope in this rhythmical way. Would anyone make a table to-day without being sure it would not be destroyed in the night; would anyone sow seeds if he had no idea what would become of them?

It is precisely in physical life that we need hope, for everything is upheld by hope and without it nothing can be done. The forces of hope are connected with our last sheath as human beings, with our physical body. What the forces of faith are for our astral body, and the love-forces for the etheric, the forces of hope are for the physical body. Thus a man who is unable to hope, a man always despondent about what he supposes the future may bring, will go through the

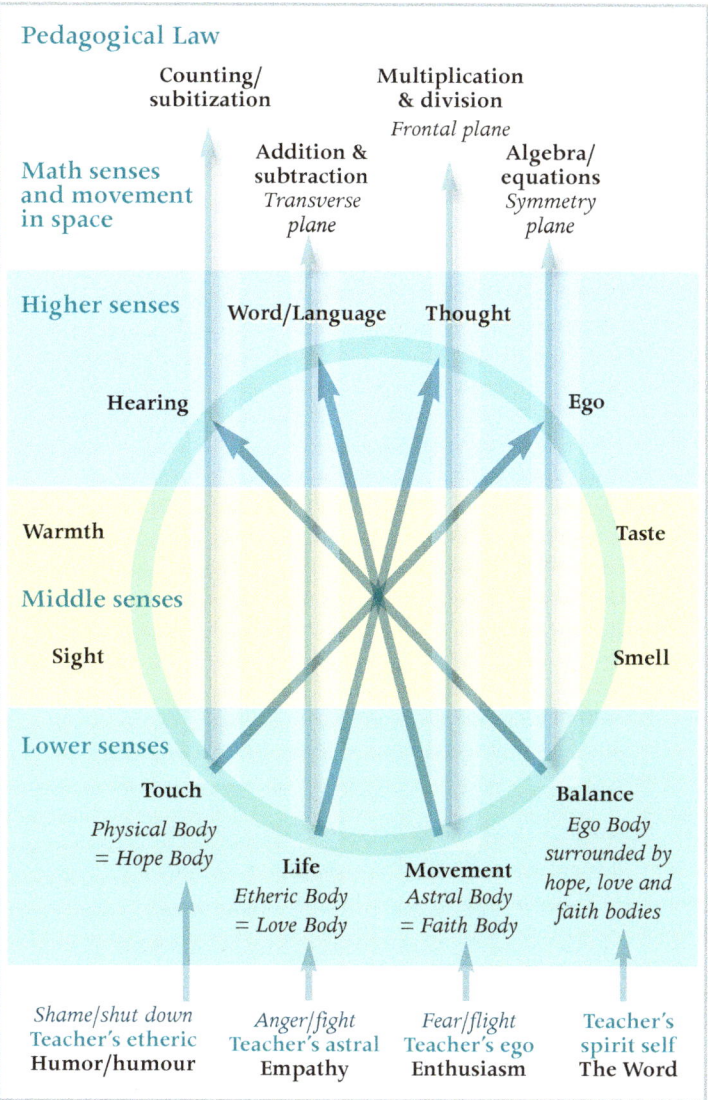

The diagram above includes material from the preceding chapters on the twelve senses as well as connections between the foundational senses and numeracy.

world with this clearly visible in his physical appearance. Nothing makes for deep wrinkles, those deadening forces in the physical body, sooner than lack of hope.

The inmost kernel of our being may be said to be sheathed in our faith-body or astral body, in our body of love or etheric body, and in our hope-body or physical body; and we comprehend the true significance of our physical body only when we bear in mind that, in reality, it is not sustained by external physical forces of attraction and repulsion — that is a materialistic idea — but has in it what, according to our concepts, we know as forces of hope. Our physical body is built up by hope, not by forces of attraction and repulsion.

He summarized as follows:

Faith, love, hope, constitute three stages in the essential being of man; they are necessary for health and for life as a whole, for without them we cannot exist. Just as work cannot be done in a dark room until light is obtained, it is equally impossible for a human being to carry on in his fourfold nature if his three sheaths are not permeated, warmed through, and strengthened by faith, love, and hope. For faith, love, hope are the basic forces in our astral body, our etheric body, and our physical body. … Are not these three wonderful words urged upon us in the Gospel revelation, these words of wisdom that ring through the ages — faith, love, hope? But little has been understood of their whole connection with human life, so little that only in certain places has their right sequence been observed.

It is true that faith, love, hope, are sometimes put in this correct order; but the significance of the words is so little appreciated that we often hear faith, hope, love, which is incorrect; for you cannot say astral body, physical body, etheric body, if you would give them their right sequence. That would be putting things higgledy-piggledy, as a child will sometimes do before it understands the thought-content of what is said.

Now we can complete this new row (Row 4) in our diagram, adding 'Love' in the column for the etheric body, and 'Hope' in the physical column. I've also added a note about the term "anticipation" as described by Molly von Heider in her book *Looking Forward*.[23] We'll have to come back to this thought later.

I want to add a row (Row 5) to our schematic, based on a wonderful chapter in *The Human Soul*, in which König illuminates the true nature of fear, shame and anger: as gifts from our higher selves. Let's add these three emotions to our diagram, in their proper place. Where do they belong?

The above painting of shame, a detail from *The Expulsion from the Garden of Eden* by Masaccio, showing Adam and Eve in distress as they are expelled from the Garden of Eden, helps us, I think, to see that shame is related to our physical body.

König gives us the information that we need to locate all three emotions when he states the following:

Fear, shame and anger are our good companions. Before us walks anger, guiding our moral judgments. At the right side goes fear, at the left, shame. They never appear unless we are in need of them. They are the three good servants of our higher self."

When Adam and Eve left paradise, they were accompanied by fear and shame, and anger walked before them.… The children of Adam and Eve have learnt to understand that paradise will again be opened to them when their souls have been transformed. When anger has changed into love, shame has turned into hope, and fear has metamorphosed into faith.

I find these thoughts so helpful, so potentially redemptive. To think of anger, for instance, as a gift from our higher self, a small helping of holy wrath that alerts us when something is unjust and needs action. But then our human task is to find action that is based not in anger, but, ultimately, ennobled by love. To correct the wrong and then to forgive.

Dr. Martin Luther King Jr. described this transformation when, during his famous "I have a dream" speech, he advanced something which to me is even more important than that well-known refrain. He said:

> We must forever conduct our struggle on the high plane of dignity and discipline. We must not allow our creative protest to degenerate into physical violence. Again and again, we must rise to the majestic heights of meeting physical force with soul force.

In a lecture Rudolf Steiner gave entitled "The Mission of Anger," December 5, 1909, he pointed out:

> For the spiritual scientist, anger is also the harbinger of something quite different. Life shows us that a person who is unable to flare up with anger at injustice or folly will never develop true kindness and love. Equally, a person who educates himself through noble anger will have a heart abounding in love, and through love he will do good. Love and kindness are the obverse of noble anger. Anger that is overcome and purified will be transformed into the love that is its counterpart. A loving hand is seldom one that has never been clenched in response to injustice or folly. Anger and love are complementary.[24]

Because König has helped us to link shame to hope, anger to love, and fear to faith, we can site them properly [Row 3 in table] with our understanding of

the physical, etheric and astral aspects of the 4-fold human being.

As teachers, don't we sometimes encounter these three emotions coming toward us, not only when we deal with our older students but perhaps even more strongly with parents? How can we help the overprotective parent, the 'mother bear', the father who begins asking a flurry of sharp questions about academics in sixth grade? How can we encourage the parent whose low expectations for his or her own child really come from the parent's own struggles — and shame — in school many years ago? Haven't many of us met a parent who has said something like, "I wasn't good at math either?"

Arranging for faith, love and hope in the classroom

If you've found the citations above helpful, I'm glad. But now I need to give a little warning: the following ideas from these lectures that I will share with you today cannot be more than my personal interpretation. So, I want to remind you to carefully research these two less-well-known lectures, work with them, and draw your own conclusions. In other words, what I'm about to present is just one possible lens.

If, in the interest of pedagogical research, we take the liberty of proceeding from the outermost, physical sheath, reversing the order to make it "hope, love and faith," I believe we can come to an archetypal fourfold pattern for 'the what and the how' that must be included in every successful lesson... regardless of the age of the students or the subject being taught, and also in dealing with parents. Let's look again at that happy main lesson we visualized at the beginning today, but now, though, in a manner that in my opinion is suggested by the preceding fundamental concepts and citations.

Please recall that after the warm-up session, we saw all the students sitting at their desks, with posture that was poised for learning. This is at heart a physical description; therefore, it points us (or at least me) to the fact that the first step in any lesson — the step that relates to the physical— is hope! Hope is where we must begin any lesson, in any context; the teacher must make sure there is hopefulness. For the tale of the queen, the student's feeling might be, "I hope we hear the end of the tale today, and that the princess marries the brave lad;" for the tutorial on quadratic equations, it might be, "I hope my homework is correct; I think it is … I'm pretty good at this."

And as we learned from König, the inverse of hope is shame. Isn't it true that in any classroom, there are quite a few students whose starting point for at least some aspects of schoolwork, is shame? To put this in 'mainstream' terminology, students who are in shame mode are in a state of shutdown. So let's be honest: very little progress can be made with a student whose first feeling is: "I'm not good at this." An example could be a student who hasn't completed her homework, and is trapped in her anticipated embarrassment. Another kernel I gained from Jaimen McMillen was the adage that, "if you want to know what you've achieved, look at the bottom third of your class." Especially with the bottom third, hope-building must be step one.

At a recent remedial teacher conference at which Joep Eikenboom was the lead speaker, an audience member asked (in so many words), "shouldn't we honor the gift of dyslexia and not impose literacy expectations that could undermine self esteem." I would argue that as educators — especially as remedial educators — it is our duty to consider that every learning difficulty that has a neurologic and/or inherited component can, if not addressed, become a part of the person's biography that induces shame in both the student and his or her parents. I emphasize: Our first task, our duty, our strongest tool as educators is always to bathe each student in hope. We'll talk in a few minutes about the 'how' of addressing this need.

What comes after "physical"? We have always heard the sequence as "physical, etheric, astral, ego" but let's look at step two in our lesson: the teacher: "begins to take them on a journey to a new land… They follow this new path blazed by the teacher for quite some time, and the minutes fly by." Did you notice all the motion words? And, aren't we supposed to incorporate the emotions of laughter and tears in every lesson? Thus, the teacher is inviting the students to follow her along in an exploration of the unknown; to take a leap of what? A leap of faith! So our second task as teachers is to deal with the students' astral bodies; to offer presentations that engage their feeling life, both sympathy and antipathy. Rudolf Steiner points us to the unfortunate fact that no education is possible without struggle and suffering. Our second task, then, is to inspire our students to have faith, and to try to keep its inverse, fear, at bay. Perhaps this why substitute teaching can be so difficult: the class has no history of trust, no habit of safely following this person into unknown territory. (Also, it's fun to see if you can run circles around a substitute!)

Now if we follow Jaimen's idea a little farther, we'll see that the middle third of a class needs extra consideration or teacher focus at this step of the process. They may have confidence in themselves (hopefulness; not in shame mode) but less readiness to follow the teacher. A student who tends to be in flight mode—or with ADHD characteristics in mainstream terminology—calls for extra connection and guiding ego presence to stay with the lesson. Well, what happened next in our idyllic lesson? They got to work on their main lesson books; the teacher walked around observing, and provided help here and there. Clearly, the teacher is now in gardener mode, lovingly walking around her classroom, giving a little more sunlight here and weeding there; the students are thinking and synthesizing. So, it seems that our third task is to tend to the students' etheric forces. Ideally at this point, they are digesting, processing all that you presented, and coming to love it and make it their own. But because antipathy or anger are the inverse of love, it's normal to see some main lesson pages rushed though or, in middle school, to be asked an occasional "Why do we need to know this?"

Our little lesson story ended when, the next day, each student was able to contribute something to the recall period of this lesson. When students can contribute to recall, this means the material is being brought into balance, and balance is the realm of the ego. This points to our fourth and final task, during which we may try to draw on a nascent part of our humanity beyond our current fourfold development: our evening meditations, and our Logos-filled speech in the classroom, can become the part of the lesson that helps students bring things into balance.

In summary, students were able to begin the lesson in a physically comfortable, hope-filled manner; with trust for the venture into new territory; found something to love in the material; and then took the fourth step of bringing the lesson into balance. That is the fourfold path for our job as teachers.

In closing this section, I would like to offer the following from the introduction by Christopher Bamford of a selection of lectures by Steiner entitled *Love and its Meaning in the World*:

> Although Rudolf Steiner does not often explicitly speak or write of love, love is the very heart and ground of all his teaching, the foundation of all he did, and all he hoped that we would do. Steiner teaches that, without love, nothing is possible; but that with love, we can do everything. Love is always the love of the not-yet. To love is to create; it is to enter selflessly into the current of time that flows toward us from the future.[25]

Combining faith, love and hope with the Pedagogical Law

The preceding suggests one way of contemplating classroom needs and rhythms: a pattern for the 'what' of hygienic teaching. To this, we must look to add the 'how' — how can we promote hope at the start of a lesson, faith when we are leading along, and then love when students are going about their work with the material?

Let's take a look at modern life in general. It seems like we've become hard-wired to fall into what a friend of mine calls the Have-Do-Be Trap… a problem/solution spin cycle. For instance, very often in early January, people decide they absolutely must *have* gym memberships and new workout clothing, in order to do exercise, in order to be in shape. Isn't that what Nike sells? You need to buy the gear so you can "just do it" and then you'll be more muscular and speedy? Or, the federal government identifies inequalities in public education outcomes (which there certainly are), so it decides that America *must have* national standards for education, in order for teachers *to do* measurable instruction, in order for the end product, which is that America's students will be successful in the global economy.

In other words, our go-to approach is to see if we can name a problem … and then plug in the "obvious" solution, which almost always involves buying something or writing up a new deal that we have to have to make the problem go away.

However, No Child Left Behind and then Common Core have demonstrated that maybe a different perspective is needed in order to lift up the way children are taught. In any event, at least for Waldorf teaching, the beginning of a powerful answer to how we can improve our approaches at each step of the fourfold lesson pattern I described, is — again, in my opinion — given to us by Steiner, if we work to combine his Pedagogical Law with the architecture of his description of our relationship to Hope, Faith and Love.

Hope and the Pedagogical Law

I recently Googled "boosting your child's self esteem" and found 107,000 web pages of advice available for parents. There is indeed a bit of truth in the common parenting concern about nurturing self esteem; it's kind of like saying, "strengthening hope." And it the role of parents to be sure that teachers are helping students to see and develop individual strengths. Encouraging words are certainly part of what is needed in the realm of hope.

My wife attributes quite a bit of her success as a class teacher to frequently expressing to her students how lucky she felt to have such a strong class, such capable math learners, etc. This was not empty "friend teacher" rhetoric; it was a conscious choice as a way to foster a hope-filled working environment.

So, when we begin a lesson, we need to work with the etheric forces — our own and what surrounds the class — to support the students' physical readiness and hopeful state. This is why that little tale of the main lesson included a brief description of the classroom as being lovely, warm and sunny, with the aroma of baking bread from the Kindergarten.

Since we know that the etheric body can also be called the habit body, the necessity of creating a hope-filled environment confers on us as teachers a duty to work on our own habit bodies; our humours or temperaments. This is the basis for the well-known Waldorf school mantra, "Who you are is more important than what you teach." My friend Mary Jo Oresti has given me what amounts to a corollary of Steiner's pedagogical law: "Every single step forward pedagogically requires two steps forward in personal development."

In *The Spiritual Ground of Education*, lecture 4, Steiner presents the following:

In a Waldorf school, who the teachers are is far more important than technical ability they may have acquired intellectually. It is important that teachers not only love the children, but also love the whole procedure they use. It is not enough for teachers to love the children; they must also love teaching, with objectivity. This constitutes the spiritual foundation of spiritual, moral, and physical education. If we can acquire this love for teaching, we will be able to develop children up to the age of puberty so that, when that time arrives, we will be able to hand them over to the freedom and use of their own intelligence.[26]

So, first, last and always we must work on our inner and outer habits. It's not about: you have to have a warm, sunny classroom with the faint aroma of bread-making in order for you to do effective teaching, in order for the students to be educated; rather, it's about you being a person who tends to the environment. If you decide to be a person who likes your surroundings a little more lovely, you will do nice touches here and there that enhance a hope-filled learning environment.

What other personal habits can we think about here? I for one know I can tend to rush along and thereby place students in a hope-deflating situation; I need to temper my choleric temperament. It's also in my nature to be a little, uh, concise with people at times, so I have to work very hard to keep potentially short and therefore shaming responses out of my repertoire during unguarded moments. I'm also relatively organized and goal-oriented; teaching gives me the opportunity to slow down and be involved in a process that takes years to even know what progress is happening. I bet we all have a few traits we could change, for our sake and the students'.

Walter Holtzapfel, in Chapter 3 of *Children with a Difference* emphasizes two key words to guide us in developing our own etheric bodies, so that we can positively influence the students' physical bodies: "humor" and… "humour". First of all, a little broad humor (h-u-m-o-r) gets things going nicely and warms up the room; an age-appropriate riddle, tongue-twister, anecdote or joke. Secondly, h-u-m-o-u-r, the older spelling of the word, which meant fluids, or what is in the air.[27]

Our knowledge of the twelve senses can also be put to work on this aspect, reminding us to build a general feeling of hope in the classroom. The four middle senses—the ones Albert Soesman refers to as the soul senses—are smell, taste, sight and warmth. Doesn't the pedagogical law make it clear that caring for this realm of the senses is vital to the success of schoolwork, or really for interactions in any setting where we are hoping for growth? I believe it does. Making sure that students are situated in a pleasantly clean classroom where snacks are healthy, where lighting is good, where account is taken of viewing and hearing angles (including consideration of eye and ear dominance), where students are appropriately dressed and the aura is sunny: that's job one.

In summary, we can strengthen hope with everything that surrounds and supports the setting, the atmosphere, for learning.

Love and the Pedagogical Law

The teacher's astral body/emotional state will strongly influence the resting pulse, classroom focus, and health of each student. In the lecture "The Art of Educating Young Children," Steiner said:

> We come to the part of a child's development based primarily on the rhythmic system. As we have seen, here we must work artistically in teaching. And we shall never accomplish this unless we can join an attitude of reverence toward the child with a love of our educational activity; we must saturate our teaching with love. While children are between the change of teeth and puberty, all our teaching must be done out of love for teaching itself, otherwise it will have no good effect on them. We must tell ourselves that, no matter how clever a teacher may be, the lives of children reveal infinitely significant spiritual divine matters. But, for our part, our love must surround our spiritual efforts toward children in education. Consequently, no pedagogy should be purely intellectual; the only guidance we should engage is that which helps us teach with loving enthusiasm.[28]

Faith and the Pedagogical Law

Next, according to the way I'm suggesting we might look at the four steps in the learning process, we need to strengthen faith, to support students' astral bodies as you lead them along with new material. This confers on us as teachers a duty to be ready with our enthusiastic ego presence. Holtzapfel puts it this way:

> What must be the condition of the teacher's ego in order for him to work in a strengthening way on the child's astral body? "Have enthusiasm! — that is what counts," said Rudolf Steiner during the holding of the Curative Education Course, when discussing the pedagogical measures to be take to stimulate a child's astral body to greater participation. The fire of enthusiasm lends strength to the ego of the teacher to work upon the astral body of the child.

During the course, Steiner also indicated that this attitude should include enthusiasm for the truth; that our students should feel that we are excited in our heart and soul for the truth in the material we present. Steiner also drew attention many times to the connections between the ego and the blood.

When evaluating teachers, don't we often use the phrase "classroom presence?" Even a very experienced educator confronts issues of self-confidence almost every day. A successful teacher has cultivated a persona or presence in the classroom that seems to work most, if not all, of the time. Every once in a while, what may seem like a power struggle will arise and a good teacher will reflect: "Could I have handled that situation differently? Did I lose control of my emotions and/or actions? How can I go back into the classroom and redeem the experience for the students, and regain my authority?"

Self-observation

Since the beginning of the twentieth century, the eastern, Buddhist-inspired practice of Mindfulness Meditation has rapidly increased in popularity in the west; scientific research has attested to its physical and mental health benefits. In addition to an extended focus on breathing, most guided mindfulness meditations will include a time for quiet observation of one's internal state, beginning in the region of the head and methodically moving downward to the feet while carefully noting areas of relaxation or tension along the way.

On January 14, 1917, Rudolf Steiner gave a lecture that, to my thinking, suggests a parallel but quite different process of self-observation. The horrors of the World War had been dragging on across Europe when Rudolf Steiner presented his 33 lectures on the causes of that conflict, providing immense detail from his supersensible research into the motives and actions of the leading personalities involved. But in the 19th lecture he appears to depart from his broad historical theme and began speaking about the causes of human spiritual, psychological and physical illnesses.

In contrast to the uplifting discussion we just had about *Faith, Love and Hope*, this lecture from Steiner is, suffice to say, not something you'd want to pick up at a moment when you need some light or cheerful reading. However, it does, all by itself, offer what I believe can serve as a complete template for a true modern approach to psychology, and it outlines an important mindfulness tool of a different sort for not just teachers, but adults in general. The information Steiner provides in this talk can certainly be very beneficial if put to the service of teacher self-examination, as I'll attempt to explain. He began this lecture, presented in Dornach on January 14, 1917, with the following:

> The nature of man is complicated, and very much of what actually goes on within the human being remains more or less beneath the threshold of consciousness, merely sending its effects up into consciousness. True self-knowledge cannot be won without first obtaining insight into the working of the sub-consciousness weaving below the surface in the impulses of soul. These, it could be said, move in the depths of the ocean of consciousness and come to the surface only in the wake of the waves they create. Ordinary consciousness can perceive only the waves that rise to the surface, and on the whole one is not capable of understanding their significance, so true self-knowledge is not possible. Merely pondering on what is washed up into consciousness does not lead to self-knowledge; for things in the depths of the soul often differ greatly from what they become in ordinary, everyday consciousness. Today we shall look a little into this nature of man in order to gain, from this point of view, an idea of how the subconscious soul-impulses in the human being really work.[29]

Subsequently, Steiner indicated that our finer bodies need to be "anchored" in three particular zones of the physical body. First: he said that the Ego body is meant to be anchored in the area of the solar plexus and the ganglia radiating from it. Isn't that a little surprising or counterintuitive?

He commented, "…the point at which we experience our ego is not the same as the point at which it chiefly works in us." And, "When the human being is in a normal state of health, the ego is chained to the solar plexus and all that is connected with it," i.e., the abdominal organs; "there it has to behave itself."

Second: "Just as the ego has its point of contact in the system of ganglia, so does the astral body have its point of contact in all those processes which are linked with the nervous system of the spinal cord …the nervous system of the spinal cord which has to do, for instance, with our reflex actions and is a regulator for much that goes on in the human body."

Third: he stated that the etheric body is to be "bound by the cerebral system and everything that belongs to it. Therefore, the etheric body has its point of contact by means of the cerebral system. Similar things can be said here, too. In our head there is a prison for our etheric body....There is much in our human nature which must be held in check; we are at least partially decent human beings because the devils in us are held in check by the divine spiritual forces. … Because of the various temptations, we do not possess all-that-great an aptitude for decency. A good many bad dispositions and moods of soul life are the result of meeting with the demons in us. … So we have three possibilities for psychological illness, and also three possibilities for escaping from the physical body."

Thus, Rudolf Steiner in this powerful lecture delineated three categories of soul problems that can result from a finer body escaping from its mooring. Of the ego body, Steiner said: "Because of its Luciferic infection, the ego tends all the time to behave in a dastardly lying manner." When the ego is released, he noted, this leads to characteristics such as spite, cunning, and haughty opinions. "When the astral body is released, this leads to volatility of ideas and lack of cohesive thought, manic states on the one hand or, on the other withdrawal, depression, hypochondria." And when the etheric body is loosened from it point of contact in the cerebral system: "…the etheric body has the tendency to reproduce itself, thus becoming a stranger to itself and spilling over into the world, carrying on its life in other things." Steiner included the Ahrimanic qualities of envy, jealousy and avarice, and of being asleep to reality in the typical manifestations of this third possibility for illness.

Three possibilities for lesson problems

How can this help us in the classroom? Don't we all have at least a few days when things go a lot less amazingly wonderfully than we thought they would; when we go home feeling defeated, muttering "I'm actually a bad teacher" or some such self-talk? Well, with this lens we might be able to spot one or more of the following as review points for the future.

One: how was my physical posture? It makes a difference if one pauses mentally every so often and lifts the head into levity and stands a bit taller and more poised. This relates to the tendencies of an unchained ego. Of course nobody will last long as a teacher with tendencies to be "dastardly" but it can happen to any of us to lapse into a little haughtiness or to be inflexible and unaware when our lesson plan is not meeting the class.

Two: how was my breathing and rhythm? Was my presentation relaxed and cohesive? Did I check my own breathing? Am I developing the 'listening ear' for how my students are receiving things?

Three, was my mind wandering, did I get too far ahead of myself or the class, get so caught up in the material I prepared that I didn't really notice the students' breathing, posture and facial expressions?

My suggestion for a Steiner based "mindfulness meditation" that can be done very briefly throughout the day is to remember to regularly take a few seconds to check one's posture, breathing, and presence or clarity of thought… to mindfully note one's own Touch, Life, Movement and Balance.

When you've read this lecture 19, I hope you'll see how it underscores the importance of working on your own postural control as a path of personal and professional development. I'll add a few highlights in Row 7 of the diagram and I'll have more to say about this later [See Section 4].

A pedagogical story

The December 2015 *Discover* magazine story "Great Expectations" recounts that in 1964, Harvard psychologist Robert Rosenthal approached Beverly Cantello and other teachers at Spruce Elementary in San Francisco, asking them to help him run a trial of a new IQ modality named the Harvard Test of Inflected Acquisition. The test, Rosenthal said, was designed to identify which children in a given classroom were poised to bloom academically.[30]

And indeed, over the next school year those students identified as being on the launching pad did jump ahead in the following school year, with those in first grade making gains of more than 27 points in their average IQ scores. But after reporting on the post-testing results, Rosenthal revealed to the Spruce Elementary teachers that he had not told the truth when beginning the trial: the test he'd given them to administer was nothing but a standard IQ test. And the list of ready-to-bloomers had really just been chosen at random. Beverly Cantello's selected third graders were among those who made impressive gains. "At first, I was offended," Cantello recalled for *Discover*. "Later I understood why he needed to fool us." Rosenthal's reasoning was this: "The bottom line is that if we expect certain behaviors from people, we treat them differently, and that treatment is likely to affect their behavior." Rosenthal called his discovery 'The Pygmalion Effect', and his research was to have many positive effects on teaching practice in the 60s and beyond.

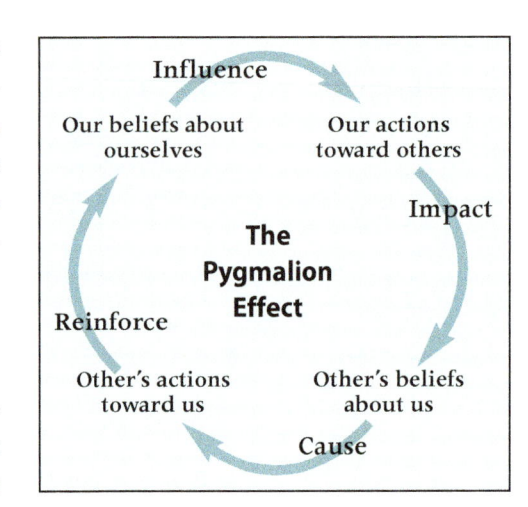

Here once again is mainstream research pointing to the practical—and completely modern—wisdom of a Steiner paradigm laden with seemingly odd terms like astral, etheric and ego bodies.

Cowboy Wisdom

Teaching children has a lot in common with training and riding horses. Take a look at this from an anthroposophic perspective: with a horse, one is dealing with a creature comprising physical, etheric and astral bodies. No ego; but a sort of group soul. With children (and this progresses over time), one is dealing with a being with physical, etheric and astral bodies, but an ego body that emerges only slowly over the K–12 span of time. In both cases one might say that the teacher is dealing with a herd mentality. Why so much time for recess and games class? Well, partially because they just need to run around and work out their herd hierarchy for themselves.

The vocabulary of modern science paints the same picture in a different way. We now know that horses don't have a prefrontal cortex, the part of the brain responsible for executive function, planning and evaluating. Humans do have a prefrontal cortex, but it does not become fully myelinated and functional until the early twenties. (More on this later.) Thus, neither horses nor young students have much capacity for time management, forethought, or conscious long-term delays in gratification.

As a recreational rider, I can tell you that teaching is just like riding: when things are going well the time flies by and you end the lesson with more energy than when you began.

A man named Buck

I was inspired to begin writing this chapter after watching the movie *Buck*.[31] Produced by Robert Redford, it's the life story of master American horseman Buck Brannaman. I strongly recommend this film to all teachers and parents, and especially as one that deserves time in a faculty meeting study. It provides invaluable reminders of how to teach with respect and compassion; how to uphold the maxim that for every step forward with pedagogy one must take two steps forward with personal development.

"Your horse is a mirror to your soul, and sometimes you may not like what you see. Sometimes, you will," says Brannaman, a true sage on horseback who travels the country for nine months a year helping riders of all ability levels, and also helping horses with people problems. *Buck* follows Brannaman from his challenging childhood to his successful approach to educating riders on how to move as one with their horses, using only the slightest effort and correction. A real life "horse-whisperer," he teaches people to communicate with horses through leadership and sensitivity, not punishment. Brannaman possesses near magical abilities as he dramatically transforms horses—and people—with his understanding, compassion and respect. In this film, the animal-human relationship becomes a metaphor for facing the daily challenges of life. Buck is about an ordinary man who has made an extraordinary life despite tremendous odds in childhood.

Buck Brannaman began his career as a trainer and master teacher of other trainers by studying and being mentored by another famous horse whisperer, Ray Hunt. Here are some things Hunt had to say in his book *Think Harmony with Horses*:[32]

> Now there are a lot of horses doing things that they don't like doing, but they are the victims — they have to do them. This is what I don't like to see in a horse. I don't like to see a horse doing things that are our ideas but not his. I believe the horse can do these things we're asking him to do and really want to do them. So you don't make anything happen. You let things happen. If you let him do it, he likes it and then it's his idea; but to do this well you're going to have to be a teacher! You're going to have to understand the horse's feelings. You will work on yourself more than on the horse to realize what is taking place.
>
> I've never been a teacher in a classroom but I don't think the teachers are going to make their kids do anything. I don't think that when students walk into the classroom the teacher meets them with a club and says: "Now kids, we're going to do this!" A good teacher not only does not need a club but doesn't even have a "have to do this" mental attitude. He knows how to approach the student and present the material so that the student is eager to learn. He can fix it up for the student and let him find it. Of course not all teachers have the same gift for teaching. I've heard so many people say: "My child really got a good start in school; he had a good teacher," while another will say: "I wish mine had gotten a good start; he had a poor teacher." Now I don't know whether these children had good teachers and a good start or bad teachers and a bad start. Both things can happen to a child. It can happen to a horse. But, if a child or a horse is having problems it's so easy to just say: "Augh, he's slow, he just doesn't understand." So the thinking is to just go ahead and work with the fast ones and let the others hassle along. Don't give any time or thought to the ones with the poor start. But maybe the other children weren't smarter, but just caught on sooner because they were less bothered, whereas the slow student was maybe just as bright, but his personality or characteristics, or the situation he was under made things more difficult for him. Perhaps he was bashful, shy, or didn't have the confidence

he needed in that teacher to get a good start. But, to a real teacher, all the students are equal. This child, the one who is having some trouble learning or behaving, gets special care from a good teacher. This doesn't mean keeping him after school. The teacher won't even make an issue of it at all. But you'll see the teacher, maybe, stop by the desk and encourage the child, help him a little bit. Then the teacher will help the others. You won't see the teacher doing much for those who don't need much help, but there will be a real good friendship with them anyway. A good teacher is able to encourage all students to develop their abilities. All students are different, and so are all horses. A lot of times you will present something to the person, or the horse, and they will do plumb opposite of what you want. But the way you presented it was without understanding.

Let's get back to teaching the horse and the ways of making him understand. Maybe by presenting what you want in a different way you'll get a different try — you'll get understanding. I'd say that about 99% of the time [when] the horse isn't doing what we would like him to do is not because he's trying to get the best of us. It's because he has no choice. The way we present it, it just doesn't come through that way to him. You'll be the one who analyzes how he reacts and you'll realize he doesn't know what you want; he doesn't understand. We have to present it to him in a way he does understand, but you can see that we have to be the teachers. We have to be the ones who really make most of the adjustments. Sometimes we make a 90% adjustment just to get the horse to make a 10% adjustment. It will be one mind and one body because his idea will be your idea, any time you ask for it. He will have learned it because you have offered it in an understanding way. You've made it enjoyable for your horse to learn. You've worked on a level he understands. You've kept his mind right and let him know ahead of time what you wanted so he doesn't have to become bothered. Make it a way of life with the horse to be the way you want — listen and learn. You listen to your horse and learn from him.

Top ten lessons from training/riding a horse that apply to teaching a class of children:

10. Never go to ride a horse that starts to move around when you're trying to mount.

9. It takes a lot of ground work (i.e., just using a lead rope) for a horse to understand what you want.

8. When a horse figures out what you want and shows it, give her a nice long break to digest it. You'll be able to see her relax her neck, perhaps make a licking and chewing motion; or you'll hear a nice long exhale.

7. A horse will pick up on your mood.

6. If a horse isn't doing what you want, it's probably because you gave a mixed signal or your mood was off. Or you got ahead of its learning curve and you needed to pause and take many steps back.

5. Horses are prey animals. It's normal for a young horse to be skittish, react to anything new in the environment, and to want the safety of a herd.

4. When a horse isn't paying attention to you, don't take it personally. But, in most cases you can give a firm reminder as long as you're not taking it personally.

3. Most horses like humans, and a horse will be happy to stop paying attention to the herd and pay attention to you if you have something interesting for it to do with you and you've built up a relationship.

2. Some aren't interested in humans. They'll do better at first if you run their lessons out of view of their herd.

1. The horse wants the rider to be the leader. It needs to trust that wherever you ask it to go and whatever you ask it to do will be safe and smart from a horse perspective. You can't, in short, be a "friend teacher."

2 Foundations for Student Capacities and Readiness

On Inner Development

Most people who become advocates for Waldorf education — parents, teachers, graduates or others — will at some point find themselves taking a stab at thinking up a good "elevator speech" about Waldorf, a few simple sentences that help open the door for someone hearing about Waldorf for the first time, or (even thornier) who may already have an impression from things heard through the grapevine.

Commonly, such mini-intros will include versions of one or both of: "lifelong love of learning" and "age-appropriate." My own attempt at finding a conversation-starter includes words to the effect that my school offers a rigorous classical curriculum based on what the young person is emotionally and physiologically ready for. (I don't get many "tell me more" looks, but at least I spoke my piece.)

What do such phrases about Waldorf really imply? What is age appropriate, developmentally appropriate, love of learning? Why did "Steiner Say" that first grade entry should wait until after the seventh Easter, or for the change of teeth to begin? How can we square the anthroposophic terminology and implications of Steiner's pedagogical lectures with modernity, how can we walk the talk behind the catchphrases we might need to offer in public? Well, I believe the world still really needs Waldorf Schools, perhaps even more in the "Screen Age" than it did in 1919. So we can continue to work on keeping it real by daily dedication to a more holistic approach to education, (a) consistently maintaining a deeper look at what's really going on with each child, and (b) providing a richer repertoire of the physical and artistic activities all children need as they wend their path of internal growth from early childhood to adolescence. That's what Sections 2 and 3 are about.

Another pedagogical story

Please place yourself in this short imaginary tale: You're house hunting, strolling around a familiar neighborhood, and you spot a vacant one that looks interesting. A "For Sale by Owner" sign hangs out front and you decide to just go take a peek in the windows because the house is out near the sidewalk. You check out the living room space. A couple of the basement windows are also in view, so you take a quick look down below before continuing your walk down the street.

What did you see? Almost with a certainty, the general impressions you got from the exterior will be matched by what you could see of the interior, and vice versa. Well-kept roof and paint, and a neat yard? A tidy and clean living room and basement. Or, roof has a little sag and siding needs work? No surprise to spot worn carpet, cracks in the basement walls or a jumble of storage items.

The same rule of thumb is true with young students. What can be seen on the outside, through movement and speech, is almost always a reflection of internal physiologic organization, a mirror of the many, many unseen factors that are vital for schoolday thriving and reaching one's academic potential.

A change in tone

The opening section of this book was offered at the level of encouragement and suggestion. That is, it's a collection of my teaching research and experiences, and of personal opinions and professional-development hints. Lenses on Waldorf teaching and possible ways one might put them to use. If you found some of Section 1 helpful, great!

By contrast, I want to present this section with all possible firmness. Being aware of and addressing—at least in some ways—the childhood developmental aspects surveyed in this second section should always be part of a teacher's work, especially in the lower grades. (And not just in Waldorf schools.) Permit me to spell this out with a logic sequence:

A. Many (but not all) learning difficulties are the result of obstacles at the level of neuromotor organization, i.e., physiologic readiness. For learning difficulties with underlying developmental delays or gaps, addressing the academic situation head-on via imposition of a program of drill/tutoring can be counterproductive until developmental barriers are identified and addressed… or ruled out. (See The Hierarchy of Learning Readiness, pages 7-8.)

B. All general education teachers need to be aware of and provide movement, drawing and painting modalities for strengthening child development.

C. All general education teachers also need to be able to look for signs that these modalities are strengthening the whole class and also know how the activities can bring to the surface signals that, here and there, further outside help is called for. (They don't need to be diagnosticians.)

The above three points are proven true because:

1. Learning requires perception and expression, which are functions of the interweaving of the neurological and motor systems.

2. "Ontogeny repeats phylogeny": (a) Human neurological and motor systems are the result of phylogeny, i.e., of the millions of years of macrocosmic evolution of life forms from simple organisms to mammals in general, to humans; and (b) In the comparatively short span of years from conception to adulthood, each individual human's neuromotor development (ontogeny) is—and requires—a microcosmic repetition of that entire history.

3. Neurologic organization is a step-wise process leading to unified wholeness. Each step tends to happen within a general month-by-month timetable in gestation and infancy, and within a year-by-year timetable for the balance of childhood, adolescence and early adulthood. Lack of completion of any step at its place in the sequence will affect all that follow.

4. Since all school-age children are marching along this timetable (but each at a slightly different point) all schoolchildren will benefit from grade-appropriate developmental activities, and some will need them more than others.

5. Thus, age-targeted developmental activities will benefit all students, and reveal individual needs. "The assessment is the therapy."

In short, the outer phenomena one can observe in children whose developmental foundations are not yet complete within a general yearly timetable should never be ignored. Unaddressed developmental hitches will lead the student to unconsciously resort to splinter skills, i.e., alternate ways of doing tasks, work-around methods that can often be maladaptive in the long run. By the age of nine or ten, little developmental problems here or there may very well become persistent barriers to learning, and they will by then have become, at best, much more difficult to go back and work on via developmental approaches offered by Extra Lesson, Occupational Therapy, Sensory Integration, Developmental Optometry, or other professional modalities. Even worse, they will tend to open the door to one or more of the three classroom cousins of shame, anger and fear: shutdown, fight and flight. In most cases where a child is not thriving for developmental reasons, some slight or greater delays in more than one or two aspects will be present; there is usually overlap or comorbidity pointing to a more holistic picture of neurologic immaturity.

But the good news is that by proactively addressing the developmental aspects that are often the roots of such problems, a lot can be done to avoid shutdown (aka "poor work habits"); fight (aka "oppositional behavior"); and flight (aka "attention deficit" forms of avoidance). Thus, the goals of this section are:

1. To provide an overview—based in modern science—of the phases of neurologic and motor development from gestation to the end of adolescence and the beginning of adulthood.

2. To provide a clear outline of how that inner neuromotor growth will be made outwardly visible, via developmental aspects that can be observed in your class every day; and to give enough detail to strongly support the basic "why" of the observation and activities portions that follow. Given the complexity of these aspects, references will also be provided for teachers who want to expand their understanding and expertise beyond a working familiarity.

3. Observational worksheets you can use to add depth and clarity to your picture of each student, and as objective tools for communicating with remedial specialists about any yellow or red flags that point to possible needs for specialized evaluation.

4. The developmental aspects outlined will be especially brought to the surface if you make time to utilize the activities provided in Section 3. However, the goal is far beyond screening for individual problems, as will be described.

You can be a "First Responder"

Regular-education teachers are not expected to take up professional diagnosis or one-on-one remediation of the kinds of developmental obstacles presented in this section. However, they can provide daily activities to help all children complete integration of their finer bodies, and they can be a vital part of a safety net for those students who appear to need additional attention. If you are a class teacher or subject teacher, I hope you'll feel empowered and informed enough to officially appoint yourself a "Developmental First Responder"… ready, willing and inspired to be on the front line of a program that helps every child in the class (because even children who are right on track developmentally will be further strengthened); and prepared to "call 9-1-1" when the professional insight and help of a outside expert might be needed. The Inventory of Readiness for Classroom Tasks form in the Appendix offers a good place to begin.

And please don't feel that you should wait until you've mastered all of the background theory before trying out some new activities in the next section. It's true what they say: "An ounce of action is worth a ton of theory." Including experiential learning in all parts of the day is a Waldorf mainstay for success — for you as well as for your students.

Neuromotor development

Leaving aside for a while all of the deeper insights one can gain from an anthroposophic study of this topic, let us first consider what modern science has to say about neurology, brain development, memory, neuromotor functioning, academic readiness, etc. There are two facets of human brain development to consider here: the structure of the nervous system—usually almost completed during childhood—and the slower process of organizing the workings of this structure. This latter aspect is closely tied to the decades-long process of myelination of the nerve system, which continues all the way through early adulthood.

Structural maturation of brain regions and connecting pathways is required for development of cognitive, motor, and sensory functions; the human brain is not a finished organ at birth. At least ten more years are needed before even its general development is completed. This maturation eventually provides for a smooth flow of neural impulses throughout the brain, which allows for information to be integrated across the corpus callosum and the many disparate regions involved in these functions.

In the embryo, humans first begin to grow the same precursor brain structures as those that simple marine animals such as sponges first acquired eons ago, and then continue to reprise the journey from sea to shore, from reptilian to mammalian to human. The hindbrain gives rise to the pons and medulla of the brainstem; the midbrain gives rise to the forebrain, and the forebrain develops to add components, leading up to the neocortex and prefrontal cortex. This final region of the neocortex has been implicated in planning complex cognitive behavior, personality, expression, decision-making, and moderating social behavior. Notably, in the light of Steiner's paradigm of the middle senses, the neocortex evolved in part from an olfactory structure in earlier organisms.

Comparing sharks with humans shows the relative size increases of certain structures, particularly the forebrain. In sharks, this region is no larger than other structures. In humans, it's massive and develops into multiple structures including the basal nuclei, hippocampus, amygdala, and neocortex. The hominid brain dramatically expanded over some three million years. In Australopithecus afarensis the skull volume was 400 to 550 mls; in modern Homo sapiens the volume is 1200 mls or more. Most of this difference is a result of neocortex expansion.

Movement patterns reflect neurology

In simpler vertebrates, as noted, development produces a hindbrain, midbrain, and forebrain; and also a right and left side (bilateral symmetry). These nerve structures first appeared in marine life some 600 million years ago. Animals at this stage of development respond to surroundings chiefly at a fear-based reflex level; fish-like wriggling movement is characteristic. In human childhood, we see these same characteristics of response and movement: reflexive responses for suckling and other aspects of touch; and for threats to balance and safety (loud noises, unfamiliar faces, etc.). Many developmental specialists use the label "trunk stage movement" for the wriggling, somewhat fish-like mobility typical of this stage. For instance, the infant crawls on his abdomen in a homolateral pattern that resembles the swaying of an elephant's trunk: leg and arm on one side extending; and on the other side, arm and leg flexing, and twisting at the waist. Notably, crawling in this manner places one eye and ear at a time toward the floor, so that vision and hearing of the surroundings are similarly homolateral, alternating from side to side.

At about eight months, mobility, communication and memory functions move to the level of the midbrain and the child adds the third dimension to her exploration of the world. She now creeps on hands and knees. The abdomen is raised off the floor and the eyes and ears are freed to develop greater depth perception and coordination. At the beginning of this phase crawling may still be homolateral but it will soon become (or should become) cross-lateral: right hand and left knee advancing, and then left hand and right knee advancing.

You may occasionally see (as I have) a first or second grade student whose struggle with learning to jump rope reveals a vestige of this trunk stage pattern. If you stand straight in front or back as she swings her rope, you can notice that one arm extends farther from the torso than the other and the rope is actually looping around at a slight angle to the child's midline. Another method of screening for trunk stage movement continuing past young childhood is to tell the child to show you "how strong she is." Offer two or three of your fingers for him to squeeze as hard as he can (with one hand at a time). When a child is still in this trunk stage, the free hand on the other side will make the opposite gesture: extended, raised from the wrist with the palm toward the floor.

Two more steps complete the movement-stages picture in development. When the child has moved from trunk stage, the off-hand in the above little screening will squeeze equally, i.e., when one had grips tightly, the other does the same. Progress! And finally, somewhere around seven or eight years old the child should achieve bilateral independence: one hand grips strongly, but the other is at rest.

In a brief few years from birth, the child moves beyond automatic midbrain responses to outer stimuli, and transforms herself into a little human who is seeing and hearing the world "in stereo" and with a greater degree of independence, discrimination and understanding. The final step in this part of the process is achieving cortical hemispheric dominance: organizing the personal left-right pathways for processing and expressing all that the world will offer.

Myelination of the brain

Recent scientific research has brought to light amazing details about human development in the first three decades of life. Perhaps even more amazing is that these twenty-first-century discoveries are highly consistent with the academic progressions recommended by Steiner early in the previous century. This is shown in the images that follow, which show magnetic resonance imaging of the progression of brain myelination from birth to maturity in early adulthood. Myelin is a fatty substance that wraps around nerve fibers and serves to increase the speed of electrical communication between neurons, similar to the way that electrical wiring is sheathed in plastic.

The development and function of myelin remained elusive for many years, but now scientists have been able to use advances in imaging to learn more. Myelination begins early in the third trimester, but relatively little myelin exists in the brain at the time of birth. During infancy, myelination proceeds quickly, leading to a child's rapid acquisition of basic motor skills and language. Myelination continues through the adolescent stage of life. Let's look at parallels between the Waldorf education's curriculum progression and this 21st century research into brain maturity.

• **Brain development by four years:** Regions responsible for sensations like touch are almost as developed as they ever will be. The part of the brain governing vision has already matured. The area of the brain governing language is immature, as indicated in orange, but continues to develop rapidly in children through age 10. The dappled yellow and red areas of the prefrontal cortex indicate that this part of the brain, which affects abstract thinking, reasoning skills and emotional maturity, has yet to develop. This lack of maturity is one reason young children can't juggle a lot of information and may throw tantrums when presented with too many choices.

Waldorf curriculum: The essential element in early childhood education is the educator, who shapes and influences the children's environment, not only through the furnishings, activities, and rhythms of the day, but most importantly, through the qualities of her own being, and relationships to the children and others in the room. These qualities, which include attitudes and gestures both outer and inner, permeate the early childhood setting and deeply influence the children, who take them up through a process of imitation.

• **Brain development by 6 years:** The brain has already begun its 'pruning' process, eliminating redundant neural links. This will accelerate in later years; one reason why learning a new language is easy for children and much more difficult for most adults.

Waldorf curriculum: Grade 1— main lessons include phonics, writing, speech through recitation and retelling stories, qualitative aspects of numbers and the four processes of arithmetic, beginnings of science through nature stories, and the literature of Fairy Tales. Grade 2—reading and writing, mental arithmetic and arithmetic using larger numbers, legends of many cultures, and fables.

- **Brain development by 9 years:** While basic motor skills are well developed by age 5, children experience a burst of fine motor-skill development between ages 8 and 9, helping to explain gains in the ability to use scissors, write neatly or in cursive, and manipulate models and craft projects. By the age of 9 the parietal lobes are beginning to mature; this creates new capacities for math and geometry skills. The pace of learning at this age increases quickly and can be enhanced with flashcards and math drills.

Waldorf curriculum: Grade 3: students are now ready to begin grammar, parts of speech, weights and measures, house-building, farming, introduction to music notation, Old Testament stories, and much more.
Grade 4: grammatical tenses, fractions, local geography, human and animal, Norse mythology.
Grade 5: letter writing, decimals and the metric system, freehand geometry, U.S. geography, botany, Egyptian and Greek mythology, ancient history through Alexander the Great.

- **Brain development by 13 years:** Linked to judgment, emotion and logic, the prefrontal cortex is among the last areas to mature. Until it does, teens lack the ability to adequately judge risk or make long-term plans. Ask kids at this age what they want to be when they grow up, and the answer is likely to change often. Deep in the limbic system, a capacity for creating emotion increases. As yet, this capacity is unrestrained by the prefrontal cortex, which lags behind. That's why teens can seem, at random times, emotionally out of control. The parietal lobes, shown in blue, are developing rapidly at this age, and the student's intelligence and analytical abilities are expanding.

Waldorf curriculum: Grade 6 — writing and speech style development, gardening as a special subject, simple interest and percentages, astronomy, world climatic conditions, mineralogy, physics, geometry, perspective drawing, Roman and medieval history. Grade 7: composition, poetry, positive and negative numbers, squaring, cubing, and equations, economics, cultural geography, physics, mechanics, chemistry, charcoal drawing, Renaissance history, and physiology of nutrition, digestion, circulation, respiration and reproduction.

- **Brain development by 15 years:** In the teen years, an abundance of neural links continue to be discarded. Underused connections will die to help more active connections thrive. As a result, the child's brain will become more specialized and efficient.

Waldorf curriculum: Grade 8 —prose, drama, algebra, world geography, meteorology, practical physics, organic chemistry, geometry, physiology and anatomy, epic prose and poetry up through modern times, world history.

- **Brain development by 17 years:** The deep blue and purple, depicting the maturing prefrontal cortex, shows why the brains of older teenagers are capable of dealing with far more complexity than those of younger children. This development leads to a burst of social interactions and emotions among older teens. Planning, risk-judging and the beginnings of young-adult self-control become possible.

- **Brain development by 21 years:** Executive functions and maturation. Although the brain appeared to be almost fully developed by the teen years, the deepening blue and purple areas here show that tremendous gains in emotional maturity, impulse control and decision-making continue to occur into early adulthood. The 21-year-old brain is mostly mature, but the areas of green show that even at the threshold of legal adulthood, there is still room for increases in emotional maturity and decision-making skills, which will come in the next few years.

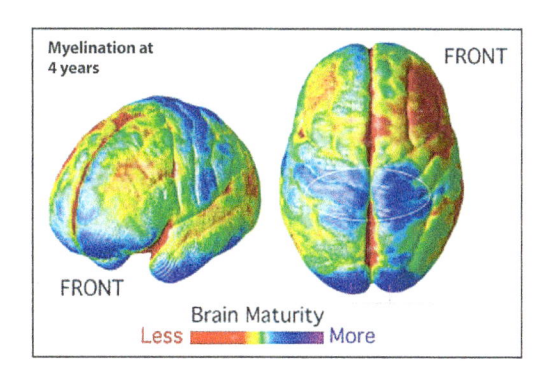

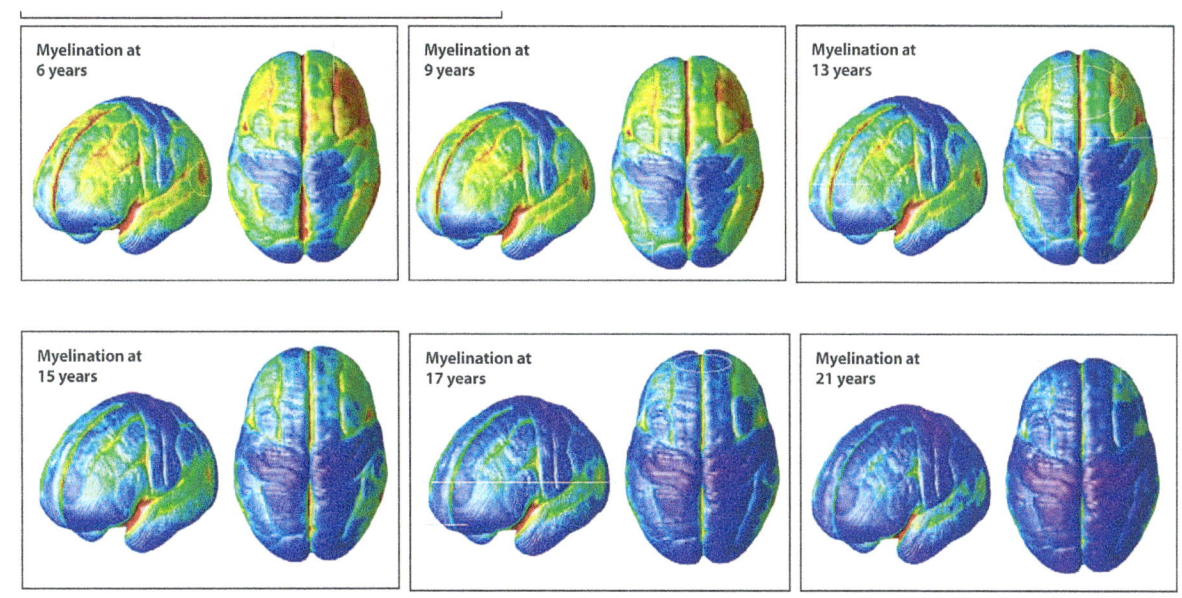

Sixteen Keys to Student Needs

From Inner to Outer to Inner

Like waves reaching the shore, the inner state of each student's psychomotor readiness for learning will rise from deep below the surface and appear to the eye if opportunities for the right school-day activities are consistently provided and carefully observed. The very same outwardly visible activities will contribute to each young student's continuing growth of psychomotor readiness The following presentation provides an accessible and effective matrix of practical ways that general education teachers can look for and address developmental highlights and benchmarks. I hope that whatever shortcomings there may be in this attempt to outline theory will be remediated by the reader applying the activities that follow in Section 3.

Keys 1 to 4: The Lower Senses

A few brief notes can be added here to the narrative and graphic from Section 1.

The Life Sense can be approached and strengthened via the four middle senses of Smell, Taste, Sight and Warmth. Nourishment in this realm is certainly called for whenever a child is not able to cope or thrive.

Some components of vision belong to the Sight Sense, and others to the Movement Sense. Peripheral vision—the response of the gaze to color and the recognition of well-known forms in the surroundings—belongs to the middle sense named Sight. But the focused, foveal vision in which there is inner sensing of movement of the eyes (part of the fine-motor keys to readiness for reading) belongs to the lower, Movement, sense.

In general, boys and girls tend to exhibit differences over time in development of the Touch and Balance Senses and the related (stereo)typical movement activities they seek; this is further explored later in this section.

The academic importance of the Balance sense, and its working together with the Movement Sense, is so extensive that we now need to explore the interplay of these two in much greater detail. In mainstream terms, spatial organization, body schema/image, proprioception, and vestibular sensing combine to provide "postural control" and are the basis for the core of consciousness, as well as the fulcrum of interaction between subject and object, between ego and others.

The lower senses and postural control: One aspect of a child's development calling for careful observation and helping attention can be summed up as the postural control system… how the network of bones, muscles and nerves can make it possible to sit at a desk, stand poised with the head upright, etc. The four lower senses can be a symphony that enable the student to breathe in and out, to shift between analysis and synthesis, between joyful movement and harmonious focus. Thus, strengthening the four lower senses is one of many reasons we as teachers must attend to our own posture: "be the change you wish to see!" There's a lot more to explore on this topic, but it will have be continued at another time.

Research on the Vestibular System and Learning: It was first reported in the early 1990s that people with damage to the balance organs of the inner ear exhibited deficits in spatial memory. This was not perhaps surprising: the vestibular system detects movement of the head in three dimensional space, performs complex mathematical computations of acceleration, velocity and position of the head, and communicates this information to higher areas of the brain. Later research has pointed to a relationship between vertigo and dyscalculia (math deficiency). In one study, researchers noted that subjects with vertigo skipped and displaced decades when counting backward by two. The subjects also displayed decreased ability to do mental arithmetic and lower capacity for central auditory processing. Other studies suggest that changes in stimulation of the balance organs of the inner ear can disrupt numerical cognition and other higher cognitive functions, resulting in an inability to manipulate numbers.

When we consider that the Math Logical Intelligence and the Spatial Intelligence (in Howard Gardner's model of multiple intelligences, see page 13) are next-door neighbors with a great amount of overlap—for instance in geometry and trigonometry—the above research can only serve to underscore the importance of taking time throughout every day for activities that provide a dose of vestibular stimulation, i.e., the kind of spinning and jumping "games" to be described in Section 3.

Keys 5 to 10 – from *Take Time*

"By working in an imaginative way with the child, his dexterity, ability to move and even inner cognitive agility can be helped." So write Mary Nash-Wortham and Jean Hunt, who began publishing their then-separate ideas about the basics of classroom enrichment and student support in 1979. In 1986 they merged their efforts to create a classic book called *Take Time*. This little yellow-covered book may be the most accessible and useful reference for identifying some of the most important keys to student thriving, and for getting down to business with focused support. (If you are a beginning Extra Lesson teacher, I highly recommend using this concise book as your first "bible" for on-the-job training.) The authors note that they have taken their therapeutic exercise recommendations and practical descriptions from the fields of speech therapy and eurythmy.[33]

I would like to add a few points about Key 10, laterality. This topic can be fraught with hoary negative connotations about left-handedness; gone are the days when primary school teachers would impose right-handed writing on left-handed students. Also, for many years it was accepted that people are predominantly either left-brain or right-brain thinkers; now that is generally deemed to be not scientifically proven. However, all phenomena are interesting, and in any event some pointers to learning style can still be gleaned without making inflexible conclusions. In other words, note with happy interest but don't judge.

For instance, one such thing to notice in this regard is hand position for writing, per the observation form that follows. Another that in my opinion is still important to know is each student's ear dominance. When one is left-ear dominant, verbal instruction goes first to the right side of the brain, then, in order to reach the language centers on the left, has to traverse the corpus callosum connecting the two hemispheres. This causes a micro-delay in auditory processing, which may in turn lead to confusion, which may in turn superficially appear to be an attention problem but probably could be better understood as a relative weakness for auditory learning and/or a preference for visual and kinesthetic learning.

Keys 11 to 13 – midline barriers, reflexes and immature gross-motor movement patterns

Why do some children move writing tasks to one side, plant an elbow on the desk and hold their chin, or squirm in their chair? What might be hindering others whose movements during circle activities just seem a little out of sync, or who struggle to play catch or jump rope? Keys 11, 12 and 13 outline some interconnected areas of inner organization that may, in ways like this, rise to the surface when consolidation that usually happens by the end of kindergarten hasn't yet been reached by entry into the grade school setting.

After attaining the combination of uprightness and postural control that makes learning to walk possible, toddlers will often progress to seeking out little jumping activities like climbing up one stair and then hopping down again. Developmentally, by creating such playful activities, the young child is working on crossing and integrating the plane of above and below; on both outer and inner movements across the horizontal midline barrier. The reality of this invisible barrier and the fact that it's not yet integrated can be observed, for example, in the manner in which a toddler will usually reach to pick something up from the floor: by squatting, bending the knees to lower the trunk, and deploying noticeably little bending at the waist. By age six or seven this midline should be integrated; flexing at the waist should be easy and automatic. Retention of this barrier can be looked for by asking

	Need / Observations	**Learning Implications**	**Example Activities**
1	**Touch Sense** Avoids physical contact, or seeks excessive contact. Trouble waiting in line, dislikes loud noises or crunchy food. etc. Can't imitate.	Connected to the Ego Sense. May have trouble connecting to others (including teacher!) Listening (attention) problems, under- or over- activity.	Shapes on back game; rough and tumble play such as bear, crawl push, ankle escape. Any games with contact, i.e., London Bridge, Nuts in May.
2	**Life Sense** Frequently tired or ill; nervous; coloring not good; insecure. Be careful to consider hierarchy of needs, i.e., is it medical, psychological, etc.	Connected to the Thought Sense. May get lost during lessons, not prepared to take things in. Approach through the middle senses.	Our ability as teachers to help a child who is chronically tired, hungry, etc., may be limited by home life. However, painting, clay work and affirmations are especially important for this child.
3	**Movement Sense** Clumsy, heavy in movements. Self-Movement Proprioception needs strengthening.	Connected to the Word Sense. This key is similar to Fine Motor Control (item 5) but includes gross motor… a more pervasive mood.	Almost any activity! Zoo Exercises; Do this, do that; Simon Says; Earth, air, water, fire.
4	**Balance Sense** Falls, dizziness, headaches, dislikes movement; or the opposite, always spinning. Balance Sense may need strengthening.	Research shows vestibular problems can be linked to math and reading challenges; including vestibular stimulation in the classroom can be a big help.	Jumping rope; balance beam games; Zoo Exercises - especially rolling; gymnastics.
5	**Timing and Rhythm** Difficulty singing or speaking a rhyme, marching or clapping with a tune.	May also have monotone speech, hearing/attention problems, reading delay. Rhythm is a pre-learning skill.	Any rhythmic activity, i.e., – rhymes & verses, singing, hand clapping games, jumping rope.
6	**Direction and Goal** Confuses directions, struggles with games like "Simon Says", contorts body while writing. Movement sense weak or disorganized, not able to support reading and writing.	Speech, writing and reading delays (i.e., can't follow the flow and direction of words); clumsiness may become a social issue.	Games like "Simon Says" Make up games requiring pointing in given directions.
7	**Spatial Orientation** Can't draw simple forms in the air, or walk them; difficulty with forms drawn on back game. Letter, number reversals. Spatial Orientation is weak; inner awareness of form and of self in space.	Will have difficulty with recognizing and forming the shapes that are letters and numbers. Learning requires imagination and ability to move from inner to outer.	Ball sequence from "Take Time", string games, jumping rope, tumbling.
8	**Sequencing** Can't remember the days of the week or months of year in order, or numbers 1 to 10, etc. Difficulty with hand clapping games, rhythmic math. Can't put things in order.	If the child cannot sequence naturally, putting letters or math problems in order for spelling becomes an ordeal.	Threading beads; sorting laundry, buttons or stones; tying shoes; alphabet song; finger games.

	Need / Observations	Learning Implications	Suggested Activities
9	**Fine Motor Control** Difficulty holding crayon or pencil; speech problems; messy writing or drawing. Jumpy eye-tracking and/or fatigue with desk work.	Depends on which area(s) of fine motor control (speech, eye, fingers) are lagging in maturity.	Copper rod exercises, jackstones in fingers, clay or beeswax modeling, tongue twisters. For eye movement, may need to consult a Developmental Optometrist.
10	**Laterality** Mixture of hand, eye, ear and foot use, e.g., in picking up and using an imaginary telescope, uses two hands, or different hand and eye. Laterality is mixed or undecided.	This may be merely a delay of a milestone that should be reached by age 7, or a longer term pattern. Processing for so-called left-brain activities will be less harmonious.	Desk placement; any games or chores that call on use of dominant side. Be sure dominant side is used, i.e., for putting dominant arm or leg first into clothing.
11	**Horizontal Midline Barrier** Writes bottom up; can't jump through a hoop or bend at waist. Horizontal Midline Barrier may still be present - incomplete relationship to above/below.	Internal movement not yet fully organized for reading and writing. This is normal to some degree up until age 7.	Jumping rope, frog hops, swinging, hanging from monkey bars, sledding.
12	**Vertical Midline Barrier** Places paper to one side, or twists torso; difficulty with ball bouncing games. Vertical Midline Barrier may still be present - incomplete relationship to left/right.	Internal movement not yet fully organized for reading and writing. This is normal to some degree up through age 9.	Any chores or games that require midline crossing, i.e., erasing board, ball shuttling/passing games, 1 & 8 drawing exercise.
13	**Retained Reflexes** Falls out of chair; contorts body; doesn't crawl cross laterally; reading problems after age 8. Reflexes that were appropriate for an infant or toddler are still in the driver's seat.	Some children with retained reflexes will develop splinter skills that get the job done, but in ways that can cause tension because of the effort; others will have learning delays.	Zoo exercises, and all crawling games, swimming, tumbling.
14	**Radius and Ulna** Experience with children will show that clumsy movement of the forearm is often present when reading and writing are delayed.	Difficulty writing and reading. Delay in learning, or tension, headaches, avoidance. Radius and ulna may not be yet fully developed for the movements required.	For radius and ulna, any activity for arm dexterity, including copper rod exercises.
15	**Imitation** Inattentive, disconnected, not able to follow and imitate. Student has been over-intellectualized and not given enough imitative activities.	Imitation in childhood is the foundation for deeper learning in early grades; it creates the foundation for gratitude, reverence and responsibility in adulthood.	Games like Simon Says; Jack in the box; Do this, do that. Also, minimize verbal instructions and maximize opportunities for the child to enter in imitatively.
16	**Anticipation** Can't wait for one's turn; doesn't follow along. Soul quality of Anticipation may need help.	Won't fully participate with the class; will lack the learning habit of waiting for insight.	Any game that involves waiting for a turn, i.e., "1-2-3 who has the ball" or Duck - duck - goose. Saving the end of a story for another day.

the school-age child to take a short run and jump through a hoop. With maturity of this aspect, the student will be readily able to leap through in the air, leading with one leg in hurdle position; otherwise she will slow down or stop when reaching the hoop, turn her torso to the side a bit, and step through one foot at a time.

Next on her developmental to-do list is crossing and integrating the plane of front and back; on movement forward and back across the frontal plane. When we observe the toddler-stage beginnings of running, well, it's definitely cute but it's not yet really running. The torso remains perpendicular to the direction she's going, the arms don't swing independently but rather are held symmetrically, bent at the elbows, parallel to the body. And legs and feet sort of stump along. But that's okay, because in the toddler/early childhood stage she'll set out on a mission to fix this barrier; she'll be eager for plenty of time outdoors and at the playground — to swing, go down the slide, run up and down little hills, etc. Some may call all of that playing; I call it self-assessment and self-guided construction work on her neurologic pathways.

Coordinating activity of the front and back areas of the brain is necessary for attention and focus. Children who still need development of this capacity may exhibit signs of attention disorders and also have trouble with reading and remembering. Activities to help close the gap will help free students who have a fight or flight mode; and it can allow children to begin storing, retrieving and expressing information, i.e., the front-back parts of reading and writing.

Forward-backward frontal plane movement occurs when seated at a desk and writing. "In paper-space awareness, the frontal midline divides the front of the paper from the back, but is also recognized as the direction of the letters, and/or as the sentence is read or written [in European languages]. This study suggests that children who have not mastered moving their body forward and backward through personal space, have letter reversals when reading and writing. They also may attempt to read, write and/or draw from the right margin of the paper-space or consistently use the back of the paper…. Many children struggle to say or do what they remember. They can't get their knowledge out of storage very well. In this case, children have poor integration between the back part of the brain, where thoughts are stored, and the front part where they are expressed."[34]

Interestingly, the decline in communication between the front and back of the brain has also been shown to be a factor in aging; research has demonstrated that exercises that promote front/back processing can help delay age-related memory decline.

Finally, by about eight years old the child should gain the ability to fluidly cross the vertical midline barrier, to be neurologically ready for academic and athletic movement in the left-right symmetry plane. This barrier is beneficial in its day, because it forces balanced growth of left and right sides of the body and brain; but normal integration should begin to take place by around six or seven, in preparation for asymmetrical tasks ahead. A vertical midline barrier can cause a student to lose his place when reading, copying, or borrowing in math.

The development of fine-motor control of vision, for instance, develops throughout childhood. In the early years, the eyes are not yet able to "track" across the vertical midline from one side to the other, i.e., to follow a near object from left to right and back. A brief, gentle screening for this aspect in rising first graders will show many who begin to blink or appear taxed by the effort, or whose eye movement halts when the target crosses the center line. This is typical, and the great majority of children who, as seven year olds, are not able to comfortably track will have naturally matured eye tracking by their ninth birthday. The "first responder" level of care for eye tracking and vision would be to take note of a student who tires or appears uncomfortable when learning to read; considered through the hierarchy of need in Section 1, a delay in fine motor control of vision might be developmental or may require the intervention of a developmental optometrist.

In general, complete ease of motion in the symmetry plane is not expected before the age of nine (even though it will arrive earlier in some). This is why most Waldorf movement educators choose to call their classes for the lower grades a games class rather than phys ed or gym: many students at this age are not yet physiologically prepared for the ease of vertical midline crossing required by most organized-sport skills. They still need to work on their frontal-plane athletic foundations.

The customary assessment given Waldorf students in second grade—whether based on the Dutch model, McAllen's "First Lesson" or a blend of these—incorporates many tools for identifying midline barriers that persist beyond their due date. In the daily classroom setting, persistence of the midline barriers can be observed in many ways; be on the lookout for the student who moves desk work to one side, who has difficulty with symmetrical form drawings, writes bottom-up or reverses many letters. You may have spotted a midline barrier in the wild, but on the other hand, you might be witnessing a retained reflex.

Independence of both halves of the body—to know right hand from left, to turn left or right, e.g., in eurythmy class—is necessary for learning to speak fluently, for the possibility of developing creativity, and for the capacity for higher-level learning.

Retained reflexes

Reflexes can be thought of as a spectrum of automatic neuromuscular responses that are beneficial or protective in the neonate and toddler. Reflex actions are instantaneously deployed by the little child at stages of growth prior to the age by which she would normally have had the experiences that lead to developing learned or situation-appropriate responses. However, an automatic movement response pattern that has not become integrated—so that it does not fire off every time its stimulus arises in the environment—can become counterproductive to independence and learning. There can be a variety of reasons a particular reflex has not become integrated "on schedule," but a shortage of traditional childhood movement is one leading cause.

It is beyond the scope of this book to provide more than a quick sketch of a few of the many primitive and postural reflexes, which are given here only by way of examples of what might be seen in typical school settings. For readers who wish to have more depth in this topic, *Attention, Balance and Coordination* is strongly recommended.[35] This book by Sally Goddard Blythe classifies reflexes as either primitive — those that are present at birth and should be integrated during the first six months; or postural — those that emerge after birth and usually become fully integrated by the time the child reaches school age. Again, any movement pattern that appears to the regular education teacher as a little out of sync is a signal to consider the kind of further screening that an Extra Lesson teacher can provide. Following are just a few examples.

Quite often in any classroom a teacher will see at least one student who, for desk work, moves writing tasks off to one side, or, instead of holding the paper with his non-dominant hand, plants that elbow and holds his head. This may be a pointer to delayed inhibition of the Asymmetric Tonic Neck Reflex (ATNR), which draws the arms to move in train with the head. The benefit of such an automatic response by an infant is that it helps develop eye-hand coordination; the infant's arms and legs extend to follow the gaze, helping it learn that its physicality includes arms, hands and fingers.

A student who moves work to one side or who plants his elbow on the desk and rests his chin on that hand has probably unconsciously developed a "work-around" pattern: a compensating way of approaching the task. Because the ATNR reflex is not yet naturally integrated, he stops it from firing off by fixing his head in place, or by placing the paper so that head rotation to only one side is needed. Most adults will continue, on occasion (and especially when fatigued), to unconsciously deploy this primitive movement response — typically, when driving a car, turning one's gaze to adjust the radio or to something happening off to the side, at which point the steering wheel magically also drifts to the side as well. The arm has moved in sync with the head.

The Spinal Galant Reflex produces a waist/hips wiggling movement when slight pressure is given along the lower back near the spine. The good news: wiggling is exactly what we need to do when we experience pressure along the lower back and need to emerge from the womb! Also, this reflex initiates the amphibian-type movements needed for creeping and crawling and the hip rotation aspect of walking and running. The bad news: if this reflex does not become integrated in early childhood, sitting at a desk in first grade will cause us to wiggle around every time our back leans against the back of the chair. So, teachers, if you have a chair wiggler, that's another signal to take note and discuss it with your school's educational support staff. Here is a list of some of the atypical movements and emotions that justify a screening by an Extra Lesson teacher or Occupational Therapist. These phenomena might be caused by retained reflexes. (There can be causes other than a non-integrated reflex for these.)

- Fearfulness
- Excitability
- Distractibility
- Fatigue
- Poor posture
- Low muscle tone
- Gravitational insecurity
- Motion sickness
- Enuresis
- Startle reaction (e.g., with catching a ball)
- Speech or reading challenges
- Desk work position

Educating the radius and ulna

Rod Rolling is one of the copper rod exercises in Section 3 (p. 64). If you do this exercise with groups of lower grades students, you will probably see an interesting phenomenon every once in a while: a student who doesn't naturally maintain a palms-up gesture with the hands when the arms lift and descend, but pronates one or both wrists (unconsciously rolls one or both palms toward the floor).

The radius and ulna might be thought of as part of the musical instrument for writing and the basis for the progression from writing to reading. And, it is often the case that a young student who has not gained easy control of the radius and ulna will have reading delays or difficulty. In other words, seeing a hand (or hands) roll out of palms-up during rod rolling is a little smoke signal to investigate.

In *The Essentials of Education*, Rudolf Steiner has some interesting things to say about the radius and ulna and their relationship to learning:

> The astral body is not natural history, natural science, or physics; it is music. This is true to the extent that, in the forming activity within the human organism, it is possible to trace how the astral body has a musical formative effect in the human being. This formative activity flows from the center between the shoulder blades,

first into the tonic of the scale; as it flows on into the second, it builds the upper arm, and into the third, the lower arm. When we come to the third we arrive at the difference between major and minor; we find two bones in the lower arm — not just one — the radius and ulna, which represent minor and major. One who studies the outer human organization, insofar as it depends on the astral body, must approach physiology not as a physicist, but as a musician. When children have reached a certain level of development, they can speak and then write what they have said. This is when it becomes appropriate to teach reading. Reading is easy to teach once writing has been somewhat developed. After children have begun work within their own being — in the nervous system and limbs, in the substance of their writing and reading, and in their inner participation in producing reading material — only then are they ready for one-sided activity. Then, without any danger to their development as human beings, the head can become active, and what they first learned by writing is turned into reading.[36]

Imitation and anticipation

It is often said that the most essential task of the teachers who work with a first grade—that is, the team comprising the class teacher and any subject teachers—is to "form them as a class"; to create a cohesive learning community; to lay a strong foundation for students who can respectfully listen, learn, value each other, help each other. One vital element in this special time—walking alongside them across the bridge from six years old to eight—is to complete the work of learning by imitation and to help this metamorphose into the capacity and desire to learn through attention to the knowledge of adults. Steiner often refers to the latter by the word "authority." Unfortunately, there is not, at least in English, a near synonym that includes the meaning of imparting knowledge, but does not carry with it the unintended connotation of a degree of autocracy.

In *The Child's Changing Consciousness*, Dr. Steiner indicates why the importance of cultivating imitation and anticipation goes far deeper than the pale paradigms of "classroom management," "delayed gratification," "executive function," and "values education" imply. First, with respect to imitation:

> Questions of ethical and social education are raised when we consider the relationship between growing children and their surroundings.... Here we need to consider three human virtues, concerning, on the one hand, the child's own development, and on the other hand, what is seen in relation to society in general. They are three fundamental virtues. The first concerns everything that can live in will to gratitude; the second, everything that can live in the will to love; and third, everything that can live in the will to duty. Fundamentally, these are the three principal human virtues and, to a certain extent, encompass all other virtues. Generally speaking, people are far too unaware of what, in this context, I would like to term gratitude or thankfulness. And yet gratitude is a virtue that, in order to play a proper role in the human soul, must grow with the child. Gratitude is something that must already flow into the human being when the growth forces—working in the child in an inward direction—are liveliest, when they are at the peak of their shaping and molding activities. Gratitude is something that has to be developed out of the bodily-religious relationship I described as the dominant feature in the child from birth until the change of teeth. At the same time, however, gratitude will develop very spontaneously during this first period of life, as long as the child is treated properly. All that flows, with devotion and love, from a child's

inner being toward whatever comes from the periphery through the parents or other educators—and everything expressed outwardly in the child's imitation—will be permeated with a natural mood of gratitude. We only have to act in ways that are worthy of the child's gratitude and it will flow toward us, especially during the first period of life. This gratitude then develops further by flowing into the forces of growth that make the limbs grow, and that alter even the chemical composition of the blood and other bodily fluids. This gratitude lives in the physical body and must dwell in it, since it would not otherwise be anchored deeply enough.

It would be very incorrect to remind children constantly to be thankful for whatever comes from their surroundings. On the contrary, an atmosphere of gratitude should grow naturally in children through merely witnessing the gratitude that their elders feel as they receive what is freely given by their fellow human beings, and in how they express their gratitude. In this situation, one would also cultivate the habit of feeling grateful by allowing the child to imitate what is done in the surroundings. If a child says "thank you" very naturally—not in response to the urging of others, but simply by imitation— something has been done that will greatly benefit the child's whole life. Out of this an all-embracing gratitude will develop toward the whole world. The cultivation of this universal gratitude toward the world is of paramount importance. It does not always need to be in one's consciousness, but may simply live in the background of the feeling life, so that, at the end of a strenuous day, one can experience gratitude, for example, when entering a beautiful meadow full of flowers. Such a subconscious feeling of gratitude may arise in us whenever we look at nature. It may be felt every morning when the Sun rises, when beholding any of nature's phenomena. And if we only act properly in front of the children, a corresponding increase in gratitude will develop within them for all that comes to them from the people living around them, from the way they speak or smile, or the way such people treat them.[37]

For the child to thrive in the move from kindergarten into first grade and beyond, a vital transformation of imitation must—absolutely must—be achieved by the teachers during the first grade year. During this school year, children become students only to the degree that they are brought along to want to follow along with and be able to listen to the lessons, wisdom or authority of the class teacher and the rest of the teaching team.

> …insofar as children between the change of teeth and puberty are concerned, authority is absolutely necessary. It is a natural law in the life of the souls of children. Children at this particular stage in life who have not learned to look up with a natural sense of surrender to the authority of the adults who brought them up, the adults who educated them, cannot grow into a free human beings. Freedom is won only through a voluntary surrender to authority during childhood.[38]

Helping 21st-century children make this transformation (from the age of imitation to the age of authority) is perhaps now more than ever a Michaelic task, because it flies almost 180 degrees against the wind of the forces now affecting childhood, viz, screen time, friend parenting, organized sports starting for toddlers, etc. A great many parents today believe that stepping aside and letting a child make choices—about food, clothing, bed time, smart phone use—is the true path to preparing the child for responsible decision making as teens and adults. In an article about nonverbal education, Dr. Michaela Glöckler sheds light on this teacher quest.

> There is yet a third hindrance vis-a-vis non-verbal education—the wish of many parents to allow their child to be free, not to follow directions. Hence, in order that he not be alienated, the three-year-old is asked what he would like to eat or what clothes he would like to wear. Whoever realizes that children of this age [early childhood] learn through example and are prone to absorbing any uncertainty in the adult's attitude (for example that he is indecisive about what he wants and therefore asks the child) will change his stance for the sake of the child. Freedom can only develop when one has achieved one's own mature insight. Of course, there are preliminary stages in the development of freedom. In the non-verbal phase of education this consists in allowing the child to imitate what he sees unrestrictedly and without reserve. He must be allowed to move freely. The house should be so organized that one does not have to prohibit the children from this or that; rather their impulse towards activity should be allowed free rein. The example comes from the grownups, but the way in which the child responds is freely experienced and freely formed. Similarly, later at school, when the children learn something because they like their teacher, the element of freedom plays an important role. Because the child likes doing something, she feels free, even if the impulse for the activity has originated from an adult and not from herself. If children have been allowed to develop through these preliminary stages, they will also be in the position after puberty, when independent thinking and powers of judgment ripen, to act out of free, self-determined insight and personal understanding. Only then is true freedom possible.[39]

Boys and Girls in Movement

Stereotypes and archetypes

You may have noticed the recent popularity of news from the gender front. Books, magazines, newspapers and online news sites seem to be playing up the good news and the bad news about changing gender roles, expectations, and fortunes.

In January 2014, the *New York Times* carried a two-page spread report on the abiding biases parents express in favor of their own sons. Harvard-trained economist and writer Seth Stephens-Davidowitz analyzed Google searches and found, among other things, that in the USA for every 10 searches for the phrase "is my daughter gifted?" there were about 25 searches for the phrase "is my son gifted?" For the phrase "is my (blank) overweight?" for every 10 searches for "son" there were 17 for "daughter." (Because of the nature of Google, comparative statistics from past decades are not available.)[40]

Indeed, the 'new news' seems to be how much of this publishing wave focuses on the topic of challenges faced by boys—and maleness in general—in the twenty-first century. Book titles in this newly popular niche include "The War Against Boys," "Boys Adrift," "Men on Strike," "The Minds of Boys: Saving Our Sons From Falling Behind in School and Life," and many others.

A common love of he-can/she-can tales (and publishers' love of publishing) may be part of the reason for this shift in focus, but there is much more than a grain of truth behind the rising concern for boys in schools today. Realities include statistics from the U.S. Department of Education,[41] which predicts that by the next decade, 60 percent of college degrees will be earned by females; and from the National Honor Society, which states that nearly two-thirds of the high school students it recognizes for academic excellence are female.[42] In the USA and elsewhere, fear seems to be the driver behind many educational

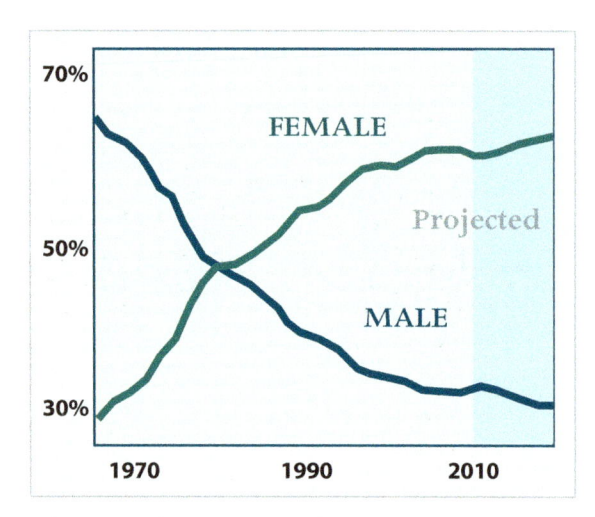

Changes in the percentage of college degrees achieved in relation to gender. U.S. Department of Education.

changes, leading us down the steps from No Child Left Behind to mandates for a Core Curriculum, taking schools to an ever-narrowing definition of their academic aims and at the same time circumscribing time allotted for, and play activities allowed in, the classroom, gym and schoolyard.

Without question, we can only feel relief that millennia of unrelenting female disempowerment (to say the least) are finally being stepped back in many areas. It subtracts nothing from this feeling to suggest that in the light of the above it may be necessary to take stock of the latest attitudes and see what might need to be re-balanced. Let us consider: are there learning-style differences between boys and girls? And if so, might the academic ascendancy of girls be, to some degree, the result of changes in 'mainstream' educational approaches during recent decades… are schools now, in general, more suited to girls' learning styles, and less suited to boys'? Has there been a downside to the rightful movement to empower girls, such that typical 'boy behavior' has been in some circles defined as a problem to be disciplined away? I think many teachers would answer "yes!" to these questions. And finally, what is the situation in our Waldorf schools? Is it more balanced?

I believe that boys and girls do have different developmental movement needs, needs that should be addressed in our Waldorf classrooms, schoolyards and games classes; that while boys and girls have many developmental-movement needs in common, there are also important differences in the ways they use movement to structurally organize their perception of and contact with the world. My goal in writing is to review perspectives on this vital topic, from a number of informative sources; to see how these seemingly disparate sources might be connected; and, I hope, to inspire further research and discussion at your school.

Differences demonstrated by modern science

In December 2013, a team of University of Pennsylvania Medical School researchers, led by professor Ragini Verma, published the results of a groundbreaking brain imaging study.

"These maps [on p. 51] show us a stark difference—and complementarity—in the architecture of the human brain that helps provide a potential neural basis as to why men excel at certain tasks, and women at others," said Verma.[43]

The University of Pennsylvania study has for the first time shown that the brains of men and women appear to be 'wired up' differently, which could explain some of the stereotypical differences in male and female behavior, scientists have said. Researchers found that many of the connections in a typical male brain run between the front and the back of the same side of the brain, whereas in women the connections are more likely to run from side to side between the left and right hemispheres of the brain.

"On average, men connect front to back [parts of the brain] more strongly than women," whereas "women have stronger connections left to right," said Ms. Verma. But she cautioned against making sweeping generalizations about men and women based on the results.

This difference in the way the nerve connections in the brain are 'hardwired' is established during the time of adolescence, when many of the secondary sexual characteristics such as facial hair in males and breasts in females develop under the influence of the sex hormones, the study found. The researchers believe that the physical differences between the two sexes in the way the brain is hardwired could play an important role in understanding why men may be, in general, better at spatial tasks involving muscle control, whereas women are better at verbal tasks involving memory and intuition.

Psychological testing has consistently indicated a significant difference between the sexes in the average ability to perform various mental tasks, with men outperforming women in some tests and women outperforming men in others. Now there seems to be a physical explanation.

"These maps show us a stark difference — and complementarity — in the architecture of the human brain that helps to provide a potential neural basis as to why men excel at certain tasks, and women at others," Professor Verma noted. "What we've identified is that, when looked at in groups, there are connections in the brain that are hardwired differently in men and women. Functional tests have already shown that when they carry out certain tasks, men and women engage different parts of the brain."

The research, which involved imaging the brains of nearly 1,000 adolescents, found that male brains had more connections within the hemispheres, whereas female brains were more connected between the hemispheres. The results, which apply to the population as a whole and not as individuals, suggest that male brains may be optimized for gross motor skills, whereas female brains may be optimized for combining analytical and intuitive thinking.

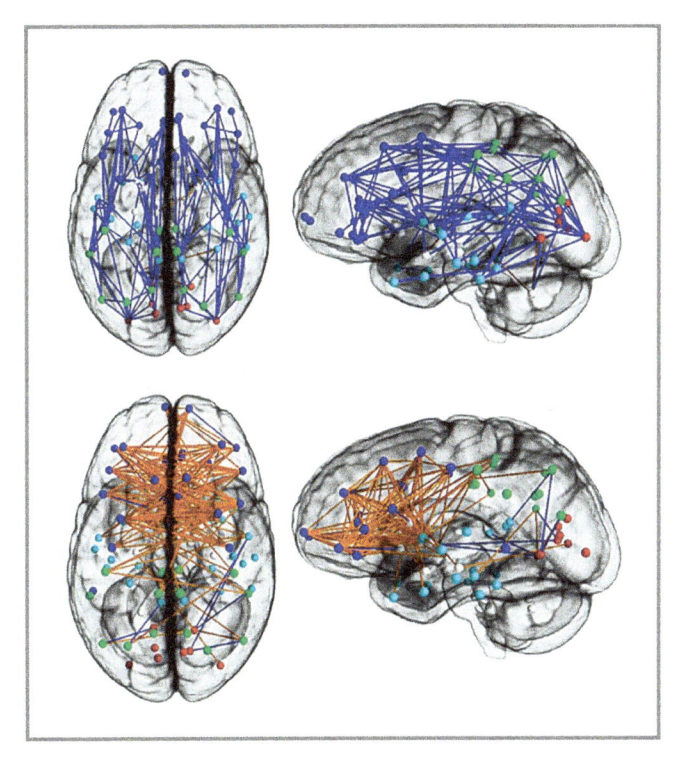

Brain networks showing significantly increased intra-hemispheric connectivity in males (upper) and inter-hemispheric connectivity in females (lowert). Intra-hemispheric connections are shown in blue, and inter-hemispheric connections are shown in orange. Credit: Ragini Verma et al., University of Pennsylvania.

Differences indicated by Rudolf Steiner

In a series of eight lectures he gave to teachers in Stuttgart in June 1921, Steiner devoted himself to the topic of differences between boys and girls. His comments on how these should be addressed during the elementary years were quite general:[44]

> We must consider the differences between girls and boys in our education leading up to this age [i.e., leading up to adolescence]. We must make the effort to develop the girls' moral and ethical feelings in a way that they are directed toward the aesthetic life. We must take special care that the girls especially enjoy the moral, the religious, and the good in what they hear

in the lessons. They should take pleasure in the knowledge that the world is permeated by the supersensible. … In regard to boys, it will be necessary to provide them with ideas and mental pictures that tend toward strength and affect the religious and ethical life. With girls, we should bring the religious and moral life to their very eyes, while with boys we should bring the religious and beautiful predominantly into the heart, the mind, stressing the feeling of strength that radiates from them.

(And about movement:)

We should encourage the inner experience the children's physical nature asks for in other areas—in the movements of arms and legs, in running, and so forth.… But this kind of physical education should be based on the development of movements not from the mere experience of the physical/corporeal but rather from the experience of soul and spirit, by letting the children adapt the physical/corporeal to their experiences.

I haven't found specifics given by Steiner on addressing gender differences in the early childhood or elementary school settings. However, the fifth lecture in *Education for Adolescents* does provide us with guiding thoughts for middle school and beyond. A few samples follow:

What we see initially is that the astral body has a stronger influence in girls than in boys. Throughout life the astral body of women plays a more important role than that of men. The whole of the female organism is organized toward the cosmos through the astral body. Much of what are really cosmic mysteries is unveiled and revealed through the female constitution. The female astral body is more differentiated, essentially more richly structured, than that of the male. Men's astral bodies are less differentiated, less finely structured, coarser.

If we bear in mind these differences between boys and girls we shall understand that the blessing of coeducation allows us to achieve much by a tactful treatment of both sexes in the same room. A conscientious teacher who is aware of his or her tasks in approaching such a coeducational situation will still differentiate between girls and boys.

Naturally, we must not take these things to an extreme, should not think of making the girls into aesthetic kittens that regard everything merely aesthetically. Nor should the boys be made into mere louts, as would be the inevitable result of their egotisms being engendered through an unduly strong feeling of their strength—which we ought to awaken, but only by connecting it to the good, the beautiful, and the religious. We must prevent the girls from becoming superficial, from becoming unhealthy, sentimental connoisseurs of beauty during their teenage years. And we must prevent the boys from turning into hooligans. These dangers do exist. We must know the reality of these tendencies and must, during the whole of elementary education, see to it that the girls are directed to experience pleasure in the beautiful, to be impressed by the religious and aesthetic aspects of the lessons; and we must see to it that the boys are told: "If you do this, your muscles will grow taut, you will become a strong, efficient young man!" The sense of being permeated by the divine must really be kindled in boys in this way.

In an era when gender/career roles were more stereotyped, Steiner also said that:

Our curriculum should be such that it allows the children to become practical in life; it should connect them with the world. Our curriculum for the tenth grade class will, therefore, be based on the following: We must, in order to do justice to the social life, have girls and boys together in the room; but we must differentiate by giving them activities suited to their sex. We must not separate them. The boys should watch the girls during their activities and vice versa.[45]

Since we know from many lectures by Steiner that he considered the astral body to be also the body of movement and emotion (and also the "faith body") and that he identified the astral body as central to thinking, the above, happily, gives us two quests. First, it provides us with a starting point for further observation and meditation, so that his recorded words become for us more than received wisdom.

Our second quest must be to find a modern-science parallel, not because we need modern science to validate its truth or falseness per se, but rather because when we can find mainstream parallels to anthroposophic findings or concepts, we add to our individual understanding and, even more importantly, strengthen our readiness to build bridges between the two and to communicate with parents and others beyond our classroom walls.

Differences in play stereotypes — boys

When I've asked workshop groups to name or briefly describe stereotypical play of elementary-age boys, it has never taken very long to come to consensus on the phrase "rough and tumble play" — wrestling/tussling activity.

There is considerable research on the topic of rough and tumble play and its connection to social and mental development. A wonderful book (*The Art of Roughhousing*) that I recommend to all parents of young children states the following:

Rowdy, physical, interactive play is by far the most common type of play in the animal kingdom. It occurs in every species of mammal and in many non-mammalian species as well. We have all seen videos of lion clubs wrestling, but you would be amazed by the vast number of species that enjoy rowdy play — elephants, whales, even ants.

Play — especially active physical play, like roughhousing — makes kids smart, emotionally intelligent, lovable and likable, ethical, physically fit, and joyful. We're not exaggerating (much). Roughhousing activates many different parts of the body and brain, from the amygdalae, which process emotions, to the prefrontal cortex, which makes high-level judgments. The result is that every roughhousing playtime is beneficial for body and brain as well as for the loftiest levels of the human spirit: honor, integrity, morality, kindness, and cooperation.[46]

And roughhousing is not just "for boys."

Almost all children love and benefit from roughhousing, but boys engage in rough-and-tumble play much more frequently than girls.... Of course, many girls roughhouse and many boys don't.... Boys as a group tend to tease, shove, and hit more than girls, even when they're having fun and being friendly.... Girls, meanwhile, are famous for what is called 'relational aggression': cruelty through gossip, dirty looks, or a cold shoulder.... Roughhousing can in fact help break this mean-girl pattern.... Through roughhousing, girls learn to be more direct about their feelings.[47]

Why is there is a continuing growth of attention deficit and hyperactivity diagnoses, especially for boys? It may be partially due to a past under-recognition of the "symptom cluster." I would assert, however, that the increase is largely due to culture shifts, especially perhaps in schools, toward defining typical boy behavior as a problem that must be restricted everywhere, forbidden on the playground, or even seen as evidence of a pathology that it would be appropriate to medicate away. Fergus Hughes, the author of *Children, Play and Development*, makes the following statement:

> There is a correlation between the appearance of this activity and the maturity of the frontal lobes of the brain. The executive functions of the frontal lobes include reflection, imagination, empathy, and play/creativity, and when these develop, they allow for greater behavioral flexibility and foresight, for well-focused, goal-directed behavior. As the frontal lobes mature, the frequency of rough and tumble play goes down, and damage to the frontal lobes is associated with a higher level of playfulness. In fact, surgical reduction of the frontal lobes of young rats results in an increased level of playfulness and hyperactivity.[48]

Whether or not a neural disorder is present, however, findings from animal research suggest that rough and tumble play not only reflects frontal lobe development but also promotes it. In other words, active, energetic, spontaneous physical play may facilitate neurological development.

Differences In play stereotypes — girls

When I've asked the same workshop groups to then name or briefly describe stereotypical play of elementary-age girls, it usually takes a little longer to reach a conclusion, but the discussion always leads to "spinning" — such as cartwheels, dancing — or the phrase "expressive movement", which covers both gymnastics and dance. Interestingly, Karl König emphasizes that folk dancing is an important activity for the development of math capacities.[49]

Googling the phrase "why do boys like roughhousing?" produces over 110,000 results. But while phrases like "why do girls like gymnastics?" (or dance, spinning movement, etc.) produce millions of results, the first several pages of link results, at least, include no pointers whatsoever to developmental reasons for this preference.

A different way of looking at the polarities

I contend that there probably is a developmental reason for these typical play characteristics: that, as a generality, boys' love of rough-and-tumble, and girls' love of spinning, expressive movement, reflect two poles of human growth and perhaps even neurologic organizing. I've reached this conclusion by looking through a sort of "binoculars" that combines ideas from Rudolf Steiner on one side, and on the other side with a gem of an insight from the twentieth-century physician and speech/auditory therapist Alfred Tomatis. I offer this lens on the polarities of boys' and girls' movement not as a definitive answer to all questions; rather, as a theory I've applied with some success in my movement program, and as food for thought and research by others as well.

Doctor Tomatis notes that the sensory cells of the inner ear and the tactile cells of the skin have the same origin. According to him, the skin and ear basically evolve from the same embryonic tissue, the ectoderm; thus the skin is differentiated ear, and we listen with our whole body. Tomatis called the ear "the Rome of the body" because almost all

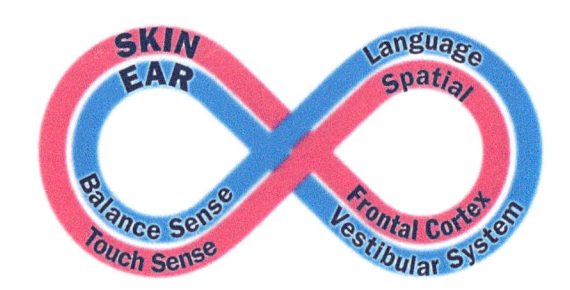

Interrelated developmental loops that can be strengthened by two polar opposites of childhood play: (1) rough and tumble and (2) spinning, expressive movement.

Developmental polarities for further exploration.		
POLARITY	BOYS (stereotypically)	GIRLS (stereotypically)
Physical structure/organ	SKIN	EAR
12 Senses	Touch sense, also Life	Balance sense, also Movement
Play characteristics	Rough and tumble play Strength	Gymnastics, spinning, dance Beauty
Type of movement	Im-pressive movement (i.e., pressing in, not "awesome!")	Expressive movement
Neurologic development	Executive function	Neurology of language
Multiple intelligences model	Spatial & Math	Language & Interpersonal
Learning style	Right brain; whole to part Visual and Kinesthetic learners	Left brain; linear-sequential Auditory and Reading-Writing learners
Learning difficulties	"On the surface" - evident in early grades. Attention Deficit - Hyperactive Dyslexia	"Hidden secret" - may not manifest until upper grades. Attention Deficit - Inattentive Type. Dyscalculia

cranial nerves lead to it and therefore it may be considered our most primary sense organ.[50]

Rudolf Steiner indicates that humans have twelve senses; that the four "physical" senses are Touch, Life, Movement and Balance. Isn't it so that in rough and tumble play, the Touch and Life senses are most engaged and affected; and that in expressive, spinning movement, the Movement and Balance senses are most engaged?

My theory is that, (A) through rough and tumble play, all children can work to develop (A1) their frontal cortex with its modulating of executive function and (A2) one of the modalities humans (mostly boys) use to establish their places in social hierarchies…. and (B) through spinning, expressive movement, all children can work to develop (B1) their vestibular system and language centers in the brain, and thereby (B2) one of the modalities humans (mostly girls) use to establish their places in social hierarchies.

A call for rebalancing movement programs

Considering changes to elementary movement programs over recent decades, perhaps the curriculum areas that have been most reduced because of institutional fears are gymnastics and rough and tumble play. It may be that opportunities for spinning, expressive movement have not been diminished to the same degree as those for rough and tumble; although most schools have cut gymnastics, there is still plenty of dance in most phys ed programs.

Gymnastics and wrestling are both sports in which injuries occur, and fear of student injuries is of course an appropriate concern for administrators, school boards, parents and teachers. I think that in the case of rough and tumble, there is also fear that boys will take the roughness too far; in some cases, general discomfort with the way that boys work things out and fear that this kind of play looks a lot like bullying (or might look that way to others). To the contrary, true rough and tumble play is, at heart, play: you know it's happening in the right way if the contestants are playful. They're laughing, they can meet each other eye to eye, and there should be flexibility and frequent reversal of winning and losing.

It has been my experience that both gymnastics and rough and tumble wrestling games can be part of a relatively safe elementary gym program, and should be started right from grade one so that the right culture of playful competition can be built over time. These interrelated categories of movement are vital ingredients for any school program that aspires to meet the deepest developmental needs of young human beings. Bringing these ingredients back, in a thoughtful, step-by-step way, will produce a number of benefits: strengthening academic readiness in general; reducing the incidence of learning challenges in the areas of attention/focus and numeracy; and deepening social-intelligence foundations.

As a plus, they can both also contribute mightily to students' athletic foundations. While not many boys go on to pursue gymnastics in adolescence or beyond, the positional and postural control built up by either gender through elementary gymnastics transfer readily to skateboarding, snowboarding, diving, and other more-popular activities. Similarly, although only a minority of boys (and a few girls) will pursue wrestling in high school or beyond, the basics built up through rough and tumble can transfer to all contact sports like football or lacrosse, to semi-contact sports like soccer and basketball… and to all arenas of life in which there is a test of wills, a need for always thinking one move ahead, and real awareness of one's own strengths and vulnerabilities.

By starting a progressive program for these two "bookend" sports in first grade, a culture of safe and playful engagement can be created and nurtured. The Appendix references many resources for such activities; gym teaching manuals from the 20th century are a treasure trove of playful, healthy ways to swing the play pendulum back to the middle.

Parallels in Academic and Athletic Development

Pioneering educators Jean Piaget, Lev Vygotsky, and many others since, have emphasized the tremendous importance of play and movement in the growth of cognitive as well as psychomotor development. Thus, age-appropriate movement programs are a necessary and effective approach for building students' awareness of themselves and the world.

Marie R. Mullan brought clarity to the question of what types of movement are "age-appropriate" and will fit the bill as dual-purpose tools for both academic and athletic growth. In *Child's Play and Play Therapy*, her exposition of movement stages in youth neatly parallels the basic ideas about childhood development that are the foundations for the hundreds of Waldorf schools all around the world.[51]

The following table shows that during the "Goodness" phase of Waldorf education young children are integrating reflexive movements and then starting the years-long progression from simple locomotion to skilled athletic capacities. In the youngest phase, movement stability is a key gateway to continued refinement of movement capacities. At the same time, language skill-building consists primarily of listening, speaking and vocabulary building; numeracy education needs to focus on counting and pattern recognition of physical objects.

During the "Beauty" phase of Waldorf education, those general, toddler-like activities such as striking objects, digging, etc., are transformed to become much more purposeful: now children are ready for, and seek out, movement activities with a more defined result. In parallel, they are ready to learn how certain combinations of lines and curves become letters, sounds, words, sentences and stories; and how certain other combinations of lines and curves represent number qualities and possibilities and can be applied to life experiences.

Foundations for Student Capacities and Readiness

A Timeline of Psychomotor Development – learning to move with control and efficiency through space and time					
Age (years)	**Prebirth to 2**	**2 to 7**	**7 to 10**	**11 to 13**	**14 and beyond**
Stage	GOODNESS		BEAUTY		TRUTH
	Birth of physical body. Standing and speaking.	Completion of early childhood development	Forces freed for picture thinking. "Nine-year change" = beginning of self-awareness & judgement.		Forces freed for critical thinking.
Qualities	Timeless...Prompt Lost in space..At home in space Subjective/non-literal..Objective/literal Imitation ....Responsibility Dependent..Independent Right brain..Left brain Nonsocial...Social Play..Athletics Nondirectional..Precision Flexible rules..Inflexible rules				
Phase of Motor Development	Rudimentary movement: reflexive movements are subcortically controlled. Mastering above/below	Fundamental movement abilities. Mastering forward/back	General movement abilities Mastering left/right	Specific movement abilities	Specialized movement abilities
Stability (postural and positional control)	Sitting and standing.	Riding a bicycle, sledding, swings & slides.	Tree climbing, gymnastics, swimming.	Sport skills and low-competitive games with sport elements ("playing at sport").	Team and individual sports.
Locomotor	Creeping, crawling, walking.	Running, roughhousing, exploration.	Tag, circle games and dances.		
Manipulative (gross and fine motor skills)	Reach, grasp, release.	Digging, throwing and catching, play with toys.	Chores. Beginning sport skills.		
Stamina and Strength (physical development)	These two physical aspects will be naturally developed through childhood work and play activities. Direct development of stamina and strength through specialized workout activities should not begin until the early teen years because they bring in premature awareness at the expense of imaginative play and work.				Conscious building of stamina and strength can begin in at this stage.

Development of capacities needed for both academic and athletic progress.
Adapted from Motor Development and Children's Play *by Marie M. Mullen.*

Finally, when the students enter adolescence, they are emotionally ripe to explore what is true and what is false in the world at large, and perhaps especially so in their parents and teachers. (Unfortunately for parents and teachers, the development of critical thinking begins with an emphasis on critical.) Waldorf educators call this the "Truth" stage, in which students are ready for a big leap with grammar, syntax, complicated mathematical rules....and for true competitive athletics with specialized skills and precise and complicated rules.

Summary

During the early years, a child is working to take up her inherited physical body and consolidate the multitude of factors that contribute to harmonious integration. Through this all-important process, the bodily inheritance can be reshaped and will become the bearer of her own ego, prepared for the life lessons that await. Modern education puts considerable emphasis on the daily, even minute-by-minute acquisition and recall of facts. But while facts can generally be learned at any age, after the tenth year it is very difficult to complete the steps in the developmental constellation addressed in this section.

Secondary psychological scars will almost certainly grow in a young student whose physiologic readiness leaves her in limbo as the academics march on. Because of this reality, the classroom and play space activities in the next section are at least as important as anything else a teacher in kindergarten or the lower grades can present.

All of the above keys to development can be tied together under the umbrella heading of Postural Control, referring not only to physical posture, but also to one's way of being — stance — in the world. The following wonderful words of wisdom from Audrey McAllen get right to the heart of observing and of helping the symphony of the senses, as well as the balance between inner and outer:

The postural system, what's that? Standing and sitting properly? Surely this is for the gym and eurythmy teachers, nothing to do with me; I'm a class teacher.

But it is for the class teacher. Quietly over the last three decades, neuropsychologists, as well as occupational and physical therapists, have studied the causes for the crop of hindrances that stand in the way of learning.... When higher levels of the brain are forced to enter into action in order to maintain posture, learning possibilities decrease. In other words, the formative forces at work on the body during the first seven years have not been freed from their organic task in order to become usable for thinking and imagination.

... [Development of the postural system] is a process of ego activity metamorphosing to a higher level ... The senses of the postural system [self-movement and balance] should be integrated by about the age of three. This is the time at which the ego of the child manifests its first stage of coming into consciousness with the possibility of saying "I", so we see how deeply these senses are related to ego development.

...If this very complicated system is not properly integrated, then what the child learns does not go into the subconscious, i.e., into the ethereal body, to mature and be available for recall. Learning is then only taken into the areas of the brain which respond to short-term memory. This means the child has to constantly relearn the same things day after day; thus the contents of the lessons do not mature into faculty.[52]

Audrey McAllen, Sally Goddard-Blythe, as well as many other researchers, consistently state that purposeful balance and posture are basic for the use of such instruments as pencils, brushes and rulers.

3 Exercises and Activities for Strengthening the Whole Class

Introduction

The following exercises and activities are highly recommended as part of a primary grades teacher's repertoire of ways to help all students be ready to do their best, every day. Experience has shown that students who do these activities are able to move ahead more solidly. Benefits of these exercises—if done regularly and with the indicated rhythm—include:

- Foundations for literacy – developmental capacities for all aspects of language.
- Foundations for numeracy the math/logical and spatial intelligences in motion.
- Readiness for deskwork enhancing focus and attention. Setting the stage for harmonious receptivity to new material.
- Bodily/kinesthetic and spatial integration.
- Strengthening the will.
- Class social cohesion and teamwork.

Many of the activities in this section are adapted from either *The Extra Lesson* or *Take Time*. (And as previously noted, the authors of *Take Time* credit *The Extra Lesson* as a foundation for their work.)

When Audrey McAllen wrote the first edition of *The Extra Lesson* in the early 1970s, there were still many active in the Waldorf movement who belonged to what I've called "the second circle from the sun": people who had known and learned from colleagues and students of Rudolf Steiner himself. And it seems to me (and to many teachers today with whom I've discussed this) that at the time she wrote her first edition, Ms. McAllen must have been able to assume that the majority of her audience would have a level of anthroposophic immersion such that she would not need to explain the spiritual scientific reasons for her presentations of the exercises.

For instance, why do the spirals go in certain directions, why are some to be done sitting and others standing, why are certain colors given for certain paintings, what are the deeper reasons for the directions of movement in the drawings and paintings?

Thankfully, in 2007, Joep Eikenboom provided a very detailed book, *Foundations of the Extra Lesson*,[53] that illuminates all these questions from the anthroposophic perspective. For Waldorf remedial teachers today, this monumental effort on his part is thus an invaluable companion to Audrey McAllen's book. However, I think it is fair and right to suggest that the whole-class exercises highlighted in the following pages of this section can be done with complete integrity by general-education Waldorf teachers, even if they have not yet read Eikenboom's book and are still in some ways unaware of the reasons for the directions in McAllen's, but if (and only if) they respectfully adhere to a literal reading of those indications and forge ahead with enthusiasm.

An expanded school program

In addition to helping you widen the horizons of what developmental activities all the students in your own class receive, I hope this book will also inspire your school as a whole to expand its program, to open up to new ideas about time and teaching resources. Here is the full spectrum of classes and services we developed for the grades at Aurora Waldorf:

- Games/Gym — two periods a week in primary grades; 6 periods a week in middle school.
- Tumbling — one (additional) period in lower school. Tumbling/Circus Arts are continued in middle school within the above 6 periods.
- Enrichment Class — one period a week of movement, drawing and painting based on *The Extra Lesson* and related sources, in grades 1, 2 and 3.
- Inservices for Class Teachers — time is budgeted for the Extra Lesson teacher to go into morning main lessons and inservice the whole-class activities described in this section.

Having three or more games/gym and tumbling classes does not increase the teaching budget because in almost all cases two (separate) grades are combined, i.e., 1 with 2, 3 with 4, etc.

Finally, if a lot of the activities in this section are new to you and you start to feel 'repertoire overload', not to worry! Section 4 provides a step-by-step approach, and a variety of ways to share the load with other teachers.

Foundations for Developmental Movement

Jumping Rope

Every Monday morning at my school, our first graders gather in the gym with their 8th-grade buddies to learn to jump rope. Jumping with long ropes and partners, skipping with individual ropes, two-in-a-rope, the "big-little hop," frontwards, backward, jumping tricks, and more! What better way to begin shedding the carry-over from weekend life and be poised for the new week school learning?

Jumping rope is such a popular childhood pastime all around the world that it may escape attention just how meaningful it can be in the life of growing children and in a school's academic program. Let's look at it through the lenses of both anthroposophy and modern science. Olive Whicher presented the following:

> Man reaches towards the stars; through bodily movement he can feel himself widened and expanded, as though his fingers could feel the distant horizon, as though as a physical-spiritual being he could permeate limitless space. But more, the most essential thing was this: the power for movement springs not only from within the body; from the world-circumference also comes the force whereby the body is held erect and enabled to move. The Will is asleep in the human body, glowing like a smoldering fire in the darkness. Left to itself it makes no movement, or at most only uncontrolled twitching of the limbs. Noble movement is called forth, through the light of consciousness, from the world surrounding man. It is well to reflect, for example, on how the small child is first called to his feet and, standing erect, makes his first steps into the beckoning world about him, where exciting shapes, cools, human faces all ask to be reached and touched by little outstretched hands.
>
> Indeed, throughout conscious life we are continually being called to activity and movement by the tasks which lie within our destiny in the world and among the human beings around us. The Will, hidden and secret, is related to the centre of the Earth, while the world of Light—the world perceptible to the senses—is spread around man and come to meet him from the wide horizons of space. The Thinking-Sensing human being can live in a world of wide horizons. And human movement—dynamic, purposeful movement, spiritual as well as physical—is brought about not one-sidedly by compulsion from either world, but through the balanced interplay of both.

Two kinds of forces, springing from two different worlds, give man the possibility to stand erect and rejoice in his freedom of movement. They are the centric, earthly forces on the one hand, and, on the other, forces of quite opposite kind and quality, which we may call peripheral forces. In the early chapters of their book *Fundamentals of Therapy,* Rudolf Steiner and Ita Wegman describe how these peripheral forces work inward from the wide distances of universal space towards the living entities on earth. In contrast to the gravitational forces of the Earth, which work between point-centres, we must learn to know and understand these other forces, carried plane upon plane, inward from world-horizons. Inasmuch as any earthly substance is endowed with life, these are forces which raise it upward — plant substance, incarnate substance-overcoming gravity. These are cosmic, ethereal forces.

Thus man needs the power of the earthly, gravitational forces: the domain of the Seraphim, Cherubim and Thrones. He needs also the cosmic, peripheral forces, which, from above, bear him upward, and here the Second Hierarchy work-spirits of Form (Exusiai), Spirits of Movement (Dynameis), Spirits of Wisdom (Kyriotetes). Man lives and moves in the dynamic interplay of these great contrasting powers.[54]

I can add two points to the above background regarding the necessity of making a grade-by-grade progression of jump rope skills and lessons. 1. It's an outbreath activity; thus, it sets the stage for inbreath learning. 2. The rhythm of the double hop mirrors the rhythm of the heart, strengthening the child's life sense and will forces. This is why jumping rope in early childhood and the lower grades should always be done with a "big-little" double-hop jump, i.e., not with a single-hop speed rope

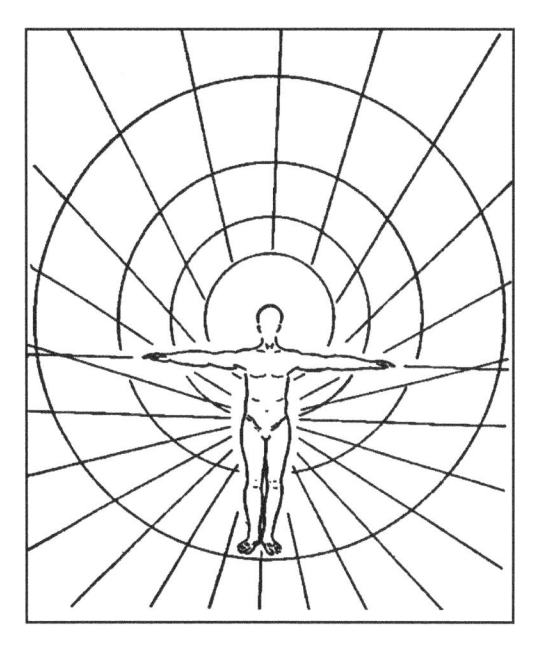

Two kinds of forces, springing from two different worlds, give man the possibility to stand erect and rejoice in his freedom of movement. – Olive Whicher

technique. Save this for the years when you hope to see a burst of worldly awakening begin.

The perfect exercise

For any age, jumping rope checks almost every box as a workout regimen. It's cardio. Upper body. Lower body. Balance. Easier on the knees than running on pavement. Terrific for interval training. Raises body temperature and pulse. Helps your amygdala calm down so you can refocus. And since it's been proven that students need exercise breaks throughout the academic day, jumping rope checks the box for something that can be done in a short amount of time with almost no logistical considerations: just ropes and space, and you're good to go.

The internet is a rich source of what can be done with jump rope tricks and skill building; a youtube video is worth a thousand words in this regard. In the following, long rope refers to a rope turned by two partners.

Recommended skills progression for Grade 1

A. Hopping over a swaying long rope until mastery of hopping in time. When rhythm and big-little hop are well-establish, begin swinging rope overhead. Use Verse 1 or 2 below, or similar.

B. Continued practice with a long rope until rhythm is pretty well mastered. Begin to use verses like #2 and 3 below.

C. Begin with single rope, by walking and swinging it over as while walking/stepping through. Progress to ability to continuously forward step around the room or play area.

D. Single rope forward jumping (*feet together*).

E. Single rope backward jumping.

F. More advanced long rope tricks — use verses like #4 below. Also introduce choral speaking of verses while jumping.

Goals by grade

First Grade. Cross jump rope; begin double dutch; two in a hoop.

Third Grade. Single rope tricks; at least half of class can double dutch.

Fourth Grade. Mastery of above. Double-hop rhythm mostly maintained through grade 4.

Fifth Grade. Continue with above but begin single-hop.

Sixth Grade through 8. All of the above plus introduce interval cardio sessions (e.g., 90 second intervals with students striving for 70 seconds jumping and 20 second rest). School circus performances include double dutch tricks.

Observe/remediate

- Sequencing — an 8 year old should know the seasons, and the months of the year in order; and be able to count by twos backward from 24 while jumping rope.
- Fine Motor Control — carefully observe speech while jumping.
- Movement stages — children still in trunk stage will spin the individual rope asymmetrically.

Sample verses

Back and forth the rope does swing
Can you do the jump rope thing?
Hop your feet and count your toes
Now you're ready and over it goes!
1… 2… 3… 4… etc.

Marco Polo was a tiny old man (*rope swaying*)
He sailed the ocean in an old tin can
The winds got breezy, old Marco got queasy
One big wave and over he went! (*rope over*)

Cinderella dressed in yellow,
Went upstairs to kiss a fellow
  (*turn sideways and make climbing steps*)
By mistake she kissed a snake, (*turn back*)
How many doctors did it take?
1… 2… 3… 4… etc.
  (*speed up rope after a few more turns*)
Dutch boy, Dutch boy,
Dressed in blue.
Show me the things you like to do
Salute the captain (*salute*)
Bow to the Queen (*bow*)
Climb on board the submarine
  (*turn parallel to rope and step up*)

Teddy Bear, Teddy Bear, turn around,
Teddy Bear, Teddy Bear, touch the ground
Teddy Bear, Teddy Bear, show your shoe
Teddy Bear, Teddy Bear, that will do!
Teddy Bear, Teddy Bear, climb the stairs
Teddy Bear, Teddy Bear, say your prayers
Teddy Bear, Teddy Bear, turn out the lights
  (*pantomime pulling cord*)
Teddy Bear, Teddy Bear, say good-night!
  (*wave and jump out from rope*)

Recommended Equipment

For individual ropes, jumpers need a rope that easily reaches their armpits when standing on the middle of the rope. A supply of good ropes for the whole school can be made for minimal cost by getting four or five colors of 100 foot coils of 3/8 inch diamond braided rope, and rolls of colored waterproof plastic tape from a home improvement store.

With these supplies, you can create color-coded lengths, such as cut the blue rope into lengths for 1st grade, green for 2nd and smaller 3rd graders, etc. If you tape around for about 3 inches where you're going to cut before you cut, and then cut in the middle of the 3 inches, it saves time and fraying.

The 3/8 inch rope is usable but not optimum for longer ropes in grades 1 and 2; a step up in weight is better.

Copper Rod Exercises
Waking Up to Learning

Copper rod exercises wake children up to learning. They can serve the developmental needs of children in first through eighth grades (and beyond):

- Physiology that supports writing and reading — radius and ulna
- Direction, rhythm and sequencing — related to body geography, spatial awareness, math
- Proprioception and balance — one of the "Multiple Intelligences"
- Working with anticipation; social skills

> **Sources:** *The Extra Lesson*, Eurythmists, and Spacial Dynamics

Materials: Plumbing supply and home improvement outlets carry eight foot lengths of 5/8" copper pipe, and plastic caps to cover the ends (use a little glue to keep them in place). Use 32 inch length rods for first through third grade, 36 inch lengths for older grades.

Setting: a gym, a resource type room with carpeting, or a classroom with desks pulled out of the way.

Mood: Copper rods are upright and dignified, meant to set a mood of noble readiness. So, don't allow them to be in any other posture (i.e., the almost inevitable sword fighting). "NO Free Play" — and free play is anything the teacher doesn't give as an activity. Check your own presence and posture frequently (remembering our two posture exercises for adults). Be prepared with a sequence of activities, but also be prepared to shorten it if the class cannot hold the mood. I strive to uphold the axiom that children will best do what I'm "hoping" if I have the strength to resist "asking." This is a class that needs to be quiet (falling rods make enough noise) and well held, using your example of proper technique for imitation. Project your physical presence, and use few, if any, verbal directions. If there is any misbehavior, take away the rod and have the student sit out to watch for the remainder of the exercises.

Beginning — for every age

Arrange the class in rows or a circle, with at least one foot of clearance between finger tips (more is preferable). Teacher (perhaps with a well-behaved helper) goes to each student and tosses a rod with upright toss. (Rod must remain in vertical orientation throughout toss and catch.) Student then takes rod and balances it on head. To distribute the rods, wait for proper mood and posture, and require precise imitation of your methods. Eye contact and arch of throw are important. Observe the catch: does the student duck or shy away from the throw?

Balanced stepping with rod on head. Verse is good up to age 9. Older children can be tasked to turn once around.

> I lift my leg, I stretch my leg,
> I plant it firm and light.
> I lift again, I stretch again,
>   my pace exactly right.
> With care I go, so grand and slow,
> I move just like a stork.
> My eyes are bright, my head upright,
>   pride is in my walk.

Head-balance drop to hands in front (later hands catch in back): Extend arms at shoulder width, hands palms-up; wait for all to imitate, then drop rod to hands. Now class is ready for focused activities.

Arm and hand exercises

All except #8 and #9 can be done from grade 1 on.

1. Rod rolling on arms: A very important developmental exercise for 1st and 2nd grade (can continue into 3rd grade without the song). With arms outstretched in front, slowly roll the rod to the finger tips, and then back to the neck. Notice if there are children who have trouble keeping their palms "sunny side up" (delayed development of radius and ulna) and quietly, indirectly encourage this awakening. Use "Skye Boat Song"[55] or "Row, row, row your boat."

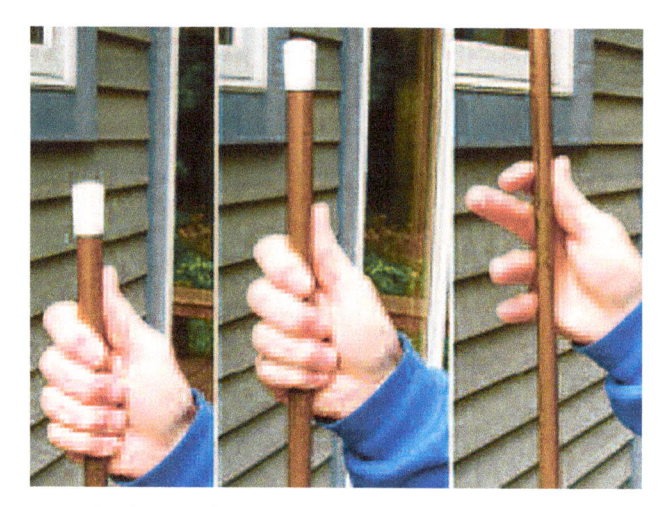

Tree Climbing with palmar grip

Tree Climbing with pencil grip

Exercises and Activities for Strengthening the Whole Class   65

2. Over and under the hands: Catch from palm to back of hand (and/or snatch on way down) using a nursery rhyme or verse for beat.

3. Finger Finder: both hands on top of the rod, then under the rod; with each syllable, successively lift indexes, middles, rings and pinkies (same order both over and under!).

Verse: Pep/per and salt ... Pep/per and salt ... Over and under and ne'er a fault. Pepper and salt.

4. Tree Climbing: exercises (pictured): Do both pencil and palmar grips, and (all students) do both left and right hands. Remind: "no tossies, sidies, pushies" to deter shortcuts.

5. Copper Rod Crocodile: (similar to Tree Climb, but in horizontal). Rod held with pencil grip near right end of rod, by right hand, horizontal in front at chest level. Hand "chews" along rod, moving it along to the right. Then repeat with left hand.

6. Stirring the Soup: suspending the rod by holding one end, make a slow stirring motion. Teacher calls on students to list a soup ingredient. (Don't call on the kids whose ingredients will be too creative!) Should be done with both pencil and palmar grips.

7. Drop-Catch: Grasp rod with palmar grip vertical near bottom end, then open hand so it drops straight down; try to snatch it just at the top tip, but without it falling away. Repeat with non-dominant hand.

8. Rhythmic Tossing, individual (starting in grade 2) or partner (starting in grade 3 or 4): Students recite verse in short-short-long rhythm, while (a) tossing side to side with a pause on the long beat; or (b) tossing across to a partner on the long beat. Rods remain in the vertical position for this to be safe.

Brave and true, I will be,
Each kind word, sets me free,
Each kind deed, makes me strong,
I will fight, for the right,
I will conquer the wrong. 1, 2, 3....

Grades 3 and up can also use the above for rhythmic recitation of the times tables. In middle school grades, this same activity can be made quite challenging by putting together two pairs of children who have mastered tossing across: one pair tosses on short-short-long and the other tosses on long-short short.

9. Rod 'Juggling' with a partner: one partner has two rods, and will make all throws to the same side (i.e. always passing the rod in right hand straight to partner's left hand, always passing the rod in left hand to partner's right hand). The other partner will always have one rod and will throw across (right to partner right, left to partner left).

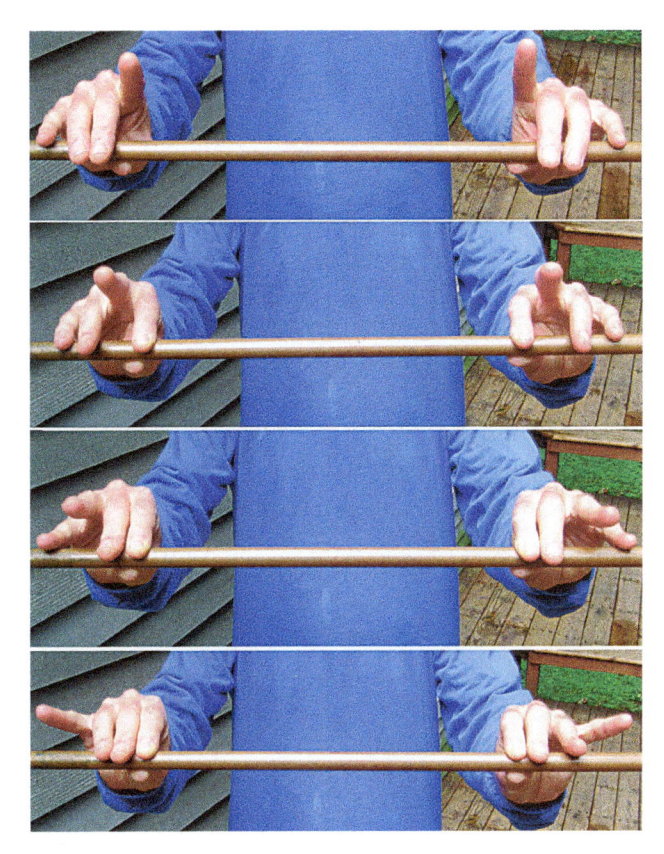

Finger Finder

To strengthen posture, focus and sequencing from grade 3 and up:

Marching speaking memory rods: Marching forward with rod held vertically in front (right hand on top), then backward with rod held behind back vertically along spine, or horizontally along shoulders (for posture). One step per number or beat. Examples:
- "Mary had a little lamb" poem forward and then backward, one step per word;
- Times tables or alphabet forward and back;
- Concentration sequence with times table, stepping forward four numbers, then three back, then four forward, etc. — e.g. 7-14-21-28, 28-21-14; 14-21-28-35…

Foot and floor exercises

All except #5 can be done from grade 1 on.

Most of these must be done on carpet or tumbling mats, in bare feet. Waking up the feet brings wakeful thinking. Also, tension in the hands can be released through foot exercises.

1. Jack and Jill Jumping sequence (up through 3rd or 4th grade.) While making one hop per word: (a) Begin standing behind rod, hop over and back with feet together; (b) Alternate feet front and back, i.e., front scissor steps; (c) Set rod to right side, hop feet together side to side; (c) Stand astride rod and hop with crossing scissor jumps, alternating right foot front, left foot front. Take note of children who can't do these without significantly turning their torsos.

2. Stepping Rhythm #1: "Jack be nimble…" stepping. Repeat several times for front and back.

3. Stepping Rhythm #2: vary pace and voice.
Stepping over stepping stones, 1,2,3. [Hold out 1, 2, 3 fingers with both hands]
Stepping over stepping stones, just like me. [point to self]
The river's very fast, [eurythmy "F" gesture] *and the river's very wide,* [arms/hands wide]
And we're stepping over stepping stones to reach the other side. [hop back feet together]

4. Snails Journey: very slowly inching over rod with bare feet. A real waker-upper!

5. Foot Toss to Hands: balance middle of rod over foot, and use foot to toss rod up to hands (rod should remain horizontal).

Additional balance games

Circle Pass (grade 3 and up): Students in a circle with right pointer finger on rod held vertical on floor. Teacher says "ready set go!" Each student steps to next rod (no leadoffs!) Make more difficult by increasing size of circle or having them step to second rod.

Drawing a Circle (grade 4 and up): grip the rod between big toe and next toe, balance on other foot, and trace a circle.

Rod Vertical Balance (5th grade): on palm or finger tip. This requires a lot of space, and students who can be trusted to not race around and collide with others.

Collecting the Rods

Remember that the mood set here can affect the mood at the beginning of the next session.

Reverse the beginning: balanced on head to drop to arms to right hand throw to teacher's right hand.

Circle Trace: students stand face left in wide circle, right hands holding rods at a downward angle, tips to the floor pointing to the center of the circle. Then all in unison inch toward the center point, making sure no one's first or lagging. When the rod tips converge at the, hands raise rods to vertical and teacher wraps arms around the stack to collect.

There are many more ways to use rods but the above is a good starter repertoire. Any verse or poem that fits can be chosen; start with old favorites so that you don't have to worry about memory. Good luck and have fun!

....

A good source for plugs that cap the ends flush, is mocap.com part #RN5/8CBK1

Crawlasthenics and Zoorobics

How much creeping and crawling does it take to help organize a child for school and life? Many child development specialists believe that tens of thousands (perhaps as many as 50,000) crawling-type steps are needed to properly myelinate the brain for academic readiness. Given today's popularity of strollers, walkers, baby bouncers, backpacks, etc., many young children will not have taken nearly that many crawling steps before entering kindergarten.

Early movement patterns and reflexes are imprinted in utero, and they assist during the birth process. During infancy they initiate protective movements and rudimentary beginnings of coordination. Many of these patterns and reflexes are meant to become integrated during the first year, then to be replaced by new, more developed abilities which will gradually progress, through imitation of gesture, into independent movement by about age seven. When the early movement patterns are not resolved or integrated in the appropriate manner and time, then the movements of an earlier stage need to be recapitulated and practiced.

In her book *If Kids Just Came with Instruction Sheets*,[56] award-winning author and lecturer Svea J. Gold documents cases where a program of crawling for children beyond normal crawling age has alleviated learning barriers including attention deficit problems. 'Mainstream' testimony to the wisdom of these developmental movements for school age children can also be found in many elementary school gym teaching textbooks from the first half of the 20th century, where they appear as tumbling agility drills, relay races and game activities.

The best of these books I have found is *Stunts and Tumbling for Girls* by Virginia Lee Horne.[57] This book, unfortunately long out of print, is the foundation for 90% of the tumbling class at Aurora Waldorf, and the source of many exercises with pictures below.

When does a child who still has reflexes or behaviors that show a need to continue with developmental movement grow "too old" to do these activities? Certainly not before nine or ten years old, and you might be surprised how older children will react pleasantly when an adult gives 'permission' for a period of childishness in a play setting.

Beyond this, many of the same movement patterns are called forth in swimming, including the wisely named "crawl stroke."

Not only that—even for children with no developmental delays, the athletic foundations developed by a steady diet of mat agilities will absolutely translate into the spatial orientation and motor skills needed in any and all future sports pursuits.

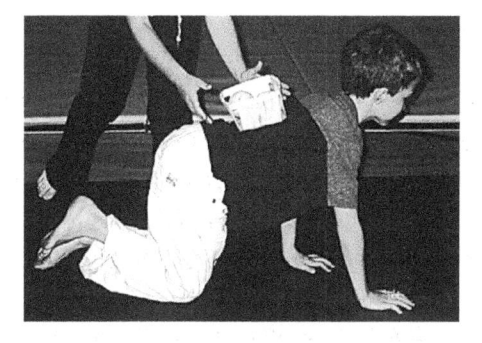

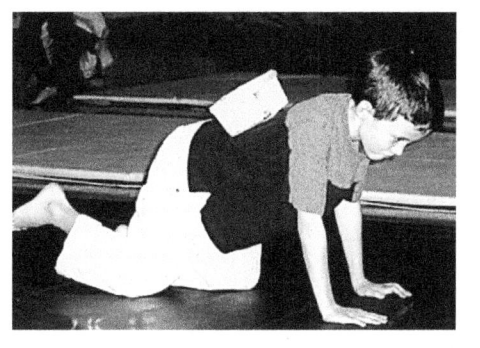

Sources: *The Extra Lesson;* AHE Publications; *If Kids Just Came with Instruction Sheets!*; *Stunts and Tumbling for Girls*; *Movement Journeys and Circle Adventures.*[58]

Materials: Tumbling mats; or if not available, a carpeted area can be used for many but not all, depending on the age/size of students. (Sometimes older and heavier children experience knee pain when creeping on carpet.) Some activities use common materials such as blocks, balls, marbles, cards, etc.

Setting: Gym or large play space; outdoors on mats in warmer climes.

Mood: The imagination of a "zoo" is suggested to enliven many of the exercises. Best results are obtained when the child "exercises the animals" for 15 minutes several times a week over a number of months. Alternating between the animals each session gives some variety. You almost cannot do these games too often!

"Baby crawling" activities

To enliven the continuation of 'just plain crawling', the following games are some of the many possibilities. See what you can add! They are appropriate for toddlers to age nine. All the games are done in a creeping position on the hands and knees. Do not immediately correct the child's movement, but do observe and then intervene after a while when necessary. Smoothness of movement: do you see chaos or lethargy? Position of hands, knees and feet: turned in or out? Does the head move? Are hands clenched or is the child up on the fingers? Are feet off the ground? How high? Does the child talk, laugh, make noises? Fatigue level: can the child participate fully for five minutes or is it less? Afterward does the child exhibit exaggerated emotion: silliness, anger, or withdrawal?

BLOCK BUILDING: Blocks are placed at one end of the room, students at the other. Child goes back and forth to get blocks. This can be a race or with the goal to build a structure.

RACE FOR OBJECTS: (Need a group of 3-5 small unbreakable objects) one person throws them to the other end of the room and parent and child race after them to see who can get the most first. Prizes may be necessary for the winners.

TREASURE HUNT: (Perhaps food such as dried apricots, slices of carrot, etc.) Food is hidden in various places around the room and the children creep around to find them. Teacher occasionally says "getting warmer" or "getting colder".

PUPPIES AND WOLVES TAG: Depending on group size, one or more students are chosen to be wolves; the rest are puppies. All must stay creeping on hands and knees. Any puppies that the wolf tags go into the "puppy pound" sit-out area.

TENT MAKING: Much creeping results from free play revolving around a tent made in the Early Childhood room with chairs and a blanket.

RED LIGHT, GREEN LIGHT RACE: Traditional game, but played with crawling toward a goal line. When teacher calls "green light" children may advance; on "red light" they must halt and hold a balance pose such as balanced on one hand and knee, plop to the mat, etc.

POTATO RACE: Roll the potato (or a ball) with the nose.

MAIL DELIVERY: Place a beanbag or a small box "from the post office" on each student's back and have them deliver it to a destination. (As a race, or not.)

FORWARD, BACKWARD AND SIDEWARD RELAYS: Relay races are a great way to maintain enthusiasm for crawling activities all the way through the lower grades.

A trip to the zoo, Part 1

The following exercises and agilities are meant to be done in a quiet way at a measured pace, and can be done in a smaller space. They may be introduced, as noted, with the imagination of a trip to the zoo, or through the woods, to the beach, etc.

BEAUTIFUL BUTTERFLY: Begin on hands and knees; with the eyes carefully following the active hand, bring the right hand slowly backward, upwards in a high arc and far forward, placing the hand on the floor. The right knee is then brought forward and placed next to the hand. Repeat with the left hand and knee, keeping the hips centered (i.e. without sitting onto opposite ankle). This exercise can be enhanced by tying a piece of red yarn in a bow knot on the child's right index finger and a blue one on the left.

BOOKS OPEN, BOOKS CLOSED: Students lie supine with arms stretched parallel to mat (like open books). On "books closed" signal, they slowly 'jackknife' up, legs straight and arms/torso in a straight line. Then on "books open" they slowly unfold back to supine. (This is identical with a gymnastic V-sit.)

EGG SIT: Sit on the floor, knees bent close to the chest. Grasp right toes with right hand and left toes with left hand. Rock back on buttocks. Extend both legs. Keep firm grasp with hands; hold extended legs in air. Balance in this position. To descend, rock forward, bend knees and drop feet to floor.

FROZEN FROG: Lying in a prone position, head to the right, right arm and knee bent forward; very slowly, one movement at a time: turn head to the left, straighten the right arm down along the side, straighten the right leg (now flat on the stomach), bend the left leg forward, bend the left arm forward (now mirror of original position). Slowly repeat the same sequence back to the other side. Three times each side. Little or no forward movement should result. Note: The above "frog" movements also appear in many Occupational Therapy manuals under the heading of "lizard" crawls.

FUNNY FISH: Lying on stomach with chin on floor, arms relaxed beside the body, legs straight together, the child slowly bends sideways at the waist, lifting and turning the head to look at the feet. Sliding torso first to one side, then to the other. Repeat several times.

POTATO BUG: Lie face down on mat or rug. Bend knees, arch back, reach back to grasp feet. Pull hard on the feet to lift the head and shoulders off floor. Rock forward onto chest and back onto thighs. Adult may need to gently help child begin rocking motion.

ROLY-POLY HEDGEHOG: Sit with feet to buttocks, knees curled up to chest and held with hands clasped around shins (as in picture for Egg Sit, but in a rounder ball). Begin a rocking forward and back motion, rocking each time all the way from top of back to heels touching and back again. This is a very diagnostic exercise for postural control. A six year old should be able to maintain posture and balance for at least eight repetitions.

SOARING EAGLE: Lie on the floor face down, then the legs are lifted with only slight bend of knees, and feet together. The arms are bent at the elbows, hands on the shoulders and the head is raised off the floor so that the child is only resting on his/her abdomen. Child balances or rocks on stomach for the duration of a poem or counting to ten. "Flying eagle in the sky… Holds his tail so straight and high… His pointed wings are strong… And guide him as he flies along."

SQUASH!: Students set up in pushup position (arms, legs and backs straight). When teacher shouts something like "ouch!", or "oof!" students briskly extend arms and legs, and collapse to the mat. (Must be done on mats or soft landing surface.)

SPEEDY FROG: On the stomach, chest down, head up. Move legs and arms to crawl forward, pushing off with the feet and pulling with the hands and arms. (Basically, an army crawl.) This is done 'correctly' when child crawls cross-laterally with full involvement of hands and feet, including pushing off with toes.

TADPOLE: Same position as Funny Fish, but wriggle forward with hands kept by side and feet together.

TADPOLE TURNING INTO FROG: Lie in a prone position, arms crossed behind the back, now wriggle forward with the help of legs and feet, including toes. (Avoid for girls over nine years old.)

A trip to the zoo, Part 2

The following exercises and agilities require space for forward motion and in most cases work well as relay races, perfect for when some more focused zoo work has been completed and you're ready to "take off the brakes" and switch to more boisterous play.

BABY FROG HOP: Take a squat position, feet pointing slightly outward. Place hands on floor with elbows slightly bent, arms between knees. Take short hops by putting hands just ahead of feet and then bringing feet up to hands.

BABY RACE: Announcing that the next activity is a baby race is almost always received with mirth; give it a try! Baby races can include regular forward crawling, as well as backward baby race, and sidewards baby race the latter two of which demand a surprising amount of motor planning.

BACKWARD INCHWORM: The same starting position as Creepy-Crawly Caterpillar described below, but pulling with the feet (moving in direction of feet).

BIG FROG HOP: As above for Baby Frog Hop, but for each step forward, leap high, fully extending. Go all the way back to squat position at end of each step.

BEAR AND FROG DANCES: Similar to Russian dancing. Start in squat position an rhythmically hop and extend alternating legs to front (Bear Dance) or side to side (Frog Dance).

CAT WALK: Take a front leaning rest position. Keep hands stationary, flex hips and walk or hop the feet up to the hands; then keep the feet stationary and walk hands forward. Keep knees and elbows straight throughout.

CRAB WALK: Take a squat position. Reach back and put both hands flat on the floor without sitting down. Support weight equally with arms and legs. Walk sideways with face up; don't allow hips to sag.

CIRCUS SEAL: Laying on the floor and holding a ball or balls as follows, roll sideways several turns along the floor in one direction and then back in the other direction. Possibilities include: ball held by the hands above the head; ball held between the knees; ball held between the ankles; ball held between the feet; or a combination of these. Alternatively, the seal can wriggle along forward.

CREEPY-CRAWLY CATERPILLAR: Lie on the back with arms across the chest, legs bent, feet on the floor, have the child carefully 'inchworm' his/her way along, pushing with both feet together (moving in direction of head), allowing the back to arch and flatten, then back, pushing with the heels.

DOG WALK: Place hands on floor in front of body, knees and arms slightly bent. Imitate a dog walking and running on all fours. Don't let feet get ahead of hands, or knees touch.

DUCK WALK: Take squat position with feet separated and knees apart. Bend elbows and place hands under armpits for wings; flap wings as steps are taken by swinging leg out to the side without raising hips.

EGG ROLL: Kneel crosswise on mats, legs slightly apart, back rounded. Fold arms, rest elbows on

Exercises and Activities for Strengthening the Whole Class 71

mat in front of knees. Push to the side with arms and knees to start momentum. Roll to the side, on to back, to other side and up to original position. This makes a complete turn. Keep body tightly curled while rolling. Get an equal push from knees and arms. At last moment of contact, push hard from the mat with arms and legs.

ELEPHANT WALK: Standing with feet slightly apart, bend forward at waist, let knees bend slightly. Clasp hands and let arms hang down in imitation of an elephant's trunk. Walk with knees slightly bent, back rounded and arms swinging; try to brush floor with hands.

KANGAROO HOP: Take a squat position, hands in kangaroo position. Spring from the floor as high into the air and as far forward as possible. Land on the feet and immediately let the ankles, knees and hips flex to absorb the landing.

KNEE WALK: Start in kneeling position, torso erect. Grab left ankle or toes with left hand, right ankle or toes with right hand; pull feet up toward backside, lean forward a bit, and hobble along.

LOG ROLL: Take a squat position. Fold arms across chest. Spring from the floor as high into the air and as far forward as possible. Land on the feet and immediately let the ankles, knees and hips flex to absorb the landing.

MOTORBOAT: Same starting position as Creepy-Crawly Caterpillar, but with feet alternating as flat back slides along floor — wood floor would be best. (Sorry, I couldn't think of an animal name for this one.)

PONY RACE: One partner, on hands and knees, is the pony, the other sits on the pony's back as they race to a line and back, and then switch roles. (Often the rider will have feet on the ground helping the effort; don't correct this.)

POP-UP SQUIRREL: Take a squat position, cross arms in front of body. Spring to an erect position, feet astride, weight on heels. At the same time, fling arms out to the side and up to diagonal position above the shoulders. Jump back to starting position and repeat as able.

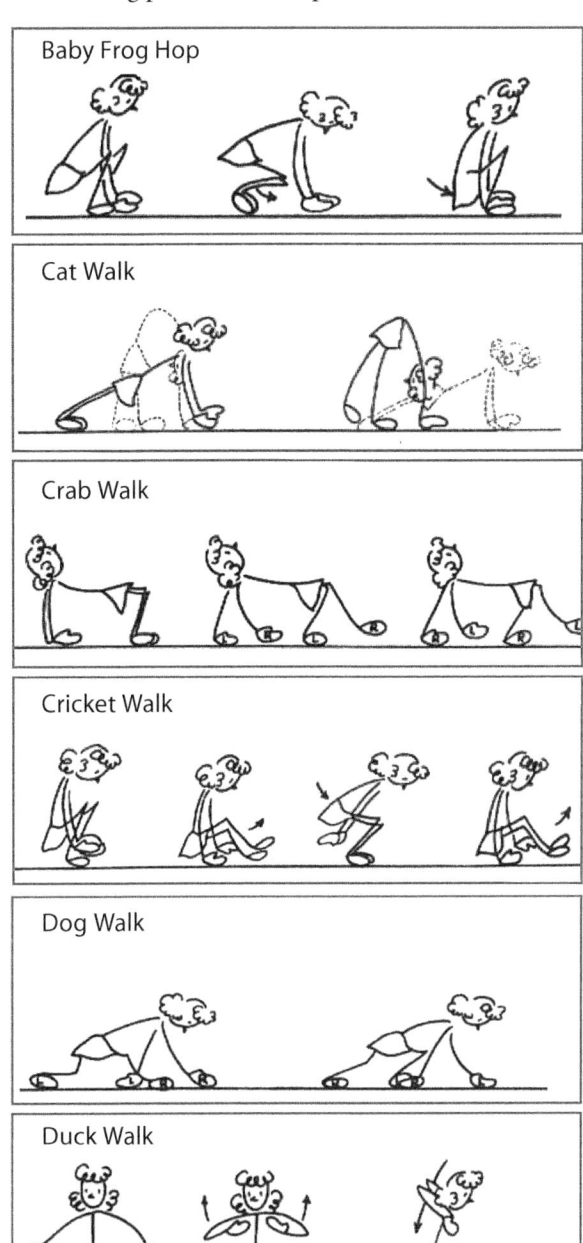

Baby Frog Hop

Cat Walk

Crab Walk

Cricket Walk

Dog Walk

Duck Walk

RABBIT JUMP: Take a squat position, hands on floor in front of feet. Leap forward by giving strong push with feet, lifting hands off floor. Land with weight on hands, and then bring feet up to hands. Within child's limits, stretch out as far as possible.

RING-TAILED LEMUR/ 3-LEGGED RACE: Crawling with one leg continually held up high behind you. Move both hands forward at the same time, taking short hops so that the body is not overbalanced.

SACK OF POTATOES: One child lies on back with the head in the direction of the race or activity, arms are outstretched to partner (standing ready to walk backward) who takes the child's hands or wrists and pulls him along the mat. After reaching a distance destination, they switch roles. To help with the race, remind children that "potato sacks don't have feet."

SLED DOG: 1 gets on all fours at a starting line; 2 is on knees behind him, and takes a firm hold of 1's ankles. They cooperatively enact a dogsled race; 1 crawling along and 2 walking on knees and perhaps shouting "mush you huskies!"

SNIFFING DOG: Crawl along on knees and elbows. This will naturally place the head near the mat. Children may be allowed to bark a little as they go.

SWORDFISH: On a good sliding surface such as a wood floor, lie on the side with the bottom side arm held out straight in front (the sword), with the head held to that arm. Use the other arm and the legs for propulsion.

TUNNEL RACE: Make more or less fair teams of six students or more; each team forms a line facing forward, with about 18 inches of spacing achieved by placing hands on shoulders of next ahead in line. On go signal, the last one in the line drops to hands and knees and crawls through the tunnel; on reaching the front she raises both hands high in the air, signaling for the one now at the back of the line to go. As the race proceeds, the lines need to move backward to maintain spacing and room for the activity.

WALRUS AND SEAL WALKS: Take a prone position. For "Seal," place hands on floor directly under shoulders, fingers to side; for "Walrus," put hands in armpits and elbows on floor. Keep ankles extended, weight on top of toes. Progress forward walking with legs and toes dragging. Remind that neither seals nor walruses have knees or feet.

WHEELBARROW: One child places hands on floor with legs straight; partner behind grasps child's ankles or knees (depending on weight and ability). After reaching a destination, they switch roles.

Little wrestling matches

These activities provide at least a triple bonus: the benefits of rough and tumble play; lots of calming deep pressure to the joints; and a ton of crawling. And fun. For each, allow time for partners to switch roles. Except as noted, all are for age six and up.

Including these types of wrestling games (and there are many others like the ones given here) in the lower grades is crucial to the progression that leads to the wrestling style for the fifth grade pentathlon and then to collegiate style wrestling in middle school. Also, there is no better way for students to learn sportsmanship than through these types of contests in the primary grades.

ANKLE ESCAPE: From the same starting positions as in Sled Dogs, this time 2 tries to prevent 1 from reaching the end line. On the go signal 1 attempts to crawl to the finish line, either by dragging 2 or by escaping from 2's grip. 2 may not stand up.

BACK TO BACK: Partners sit back to back and hook arms at the elbows. They attempt to push opponent back to a goal line. Must keep butt on mat.

BACK TO BACK TEAMS: Two teams of equal size and numbers sit back to back. Each team hooks together at elbows (i.e., not with teammate on each side) and on go signal they attempt to push the entire opposing team back across a line.

BALANCE BEAM BRIDGE: Standing on a low balance beam (no higher than a few inches off the mat or rug), two partners face each other and take right hands; they attempt to pull or push to cause opponent to step off beam and touch mat/rug with one or both feet. If you don't have small balance beams, you can substitute a rope.

BEAR WRESTLING: A raised playing area, and an apron area is needed — can be carpet or mats, depending on age/weight of children. All children crawl around in the bears den (raised playing area) like bears; they must stay on all fours. They try to push any/all other bears out of the forest (onto the non-playing area) using only their shoulders or hips. The playing should be large enough so that at the beginning the space will allow a little free roaming but not a speed-crawling charge. This could probably be played outdoors if you want to take a few mats out there.

BEAR TUG OF WAR: Partners kneel, facing each other across a line. They hold each others' lower arms, say ready-set-go, then try to pull opponent to their side of the line (must stay on knees).

DINOSAUR WRESTLING: Students spread out around playing area, stand with feet at shoulder width, bend down and get a firm grip on ankles by reaching hands between the legs from the front and continuing back so that wrists are behind achilles and fingers are wrapper around outside of ankles. On go, they stomp around, attempting to eliminate others from the game by knocking them over or causing them to let go of one or both ankles. Any who let go, even without being contacted by another, are out of the game.

MOUSETRAP: Divide class into groups of three of similar size. In turn, two make a mouse trap by facing each other and linking arms around the "mouse", who attempts to wriggle and escape from the trap. Appropriate only for grades 1 or 2.

PANCAKE ESCAPE: Two partners of equal size. One lies prone on mat, the other perpendicular (belly to back) on top. The bottom attempts to wriggle or crawl out from under while the top strives to maintain control.

STUBBORN COWS: A little wrestling match for two children (or a child and an adult who of course lets the child win). Opponent 1 (the child if an adult is the partner) is on hands and knees on the floor; opponent 2, on knees, places hands on 1's shoulders, providing gentle, firm resistance as 1 pushes forward to get out of the barn, creeping on hands and knees. Note that 2's thumbs should be held next to the index fingers so they don't pinch into 1's shoulder blades.

Games on the mats

Here are a few more ways that you can help children to have lots of fun during their foundational years.

THE CAT IN THE ATTIC: You will need a large rectangular curtain or parachute, draped over the carpet or mats. Divide the class into two side-by-side lines, one line on each side of the curtain, then pick one child to be the mouse who runs "under the attic floor," and one child to be the cat who crawls over the top. The mouse starts under at one open end and attempts to get "all the way to the other end of the attic" while the cat tries to find and tag him (through the curtain). The students on the edge of the curtain are to help the mouse in this endeavor by holding the curtain about a foot off the mat and shaking it to disguise his whereabouts, and they can also give false clues from time to time.

DOGGIES AND WOLVES TAG: On the mats or on the floor, choose a few to be wolves who chase the little doggies; if caught, doggies must either (teacher choice) go on back waving wounded paws in air until a free doggie rescues them, or Sit out in the dog pound.

SANDWICH: Half of class at a time is sandwiched under a big mat; the other half log rolls across on top of the mat. Appropriate up through grade 3 if you have a mat or mats thick enough to cushion their body weight.

SLUGS: Children do roly polys without stopping. The hungry giant(s) are looking for slugs (those who stop). If you're caught, the giant pulls them to his pot; they must stay limp the whole time. Hungry giants, making a stew, finding flat slugs just like.... you! Fee fie foe fum, hungry giants here we come. I found a flat slug to throw in the pot, I like to keep looking 'til I've captured a lot!

RULER OF THE SEA: All the children wait in a crawling position off to one side of the rectangular playing area. Teacher or chosen student, also in crawl position, proclaims: "I'm the ruler of the sea... you are all sea worms... and the sea is stormy!" On the word "stormy" (and not a moment before) children attempt to wriggle across the "sea" without being caught by the ruler. Those who are caught become 'subjects' in succeeding turns, at the start of which the ruler repeats the "I'm the ruler" phrases, but adds what her subjects are to do (examples: sea weed would be on knees, arms waving but not moving from the mat position; sharks would be on bellies slithering around and making snapping jaws movements with arms; crabs would be doing the crab walk) and changes what the children trying to cross the sea are to do. When there are a number of subjects such that the crossers have little chance, declare a 'jail break' and start a new round.

Balance, Ball, and Beanbag Activities

Resources and background

Waldorf class teachers who are seeking creative approaches to the goals of strengthening eye-hand maturity, group harmony, balance/vestibular, spatial awareness, classroom focus, and other aspects of literacy and numeracy foundations can find a wealth of background information and practical how-to's about beanbag and ball activities from many sources. I will highlight six of these resources and give you a "starter kit" repertoire for ball activities.

Waldorf-related

The Extra Lesson: Directions and considerations are given for the Above–Below and Left–Right Ball Exercises, as well as for the Bouncing Ball Exercise.

Take Time: Included in this book is a routine titled "Spatial Orientation and Movement — a series of 8 specific exercises with a bean bag." The authors note that mastery of forms in space must precede getting down to shapes and forms that create letters on paper. "The child must make an inner action to bring about the outward movement; this requires imagination and the ability to move from inner to outer."

Games Children Play: This book from Waldorf author, lecturer and mentor Kim Brooking-Payne includes two lovely beanbag activities for ages of about six or seven. These are: "There Was a Little Mouse" and "We Move Our Hands." Although these aren't identical to the above routine in *Take Time*, I think that for teachers who can't find a copy of *Take Time*, these two games provide a near equivalent.

Complementary modalities

I recommend that you take a look on youtube at all three of the following non-Waldorf programs and get a good sense of each, and then, blending elements into your work, make your own mixture of balance, musical and group learning activities. (And perhaps taking the remedial claims of each program with a grain of salt.)

BELGAU BALANCE BOARD and **BALAMETRICS:** In his 1966 typescript book *A Motor Perceptual Developmental Handbook of Activities for Schools, Parents and Pre-school Programs*, educator and researcher Frank Belgau pioneered a program of throwing–catching, balance, and related activities for helping students with learning challenges. In the years since, Belgau's son Eric co-wrote the book *A Life in Balance*; the modalities that they developed have been carried forward by practitioners around the USA. The Belgau Balance Board and other "Balametric" therapeutic equipment continue to be sold as of this writing. A number of the Belgau activities bear similarity to the Bal-A-Vis-X program with which many North American Waldorf schools today are more familiar.[59]

BAL-A-VIS-X: According to its website, this program offers a series of some 300 exercises, most of which are done with sand-filled bags and/or racquetballs, often while standing on a Bal-A-Vis-X balance board. "Requiring multiple thousands of mid-line crossings in three dimensions, these exercises are steadily rhythmic, with a pronounced auditory foundation, executed at a pace that naturally results from proper physical techniques." Bal-A-Vis-X offers extensive training programs; however, there are many youtube videos that can help teachers see the basics.

DALCROZE EURHYTHMICS: Also known as the Dalcroze Method or simply eurhythmics, this approach was developed in the early 20th century by Swiss musician and educator Émile Jaques-Dalcroze. Dalcroze eurhythmics teaches concepts of rhythm, structure, and musical expression using movement; it focuses on allowing students to gain physical awareness and experience of music through training that takes place through all of the senses, particularly kinesthetic.

Throwing and catching — step by step

Here is a sample progression of games and activities to use in addressing the skill-building needed for developmental and athletic foundations in grades 1, 2 and 3. Depending on a school's program, elements may be carried by the movement program as supplements to main lesson movement, on the playground, or any blend of those. For the games class or playground, physical education books from the mid-20th century have many similar fun skill-builders.

Beanbag activities from *Take Time* and from *Games Children Play*: as noted, there are important reasons to provide a steady diet of this activity in the first half of first grade, and on through early second grade, as part of throwing and catching skill building.

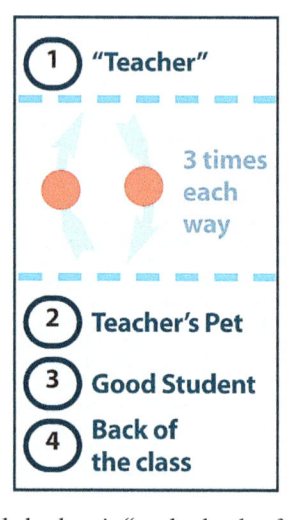

"TEACHER": a game to introduce partner throwing and catching: Arrange students in rows of four (or three if needed for numbers to work out). Student at front is first to be the "Teacher," who stands at a throwing line, facing his row. The first child facing the teacher is the "Teacher's Pet," the next is the "Good Student" and the last is "at the back of the class." Across a distance appropriate for age/skill level, the Teacher and the Teacher's Pet play catch with an 8-inch gator-skin foam ball, attempting to get three good throws and catches. If the Teacher's Pet gets three good throws and catches, she becomes the Teacher, the Good Student becomes the Teacher's Pet and the Teacher goes to the back of the class. If either the Teacher or the Teacher's Pet give a poor throw or fail to catch a good throw, then that player goes to the back of the row; it is possible for a Teacher to remain at the throwing line for several turns, but watch for those who might overstay their welcome with the group. In grade one, restrict activity to two-hand underhand throws, and begin with a throwing distance of about six feet. The foam ball is the best way to begin this activity, but later in first grade and on into second grade, you can switch to a bean bag; in second grade you could switch to a tennis ball or anything else that raises the challenge to keep it interesting.

BALLIE ON THE WALLIE, AKA SEVEN-UP: Skill steps in this traditional game will hold students' enthusiasm throughout the primary grades. It can be played with or without a wall—anywhere there's a flat, smooth surface—and all you need is a tennis ball for each kid. You can find many versions of this game online; here's a progression I use. It makes it more fun for young students if you make up names for the skill levels listed, e.g., call level 1 "nursery school" so that when they miss at a level they have to start at the beginning and "go back to nursery school." (An opportunity for good-humored kidding is at least a small job benefit during a teaching day!) Also, set the number of good catches in a row needed to move to the next level; seven is traditional but a few more can be a little more challenging. All skills require a toss to the wall or floor, one bounce, and a catch.

1) Twosies: with two hands.
2) Onesies: with one hand; then the other hand.
3) Crossies: toss from one hand, bounce, catch with the other.
4) Clapsies: add a hand clap to the above.
5) Add more tricks: build up a sequence of things to do between the toss and the catch, e.g., clap hands, touch nose, slap knees.
6) If you do have a wall to use for this game, in the second half of second grade and on into third grade, you can add a level of difficulty by having students bounce their ball to the floor so it then bounces

off the wall and can be caught in the air. In other words, the game can be played as wall–floor–catch or as floor–wall–catch.

Above / Below and Left–Right exercises

From *The Extra Lesson*: For age 7. This series of exercises provides large-motor and fine-motor midline crossings in addition to the eye–hand components.

BAL-A-VIS-X OR SIMILAR: As a morning break activity, this program is perfect: it offers important developmental and social challenges, and can be done in a short period of time with minimal equipment. Third grade and up.

BOUNCING BALLS EXERCISE from *The Extra Lesson*: For age 8 and up. McAllen notes that it brings flexibility between the stretching and lifting element, and requires will forces and concentration. This should be done before the following variation.

PARTNER BOUNCING: Once Ballie on the floor (or outdoor surface) has reached general success (and usually not until well into the first-grade year), begin putting the class in pairs. Across a distance of about four feet, they begin with bouncing one tennis ball back and forth. When mastery is reached (perhaps ten or twelve in a row without a drop) they may begin mastering two balls: first, one ball from each side, and second, two balls bounced across in turn by each partner. Another level of complexity can be added by using two balls, one of which must always be tossed in the air, and the other of which must be bounced across.

PARTNER "JUGGLING": The above sets the stage for this third-grade activity. One partner has one beanbag, the other two. Across at first just a foot or so (or even handing off if necessary to get going), the partner with two beanbags tosses straight across toward partner's empty hand, while at the same time the partner with one tosses diagonally toward that throwing hand. Now the one-beanbag partner has a beanbag in the opposite hand and will now throw on the other diagonal. When the above is mastered with beanbags, pairs can switch to tennis balls. This activity helps establish the cadence needed for juggling.

CHIME BALLS CIRCLE: A calming, focus and social activity for main lesson or extra main, second half of grade 2 all the way through 8th grade. Class sits cross-legged in a circle; teacher has a supply of at least three Chinese baoding balls (but always use tennis balls the first few times when you introduce this activity or need to re-group). Starting with one ball, the ball is to be rolled across the floor from student to student in a pattern given by the teacher, until it returns to the teacher. I recommend using the number patterns provided in *The Extra Lesson* for the Counting Star Exercise. Example: with 19 in class including the teacher, roll to the fifth person, which gives 1 (the teacher), 6, 11, 16, 21, 2, 7, 12, 17, 3, 10, 15, 4, 9, 14, 19.

CROSS-STEP BALL BOUNCE: A variation developed by the Association for a Healing Education trainings; appropriate also for age 8 and up. With one small playground ball, or a tennis ball, student straddles a rope or line with left foot to the right of the line, right foot ahead, to the left of the line, and the ball held in the left hand. To begin: bouncing the ball to the floor on the right of the line, catching it with the right hand, and then stepping with the left foot ahead and to the right of the line. Then the starting position is reversed, and the exercise continues for at least twenty steps, always with the toss coming across to the side of the line not occupied by the foot that leads. Once this skill is mastered, add speech: a times table, the alphabet forward or backward, etc.

TRIGON: A ball game played by the ancient Romans, named for its three-cornered form. Three players stand in a triangle and pass a ball or balls around in a given direction, catching with one hand and throwing with the other. This traditional ball game the provides a skill-building precursor to Bal-A-Vis-X types of circle exercises. Arrange class in groups of three. (One or two groups of four may be used to make numbers come out right.) Have group begin with one ball or beanbag and go from there…to three balls at the same time, up to three dissimilar ball or objects such as a tennis ball, a quoit and a basketball, one or more of which might be bounced instead of tossed. Third grade and up.

Equipment notes

Tennis Balls: If you have a school parent who belongs to a tennis club or plays a lot of tennis, most players' surplus balls long before they're (the balls) too tired to be useful for school use.

Juggling Balls: Tennis balls can be easily made into juggling balls by cutting a 1-inch slit, funneling in about two tablespoons of rice, and then glueing the slit with Seal-All brand glue.

Gator-skin foam balls, 8-inch dodgeballs with a resilient outer skin and a soft inside, are readily available in any phys ed supply catalog. Best ball for beginning games of catch and for the Space Ball game developed by Spacial Dynamics.

Quoits, aka Rubber Deck Rings: Also available from any phys ed supply company, quoits are a good item to have on hand in quantity, because they add interest to catching games and require a lot of wrist action to throw.

Baoding Balls: Chinese health balls, they have a chime or chimes inside a hollow iron shell, and they make a nice quiet ringing sound as they are rolled across a smooth floor.

Clay Activities

I first saw this progression of clay exercises at a workshop provided by Waldorf remedial teacher Nettie Fabrie. It requires will forces, helps awaken thinking, and strengthens posture, fine motor control, rhythm and breathing. Working with shapes is especially good to balance an overabundance of growth forces and dreaminess.

Students stand in a circle, with a container of soft clay in the middle (or several containers for quickness of dispensing). A few at a time come to the middle, each taking a lump of clay that is "bigger than a large grape, and smaller than a golf ball" and return to stand in their spots in the circle. Let them know that they're not allowed to return for more, or to give any back. To some extent, students will reveal their personalities in how much clay they choose to take.

Students should begin work as soon as they get their clay. They are to use only their fingertips for shaping. I suggest you give a hint that the first order of business is to smooth out the clay, because cracks will quickly harden and become difficult to eliminate.

An important part of this exercise is to have students stand with feet slightly apart, weight distributed and with good posture maintained. Once all have clay and are underway, expect/require silent work no matter how large the class. Occasionally, a student whose work is very good can be given the honor of walking quietly around inside the circle to show others his or her achievement in progress.

First lesson: model a ball/sphere with the fingertips of both hands, in front.

Second lesson: a sphere with writing hand, in front.

Third lesson: a sphere with other hand, in front.

Fourth, fifth and sixth lessons: a sphere as above, behind the back. Let them get a little start with the clay in front, and allow occasional looks at how their work in the back is coming along.

Rhythm: Three or four times a week for a few weeks, or once a week for up to twelve weeks. Especially good for morning circle activity.

The preceding can be done in first grade or later. Then, in mid-second grade, if the sphere sequence has been done well a few times, progress to cubes; in third grade, to pyramids. I have also brought this activity back in sixth to eighth grades in a more mentally challenging mode by having students start a sphere as usual, after which I tell them to turn it into a Platonic solid, for which I describe the facets but don't name the end result, for example, "six equilateral triangles" or "four squares and eight equilateral triangles."

When students have finished to your satisfaction, clay is returned to the container and pressed back into the supply.

A similar activity is described in old-time books of party games: the participants are each given a mystery object (either each the same object, or each a different object) such as a bolt or nut to briefly hold behind their back without looking; the mystery objects are re-gathered by the leader, and players then take an amount of clay they think will be needed to duplicate it. After a few minutes of modeling, they put their clay creations on a tray next to the mystery object(s) and the best rendition wins a small prize. I've used this as a one-time game in older grades up to the eighth grade.

Foot Circles

Method: Students stand side by side just at the edge of the paper, with enough space on each side for the activity, but close enough to adjoining students so that they can rest hands on each other's shoulders for balance if they wish. The end result desired is a good size red circle on the right, half overlapped by a similar size blue circle on the left. Size should be as large as student can make without reaching too far and losing balance. Most students will naturally make about a 12 inch diameter circle; encourage a good size without correcting. *Easier version:* Begin by having students stand with feet shoulder width or a little more apart. First, trace right foot with red crayon; then left foot with blue crayon. Shade each in with diagonal strokes. Then have students practice the circle drawing in the air just above the paper, a large counterclockwise circle with right feet—no crayons yet. Observe and correct those who use left foot; or who trace clockwise. When the whole class is moving rhythmically together with this warmup, then give permission to place the red crayon between the big toe and the next toe, to balance with neighbors if desired, and to begin drawing in a continuous counterclockwise circular motion keeping the red foot outline in the middle. Have them keep working until you signal to stop (several minutes). When the time seems right, have class stop, sit and rest in place; then repeat above clockwise with left foot, first in air, then with blue crayon. Finally, have each student, in open space above or below circles, write his or her name, with free choice of foot and crayon. For *harder version*, omit the foot outlines so that size and placement of the circles is more challenging.

The hand-tracing exercise from the Extra Lesson can also be used.

Foundations for Writing and Reading

Strengthening the Pencil Grip

Every teacher knows there are only so many "battles" one can take up in a given day, and quite often the effort to steadily encourage the attainment of a nicely functioning pencil grip by all or even most students in a class tumbles down the list of priorities to somewhere below tied shoes, raising a hand to speak, and so many other small but important details that fill our careers. Attainment of a grip suitable for cursive writing, form drawing, and painting is best worked on in kindergarten and grade one. Before this time, a palmar or fist grip may be more in line with the child's stage of development; after a grade or two, many occupational therapists believe, only the most counterproductive habits should lead the teacher to make an attempt for change.

A tripod grip is the "gold standard" of pencil grips: the *heel of the hand* steadies on the work surface; the *pinkie and ring fingers* act as a stabilizing base; and *thumb, pointer and middle finger* encircle the pencil as a triumvirate that maximizes mobility and ease. The tripod is not the only possibility for a smoothly functioning grip. Teachers need to observe: is the grip (and the writing) tense, or relaxed and smooth? Does the student tire, or can the student write without strain for a good length of time? Remember that Rudolf Steiner suggested that the first avenue to helping ease tension in writing is writing with the feet!

To see why helping students with their pencil grips might still be a very worthy educational effort (even in our Texting times!) and how it can be worked on with less psychological effort and more success, imagine that we will be taking our writing hands "down the hall" for music class and then gym class.

The Tripod Grip: My three friends will learn to serve to help me draw straight lines and curves

Music, gym and the pencil grip

When we enter the music room, the chorus lesson begins by getting the altos in one section of the riser, the tenors in another, and so forth. The teacher reminds us to plant our feet firmly, stand up in a straight and stable way ... and to keep our jaw and the lower half of the head nice and loose, with the lips and tongue also relaxed. She begins with some scales or other "musical agilities," helping the physical readiness of the students to sing on pitch and with good tone. Tight jaws, pursed lips, or tense tongues will all lead to pitch and tone problems and weak music.

Next, it's off to the gym for our writing hands. This teacher has them form a circle and do some pushups, situps, calisthenics and other strength and agility exercises. Then he leads some stretches. He's gathered up the class in this way to that they are not only warmed up and attentive, but also physiologically better prepared for the exertions ahead.

In all of the above that our "finger students" have just experienced, we can find a rhythm between stretching and lifting movements as described by Audrey McAllen; an alternation, or breathing, between tension and relaxation.[60]

This rhythm is vital to integrating the postural system, particularly the senses of balance and self-movement. Dr. König, in his lectures on arithmetic, emphasizes the essential role of these senses in the development of mathematical capacities.[61]

Back to the drawing board

Looking at a "proper pencil grip" for writing, form drawing and painting — and at how to help its achievement by our students — we can find everything mentioned above. First of all, the wrist is like the feet, gliding on the working surface as a grounded base for the fingers. The pinky and ring finger are like the legs, poised to stabilize those fingers that move the pencil. The relaxed jaw and lower head from our music warm-up correspond to the open, C-shaped position of the hand shown in the sketch. And finally, the pencil, pen or brush are in the position of the tongue, articulating the words or pictures. Only when the other members of the chorus have gotten to their places for harmonious movement, will it be possible for the thumb, pointer and middle finger to carry the most beautiful melody.

For a more practical and scientific background on the reasons for this tripod or classic pencil grip being the most functional and non-tiring, many fine references written by experienced occupational therapists can be found on the internet.

Agilities and warm-ups

Both fine- and gross-motor capacities, together with hand flexibility and a flexible attitude, must be strengthened if all students are to be enabled to gain the ability for a tripod or other nicely functional grip. The copper rod series earlier in this section includes many such activities that can be lead by a class, gym or eurythmy teacher. The "Pepper and Salt" copper rod exercise is one good example.

There are also many desk or classroom activities that may be done without supplies. Two of my favorites are:

Finger Finder Partner Game: "A" interlaces fingers, with thumbs pointing down, then rotates wrists so fingers are on top. "B" points to a finger without touching it, and "A" attempts to raise and wiggle the selected finger without moving any other finger.

Crab Walk across the Desk: Student reaches right hand to far left side of desk; stretches fingers out as far as possible; plants pinkie firmly and pulls fingers back together (leaving pinkie in place); plants thumb firmly and then stretches fingers back out so that pinkie is reaching as far as possible for the next step; and so on to the other side. Then left hand takes the same walk, from right to left. Repeat.

The Thumb Twirling Exercise from *The Extra Lesson* is also an invaluable warm-up for writing, drawing and painting. In conclusion, I think you will find that a steady diet of copper rod exercises and other finger-awareness and dexterity-strengthening activities will make the achievement of the tripod pencil grip easier and more successful. Beginning these approaches and expectations right from first grade, before other habits become implacable, will save you from many a battle in the years to come!

Crab Walk across the Desk

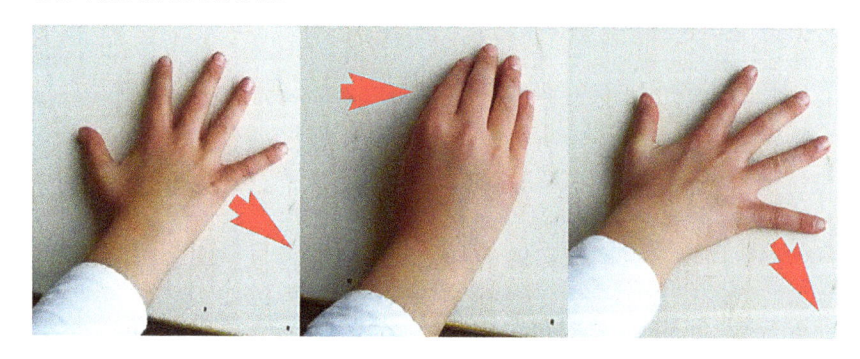

Painting Handwriting

In 1921, when the first Waldorf tenth grade was about to begin, Rudolf Steiner gave eight lectures to the teachers of the Waldorf School in Stuttgart (now collected in *Education for Adolescents*). The first six of these provide a concise review of Dr. Steiner's guidance for teaching the elementary grades; before taking up the topic of teaching adolescents, he went back over what children between seven and fourteen need in order to be well prepared for the next phase of school.

During these lectures, he stated: "We really ought to get people to write in a way that is akin to painting. Writing in that way is far more hygienic.... We should cultivate this painting-like writing. It pushes the actual mechanical activity into the body, and the writer's connection to the writing is brought to and beyond the surface." I believe he was probably indicating a "painterly" style of handwriting—i.e., with a pen or pencil, not the use of a brush per se.

In a brief chapter in *The Extra Lesson*, "Reintroduction to Formal Work in Reading and Arithmetic," McAllen stated: "In view of the reading methods which some children have experienced before coming to us, it is essential that a new child of any age should experience the letters as pictures." Then in "Writing a Story," she suggests painting writing—with a brush, in Copperplate style—as a valuable exercise for activating the lifting system, hand and eye, and recapitulating the Waldorf first grader's introduction to the beauty of written language.

I've worked with these indications with grades 1 through 8 and have found that much can be accomplished and enjoyed by progressively working with every grade on the art of painting handwriting. This can be used for its own sake as a whole-class developmental exercise and as a beautiful enhancement for Main Lesson books. It can also be used in lessons with individual students. Working to attain control for thicker and thinner parts of the alphabet educates the radius and ulna and requires quite a bit of patience.

A main lesson book title in the 8th grade

An excerpt from Steiner's July 15, 1921, lecture:

> In handwriting, physical activity plays a predominant part. We should really go into details. Let me single out the subject of writing and show you the role physical activity plays. There are two types of people in regard to writing. (I believe I have already mentioned this to those of you who have attended previous lectures.) There are those who write as though the writing is flowing from their wrists. The forming of the letters is carried out from the wrist. Future business people are actually trained to write in this way. Their writing flows from their wrists, and this is all there is to it. That is one of the two types of people in regard to writing. The other type is disposed to looking at the letters. These people always contemplate what they write, deriving an almost aesthetic pleasure from it. These are the painter type, and they do not so much write from the wrist. Those of the first type do not paint. I got to know the special training for people preparing for business. They are encouraged to

put a flourish to the letters. Their writing is characterized by continuous flourishes emanating from a swinging motion of the wrist. Taken to an extreme, this kind of writing will lead to something that is really quite awful. I know people who carry these swinging motions with their pens in the air before they begin to write—a quite terrible thing.

We really ought to get people to write in a way that is akin to painting. Writing in that way is far more hygienic. When writing is accompanied by an aesthetic pleasure, the mechanical aspect is pushed into the body. It is the inner organism rather than the wrist that is writing. And this is most important, because the mechanical aspect is then diverted from the periphery to the whole of the person. You will notice that when you teach children to write in this painting way, they will also be able to write with their toes. This would, in fact, constitute a triumph, a success—when a child is able to hold a pencil between the toes and form adequate letters. I do not say that this ability should be developed artistically. But we do have in such an instance a shifting of the mechanical activity to the whole human being. You will agree that in this regard most of us are extremely clumsy. Can you think of anyone who is able to pick up a piece of soap from the floor with his or her toes? To do this at least should be possible. It sounds grotesque, but it points to something of great significance.

We should cultivate this painting-like writing. It pushes the actual mechanical activity into the body, and the writer's connection to the writing is brought to and beyond the surface. The human being is imparted into the environment. We should really get used to seeing everything we do, rather than doing things thoughtlessly, mechanically. Most people do write mechanically, thoughtlessly. Because writing is a many-sided activity, we can, in a certain way, consider it as a significant aspect in our lessons. In arithmetic, on the other hand, the actual writing has a subordinate position, because with that subject it is the thinking that preoccupies the student.[62]

Top Left: One of many possible sample alphabets in the Roundhand, or Copperplate, style.

Top Right: Alphabet practice

Left: Begin with simple lines and curves. A complete series of exercises and other penmanship resources found at www.zanerian.com Resources for alphabet styles can also be found at the website of the International Association of Master Penmen.

Materials

McAllen indicated a fine #1 brush. I've had more success with a #6 round. A quality brush such as the Princeton Golden Taklon keeps its shape and flexibility. Watercolor paint should be a bit on the thin side. In the lower grades, students will need helper guidelines for each row of exercises or lettering.

Shaded Drawing

In her description of the "Shaded Drawing Exercise," Audrey McAllen points to the connection between the diagonal line and the will, and notes that shaded drawing calls on attention and patience.

I might add that helping children break away from the mental fixedness imposed by drawing outlined shapes is an important and noble teaching pursuit. Flexible thinking and the willingness to wait and see what might emerge from the interplay of filled and unfilled space: these are attributes that underlay success in so many realms in life.

Following are three suggestions for building up this artistic method through a progressive series of whole-class or individual exercises over time. *The Extra Lesson* indicates that the entire drawing is to consist of short diagonals drawn from top right toward bottom left. However, I believe it is appropriate to allow left-handed students to instead shade from top left to bottom right. In either case, from upper to lower.

Exercise 1. Filling a page with 'raindrop' strokes: Have each student fill a Main Lesson Book page or a form drawing sheet with diagonal dashes. The first lesson could be done with just one color, and the second (as shown above) as a color study with two colors, one on each side of the sheet. If you use blue for the first lesson, you can give the mental image of filling the page with raindrops. It is important with this exercise that dashes be placed randomly around the page, not just drawn in rows. In this way, an image is built up over time.

Exercise 2: A simple landscape with "raindrop" strokes: Again using stick crayons, have each student create a landscape scene, such as a mountain with trees. This will strengthen the students' ability to build up an image over time. As mentioned, no outlines of shapes are to be drawn.

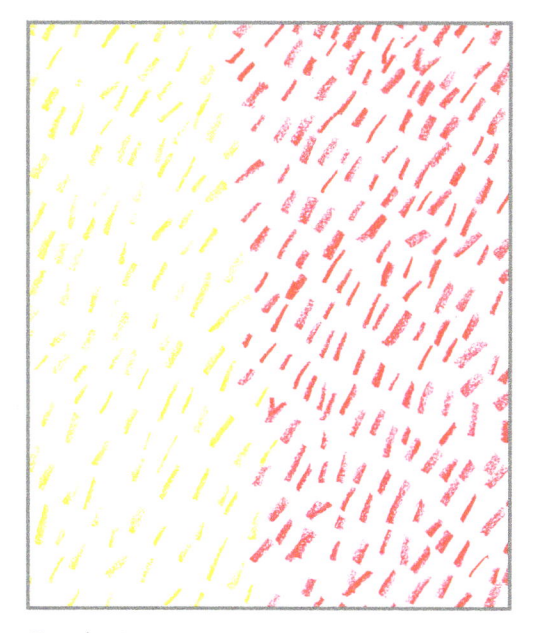

Exercise 1

Exercise 2

Exercise 3. Recapitulating the introduction to the alphabet: In the chapter titled "Reintroduction to Formal Work in Reading and Arithmetic," McAllen describes what I find to be a very common need to repeat activities that bring a living and pictorial relationship to reading and writing. For ages up to 9 years old, the exercise shown here is another way to repeat the introduction to the letters given in first grade. Have the student create a book presenting each letter as a picture, as shown; four letters to a page works well for size. This can be worked on steadily over a period of time as desired; it is an excellent "one-a-day" homework assignment.

Exercise 3　　　　　　　　　　　　　　*Additional examples*

Foundations for Arithmetic

The Connections between Math and Movement

In contrasting anthroposophy with other streams of spiritual and scientific inquiry then being pursued in Europe, Rudolf Steiner explained that on one hand there were many seeking spiritual knowledge whose methods were so almost exclusively skyward looking that it was as if they were at the misty top of a lofty mountain, and they were not really able to have a clear viewpoint of life on earth, nor were they disposed to bring what they could see from on high down to practical matters below. On the other hand, modern science was even then becoming more and more deeply materialistic and atomized, seeking to dissect and explain away every mystery.

Anthroposophy, he said, is meant to develop in humankind something quite different: following a path of meditative exercises to a viewpoint halfway up the mountain, and standing where knowledge can remain grounded in the practical but also awake and true to the spiritual in earthly life.

Steiner often lectured on the development of sense-free thought through mathematics. In *Sunspace: Science at the Threshold of Spiritual Understanding*, Olive Whicher begins the chapter "Mathematics and the Freedom of the Human Spirit" with a biographical description of Rudolf Steiner's awakening to mathematics in youth, and then of the deeper purpose of mathematical education he described in many lectures. She cites Steiner as follows:

> Whoever reads my *Philosophy of Spiritual Activity* will, I believe, find that in it there rules a kind of thinking which is akin to mathematical thinking. It is strange, but true; it is a mathematical thinking by means of which this *Philosophy of Spiritual Activity* aims to find the origin of the human impulse towards freedom and morality. The manner in which this book attempts to deal with moral and ideal questions is qualitatively no different from the manner in which the soul is active in mathematics.... There are few people in the world who have the right respect for the true mathematical process.

Being unable to grasp number concepts always induces tenderness and fear of the unknown.
– Audrey McAllen, *The Extra lesson*

Olive Whicher offers further insight:

> ...and by this he means a condition of soul into which one can come, through *the inner experiencing of space* in the activity of mathematical thinking. Rudolf Steiner describes how it is possible to grasp and experience inner questions with the same clarity and certainty with which one can prove the theorem of Pythagoras [Emphasis is in the original].[63]

As I noted earlier, Karl König demonstrated that the senses of life, self-movement and balance are the basis, respectively, for addition/subtraction, multiplication/division, and equations. I suggest that this implies something else as well: that the same can be said for the three planes of space:

- Addition and subtraction are the result of and depend on inner movement in the plane of above and below;
- Multiplication and division are the result of and depend on inner movement in the plane of front and back; and
- Algebra/complex equations and higher math are the result of and depend on inner movement in the plane of left and right.

Inner qualities of the three planes

While the various qualities of outer movement are readily visible, we can also consider that there are some characteristics of inner movement that relate to each of the three planes. The surface of above and below includes the social realm, where we meet each other, shake hands, embrace. The plane that gives rise to front and back has to do with the human will: moving forward tentatively or with strength, standing still, or stepping back. The third plane, of left and right, is the space for thought and deliberation, where we "cut through" the clutter, discriminate, analyze and balance all considerations.

When we picture the spectrum of development from infancy to adolescence we can see that inner movement is not born all at once along all three planes, but rather follows the sequence just described. The infant awakes to the world of others, then exerts the will to move around, and then acquires the ability to properly weigh choices over a span of years.

Math is inner movement

Students need to become at home in the house of numbers and very flexible in their inner ability to move them around. Through practiced inner movement they can learn, for example, to pick up the numbers 6 and 18 and know that different operations can carry them home to 24, or 12, or 3, or 108.

In eurythmy and in Bothmer gymnastics, we call upon students to be true to these planes in their movements; we are not (hopefully) being pedantic about this, but rather are asking them to stand within the gift of their human stature. The eurythmic and gymnastic education developed right at the beginning of the Waldorf School movement strives to overcome the separation between movement and our place in the universe, to exemplify the possibilities for movement with dignity and grace.

Whether the movement is in eurythmy class, a gym class lead by a practiced Bothmer gymnast or Spacial Dynamics graduate, or in morning main lesson classroom movement, hopefully all teachers are guiding students toward gestures that are true and moral, just as mathematics is a reflection of the truth and morality in the universe. Instead of mechanically raising the arms into the horizontal position and simply feeling it to be horizontal, a student can feel that the plane in which the arms stretch and repose belongs to the universe and that the outward gesture is filling out what his/her body has been created by. This is a very subtle distinction, but with dedicated effort on the part of teachers it can transform the whole quality of a person's movements — and thinking processes. In summary, we hope to help children become at home in the house of numbers, and human space is the creative force of that house.

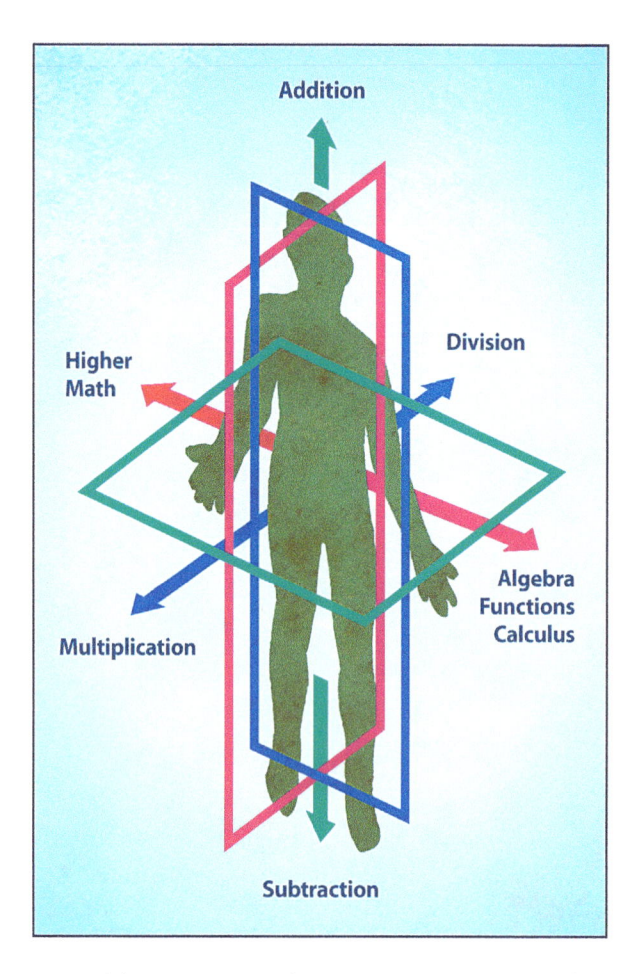

Strengthening Arithmetic Foundations

The three Rs are not equal

Waldorf class teachers have exponentially more daily opportunities to take the pulse of each child's language skill acquisition than is possible for math. From the morning greeting and choral verse to the final handshake, almost every hour in the classroom will provide many moments for formative assessment of grammar, vocabulary, speaking, reading and writing. But the number sense and its progress usually appear only during a fraction of the school day — and sometimes not every day.

This disparity of experience is probably even greater in most homes, because parents who regularly read to, and then with, their little children will easily form a general idea about progress. But especially in households or extended families where there is some skepticism about the Waldorf path to reading, daily story time might slide toward the dimension of analysis. Isn't it true that, compared to arithmetic, there is a lot more parent awareness of and nervousness about reading in kindergarten and the younger grades?

I'll try to present here some ideas and suggestions for helping teachers (and parents) assess and support the foundational, pre-arithmetic skills that are essential to numeracy development in Kindergarten and the early grades. I'm hoping readers will try some of these for themselves, and then kindly email me feedback. Ideally the following might begin a shared research project.

Rudolf Steiner helped us consider an essential difference between reading/language development and arithmetic development when he pointed to language as conventional thinking, and math as sense-free thinking. That is, in whatever native language one resides, the names of things are evolving but agreed-upon indicators; say the word "chair" in English and a mental picture of an object with four legs is pretty much a given. Thus, within the context of a spoken phrase or sentence, surrounding objects and activities (referents) allow for daily addition of vocabulary and grammar. In a written sentence, a child learning to read can gain clues to unknown sight words from the surrounding known ones, as well as from the theme and pictures.

In mathematics, however, referents and context are nearly absent, or require more mental willpower to access. As the grades curriculum progresses from manipulatives to arithmetic to math to algebra and beyond, students who have not mastered a preceding step are in great danger of forever losing the joy of numbers, self-defining as non-competent, and quietly shutting down — and perhaps without the classroom acting out and attention seeking that students with reading difficulties often provide us as a "helpful hint" to their need for extra support. Going a little deeper in this vein, note that in a lecture on Sept. 9, 1922, Dr. Steiner stated: "Even with the most careful self-examination of which the soul is capable we cannot, by using only the capacities and powers of our ordinary consciousness, grasp the real nature of thinking and the formation of ideas."[64] As noted in an excellent online article about early-grades numeracy foundations: "Children start elementary school with variable mathematics skills. Some children understand the fundamentals of numbers and mathematics, while others struggle with basic counting, number recognition, understanding of symbols, quantity discrimination, and concepts of addition and subtraction. Often, this set of early numerical competencies is referred to as number sense or early numeracy competencies. Students need to establish and understand them before moving on to more complex mathematical tasks. This article describes important early numerical competencies and provides a description of how these competencies can be taught to students who struggle with mathematics."[65]

Gender and learning-style differences

It is well known that the prevalence of dyslexia among boys is 2 to 3 times higher than it is for girls. What is less known is whether there may also be gender differences in early maths learning styles and attitudes. Although most studies do show that girls' achievement rates are equal to or slightly above those of boys, there can be attitude differences beneath the surface. According to an article published by the National Council of Teachers of Mathematics:

> Research consistently shows that, even from a fairly young age, girls are less confident and more anxious about math than boys. Moreover, these differences in confidence and anxiety are larger than actual gender differences in math achievement. These attitudes are important predictors of math performance and math-related career choices.... Some researchers have found that boys tend to use more novel problem-solving strategies, whereas girls are more likely to follow school-taught procedures. In general, girls more often follow teacher-given rules in the classroom, and it could be that this "good girl" tendency inhibits their math explorations and development of bold problem-solving skills. Such differences may contribute to gender gaps in mathematics as content becomes more complex and problem-solving situations call for more than learned procedures.
>
> Boys tend to be stronger in the ability to mentally represent and manipulate objects in space, and these skills predict better math performance and STEM career choices. Some researchers have found that spatial skills can be improved through training, and one study even found that the gender gap in spatial skills was eliminated with training.[66]

Being at home in the house of numbers

People sometimes describe Waldorf kindergarten as "nonacademic," but the truth is, with regard to language skills development, the Waldorf kindergarten strengthens key factors like auditory processing, comprehension, verbal recall, speech articulation, and an expansion of shared vocabulary... vital facets of language development that make the later steps in the academic process more readily achievable. Comprehension is built up in early childhood programs through the pictorial imagination necessary for reading comprehension in the grades and beyond.

What might be parallel factors for strengthening the young student's path to mathematics? Are there important accomplishments that need to come before computation, in the same way that, in the Waldorf approach, speech comes before writing and writing comes before reading? What is needed so all students can reach the state described by many Waldorf teachers as "being at home in the house of numbers?"

What comes before the four operations

In *Number Sense Routines*, author Jessica Shumway sets out a clear and methodical approach to assessing and addressing pre-arithmetic skills in the classroom.[65] An online review of this book notes: "Just as athletes stretch their muscles before every game and musicians play scales to keep their technique in tune, mathematical thinkers and problem solvers can benefit from daily warm-up exercises. Students with strong number sense understand numbers, ways to represent numbers, relationships among numbers, and number systems. They make reasonable estimates, compute fluently, use reasoning strategies (e.g., relate operations, such as addition and subtraction, to each other), and use visual models based on their number sense to solve problems. Students who never develop strong number sense will struggle with nearly all mathematical strands, from measurement and geometry to data and equations. Jessica Shumway has developed a series of routines designed to help young students internalize and deepen their facility with numbers. The daily use of these quick five-, ten-, or fifteen-minute experiences at the beginning of math class will help build students' number sense. The author shows that number sense can be taught to all students."[67]

The following material summarizes the progression of ten mastery steps Ms. Shumway's extremely practical book delineates, and for which it provides many fun and useful activities.

1. Subitizing: able to perceive and accurately report small quantities of objects without counting.

2. Magnitude: able to tell you which of two sets of objects or dots has more without counting.

3. Counting: able to count accurately; counting on—i.e. from 1 to 50 by ones, with one-to-one correspondence (by end of kindergarten); from 20 to 60 without starting over; from 0 to 24 by twos.

4. Ordinal & cardinal numbers: able to place/find numbered objects in the correct order; to restate how many in a set of objects, without having to recount them from the beginning.

5. Hierarchical inclusion: knows that a set of objects builds or reduces by one at a time, and that smaller numbers are part of bigger numbers

6. Part-whole relationships: once hierarchical inclusion is mastered, then able to progress to deconstruct component parts of a number, e.g. that 6 can be made up of 4 and 2, or 5 and 1.

7. Compensation: able to make trade-offs in part-whole relationships, e.g. if 7 + 3 = 10, so does 6 and 4, because 6 is one less than 7, and 4 is one more than 3.

8. Unitizing: able to recognize how groups of numbers are constructed and patterned. Able to separate a given quantity of manipulatives into simple unequal subgroups; into simple equal subgroups. Able to construct equal manipulative groups to total a given number, e.g asked to construct "16" could make two groups of 8, or 4 groups of 4, etc.

9. Number bonds: has reached automaticity for all number bonds —for two single-digit numbers up to sums of 12; for two single-digit numbers up to sums of 20 (by end of first1st grade); for any combination of one and two digit numbers up to sums of 30. Knows times tables for all numbers up to 12 x 12.

10. Four operations: able to recognize what is being asked for with written and word problems. Note that security/automaticity in all of the preceding nine steps are required before a student can begin arithmetic with ease and joy.

Recommended resources

The following are also recommended for further reading on the topic of math foundational considerations and approaches:

- *Number Sense Routines: Building Numerical Literacy Every Day in Grades K-3*, Jessica F. Shumway, ISBN: 978-1571107909
- *Diagnosis and Remedial Teaching in Arithmetic*, Fred Schonell and Eleanor Schonell, ISBN: 978-0050003459 (also at: www.movementforchildhood.com/uploads/2/1/6/7/21671438/schonell_math.pdf)
- *Knowing and Teaching Elementary Mathematics: Teachers' Understanding of Fundamental Mathematics in China and the United States* by Liping Ma describes the nature and development of the knowledge that elementary teachers need to become accomplished mathematics teachers and suggests why such knowledge seems more common in China than in the US, despite the fact that Chinese teachers have less formal education. Routledge, (2010) ISBN: 978-0415873840
- *Addition Facts that Stick: Help Your Child Master the Addition Facts for Good in Just Six Weeks* by Kate Snow. The Well-Trained Mind Press; ISBN: 978-1933339924
- *Effects of Daily Practice on Subitizing, Visual Counting, and Basic Arithmetic Skills* http://www.optomotorik.de/pubs/ovd39-2.pdf. See also "Subitizing: Vision Therapy for Math Deficits" at http://www.lookingforlearning.com/abstracts/40-4Art2.pdf

Table 1: Early Childhood and Primary Grades Number Sense Steps

A step-by-step path to building the foundations for success – and for identifying gaps that will forever limit success

Step	By Gr.	Description	Activities for Learning & Observation
Subitizing	K	Able to perceive and accurately report small quantities of objects without counting	Dot cards, dominoes, dice
Magnitude	K-1	Able to tell which of two sets of objects or dots has more without counting	Two-sided colored-dot flash cards; number guessing game
Counting – Able to count accurately	K	From 1 to 50 by ones, with one-to-one correspondence (by end of KG)	Finger holding game, object counting, drum beats, board games, interview, counting frame, number line
	1.5	From 20 to 60 without starting over	
	1.5	From 0 to 24 by twos; to count on with ability to restate starting quantity after a pause or distraction	
Ordinal & cardinal numbers	1.0	Able to place/find numbered objects in the correct order; to restate how many in a set of objects, without recounting them	See Table 2
Hierarchical inclusion	1.0	Knows that a set of objects builds or reduces by one at a time, and that smaller numbers are part of bigger numbers	Play with manipulatives
Part-whole relationships	1.5	Once hierarchical inclusion is mastered, then able to progress to consider parts of a number, e.g. that 6 can be made up of 4 and 2, or 5 and 1	Object counting with addition to/subtraction from a previously counted group
Compensation	1.5	Able to make trade-offs in part-whole relationships, e.g. if 7 and 3 equals 10, so does 6 and 4, because 6 is one less than 7, and 4 is one more than 3	See Table 3
Unitizing – Able to recognize how groups of numbers are constructed and patterned	1.5	Able to separate a given quantity of manipulatives into simple unequal subgroups	See Table 3
	2.0	Able to separate a given quantity of manipulatives into simple equal subgroups	
	2.5	Able to construct equal manipulative groups to total a given number, e.g asked to construct "16" could make two groups of 8, or 4 groups of 4, etc.	
Number bonds – Has reached automaticity for all number bonds	1.5	For two single-digit numbers up to sums of 12	Dot cards, flash cards, counting frame, number line, worksheets
	2.0	For two single-digit numbers up to sums of 20 (by end of Gr. 1)	
	3.5	For any combination of one and two digit numbers up to sums of 30	Flash cards, number lines
	4.0	Knows times tables for all numbers up to 12 x 12	Rhythmic counting, flash cards, daily worksheets
4 Operations	1-3	Able to recognize what is being asked for with written and word problems	See Table 2

Table 2: K-1 Number Sense Screening Record

Student_____ Date_____ Teacher_____

Step	Activities	Observations
Subitizing	1. Arrange deck of 10 dot cards in a row 2. Point to each and count them off, forward and back 3. Visually match card flashed by teacher 4. "Flash card" activity - if student can name one card at a time, then check for two cards side by side (for a total).	
Magnitude	1. Blue & red dot cards 2. Number line - have child point on a number, then ask for "three bigger", "two smaller", etc.	
Counting	1. Verbally from 1 to 30 by ones; and from 20 to 40 without starting over. Then from 0 to 24 by twos. 2. Number line - have student point to 6, then continue to 20. 3. Beads - estimate how many red beads in a bowl, then count them into a smaller bowl placed on the right. Then estimate how many blue beads, and count them into a bowl placed to the left. Observe hand use as well as accuracy.	
Ordinal & cardinal numbers	1. Set out a row of 12 numbered cups. Ask student to find the 5th cup, the 3rd, etc. as ability allows. 2a. Set out a row of 7 blocks, have student count them out loud, then say "Let's remember how many." 2b. After next activity, come back to them and say "I'm going to add n more; now how many do we have?" 3. Have student turn around, and hide an object under one of the cups. Then ask for a guess which number cup it's hiding under. Provide clues re: higher or lower and observe until found. Repeat once more.	
Hierarchical inclusion and part-whole relationships	Use objects in #2 above. 1. Add or take away one or two objects and ask what is there. Also ask "how many more/less are needed for n ?" 2. Ask student to give you three, give you five etc. Observe that he/she does not confuse this with giving you the third or fifth.	

Table 3: Grades 1 - 2 - 3 Number Sense Screening Record

Student_____ Date_____ Teacher_____

Step	Activities	Observations
Compensation	Able to make trade-offs in part-whole relationships, e.g. if 7 and 3 equals 10, so does 6 and 4, because 6 is one less than 7, and 4 is one more than 3.	
Unitizing Able to recognize how groups of numbers are constructed and patterned	Able to separate a given quantity of manipulatives into simple unequal subgroups	
	Able to separate a given quantity of manipulatives into simple equal subgroups	
	Able to construct equal manipulative groups to total a given number, e.g asked to construct "16" could make two groups of 8, or 4 groups of 4, etc.	
Number bonds Has reached automaticity for all number bonds	For two single-digit numbers up to sums of 12	
	For two single-digit numbers up to sums of 20 (by end of first grade)	
	For any combination of one and two digit numbers up to sums of 30	
	Knows times tables for all numbers up to 12 x 12	
Four operations Able to recognize what is being asked for with written and word problems	Addition	
	Subtraction	
	Multiplication	
	Division	

"Math Explorers Club" - a starter kit of whole-class activities for math foundations

Math strengthening activities from *The Extra Lesson*
All exercises for Body Geography
Tracing hands (and feet)
Form drawings: Counting Star; Interpenetrating Triangles; Expanding and Contracting Triangles

Dot card addition
- Goal: Consolidate number bonds
- Supports: Subitizing; counting; arithmetic
- Materials: Dot cards with numbered backs - one set per student. Teacher also to have a set.
- Description: At desks. Have students sort their decks from 1 to 10 in a straight/side-by-side row at the top of desk space. Teacher holds up a dot card, and has students place their (same) card in middle of desk space. Then, teacher says: "What card do we need to get to x?" (i.e. a five card is out, and the total needed is nine; therefore a four card is to be found and placed next to the 5-dot card.) Then, students can be asked to turn these two cards over to the numbered side and recite, i.e. "4 plus five or five plus four equals nine."

Dot card concentration
- Goal: Play
- Supports: Subitizing; spatial intelligence
- Materials: Dot cards with blank backs - two or four sets per playing group.
- Description: Children can play in groups of two or three. Shuffle all cards and then put them face up in a grid arrangement (if 2 sets/20 cards, then 4 x 5 grid; if 4 sets/40 cards then 5 x 8). After cards arranged and studied for a minute, turn them all over - face down. The students in turn try to find pairs and if successful pick up and add to his/her pile. Winner is one who finds the most pairs. Can be played either as single-pick turn, or as a player keeps picking as long as he/she finds a pair.

Dot card number bonds
- Goal: Consolidate number bonds
- Supports: Subitizing; counting on or off; arithmetic
- Materials: Dot cards with numbered backs - one set per student. Teacher also to have a set.
- Description: At desks. Have students sort their decks from 1 to 10 in a straight/side-by-side row at the top of desk space. Teacher calls out a number and asks students to set out two cards that add up to that number. When students have completed this task, then call on a few students to describe the pairings they found.

Blindfold counting with feet
- Goal: Play
- Supports: Inner picturing and movement
- Materials: Blindfolds, stones
- Description: Work in pairs, one child blindfolded in chair, other seated on floor. Seated child sets out a pile of 10 to 20 stones, for the other to count using feet.

Fingers behind back addition
- Goal: Inner picturing
- Supports: Digit awareness; number bonds
- Materials: None
- Description: Teacher stands behind student; student puts both hands behind back with fingers loosely extended. Teacher gently grabs/holds a combination of fingers from each hand (e.g. 3 fingers on the right and two on the left) and asks the student "How many?"

Activities to introduce in Grade 2

Double Digit War - Card Game
- Goal: Play
- Supports: Place value, bigger/smaller
- Materials: One deck of cards for each pair of players, with face cards removed; one sheet of paper for each player, marked & lined for tens and ones column
- Description: Groups of two: Players shuffle and split deck so each has a half-deck pile. Game is played just like regular "War" (i.e. higher number takes both cards) except that each player looks privately at his/her first card and then in unison they slap their first cards onto their respective mats, choosing to slap it into the tens column or the ones column. Then, more or less in unison they take the second card and place it in the open column.

Playing cards concentration
- Goal: Play
- Supports: Memory; spatial intelligence
- Materials: Playing cards - one deck per playing group.
- Description: Children can play in groups of two or three. Adjust number of cards to be used for group size and ability level, i.e. perhaps remove all face cards. Shuffle all cards and then put them face up in a grid arrangement. After cards arranged and studied for a minute, turn them all over - face down. The students in turn try to find pairs (either any two of a number, or two matching color numbers) and if successful pick up and add to his/her pile. Winner is one who finds the most pairs. Can be played either as single-pick turn, or as a player keeps picking as long as he/she finds a pair.

Review Exercise Worksheet

This worksheet is provided as a way to review, distill and highlight the connections between the whole-class activities in Section 3 with the developmental considerations described in Sections 1 and 2. Procedure: start with any of the activities in the list, or use a blank line for a similar activity from your own research. Then, fill in the row using a rating scale for the developmental aspects that activity addresses or involves. (You could either just star the most significant aspects in each row, or make up a coding system to indicate none/a little/a lot.

	Touch	Life	Self-movement	Balance	Timing & Rhythm	Direction & Goal	Spatial Orientation	Sequencing	Fine Motor	Laterality	Midline Barriers	Imitation	Anticipation	Reflexes	Radius & Ulna	Inbreath	Outbreath
Ball Activities																	
Ball Twirling																	
Clay Ball																	
Copper Rods																	
Cross Step Ball Bounce																	
Cubes - Fingers & Toes																	
Foot Circles																	
Jumping Rope																	
Left-to-Right Painting																	
Painting Handwriting																	
Shaded Drawing																	
String Games																	
Tracing Hands & Feet																	
Zoorobics																	

4 The Values of Organized Play

Introduction

There are always some parents, administrators, boards, and even teachers, who see "physical education" as a sideshow, an outbreath, a non-academic interval that just "lets the kids run around for a while" but you and I know better! Just as the Waldorf school history curriculum retraces the path of humanity's progress, the lower grades movement program can draw on a rich history of play and games from around the world.

With a little digging on used-book websites, one can find many out-of-print books filled with the history of childhood-focused movement—treasuries filled with competitive and cooperative games, with names like Haley Over, Jackstones, Rounders, or Venconmigo. Garrison Keillor in his book *Lake Wobegon Days* refers to happily playing something called "Pom Pom Pullaway" at recess in the sixth grade in 1954. A list of some recommended book resources is at the end of this chapter.

Three phases of movement

In Section 2, parallels between academic and athletic development were described in both anthroposophic and mainstream terms. The timeline chart (page 57) represents the first phase, labeled "Goodness," as the time for mastery of rudimentary and fundamental movement through crawling, grasping, digging, swinging and all sorts of free play—play that has no real rules or defined outcomes—or very flexible rules.

The second phase, "Beauty," starts at about 7 years and is described as the time for mastery of general movement skills. The third and final phase is labeled "Truth," being a time to take the general movement skills one has established and to apply them and refine them for specialized athletics, inflexible and often complicated rules, etc.

During the past decade or more, the correlations between self-directed free play and school readiness for the young, and between organized sports/exercise and academic readiness for upper grades, high school and beyond, have been noted and described in great detail, in hundreds of news stories and scientific studies. For these two poles of the movement spectrum (i.e., for young childhood play and for organized adolescent/adult sports and exercise) the pendulum of recognition and curriculum design has recently begun to swing back in a positive direction.

But the middle category of physical education—equally important—has received little if any popular attention, and especially outside of Waldorf schools. It could be called "organized play" and/or "organized games"—the realm of movement most appropriate for ages 7 to 11 or 12, the realm of games that have been played all around the world during this phase of life for hundreds or even thousands of years. These offer the best way to build the bridge from free play to true readiness for specialized athletic skills; they create the space where generalized movement and developmental foundations can be given their due. Athletic—and academic—foundations can be joyfully built through "old time" schoolyard and backyard games.

This middle category of movement is barely mentioned in the news or modern books, but fortunately it's well documented in dozens of books for teachers and recreation directors that were published between 1910 and 1950.

Perhaps the best of these books is *Games for the Playground, Home, School and Gymnasium* by Jessie H. Bancroft, an Assistant Director of Physical Training in the New York City public schools. The following lengthy excerpt is from her introduction to this invaluable book. Although her language style may now seem a little antiquated, the information she provides is perhaps even more significant and helpful a century later.[68]

The Use of Games

extract from *Games for the Playground, Home, School and Gymnasium*

BY Jessica H. Bancroft

THE USE OF GAMES for both children and adults has a deep significance for the individual and the community through the conservation of physical, mental, and moral vitality.

Sense perceptions: Games have a positive educational influence that no one can appreciate who has not observed their effects. Children who are slow, dull, and lethargic; who observe but little of what goes on around them; who react slowly to external stimuli; who are, in short, slow to see, to hear, to observe, to think, and to do, may be completely transformed in these ways by the playing of games. The sense perceptions are quickened: a player comes to see more quickly that the ball is coming toward him; that he is in danger of being tagged; that it is his turn; he hears the footstep behind him, or his name or number called; he feels the touch on the shoulder; or in innumerable other ways is aroused to quick and direct recognition of and response to, things that go on around him. The clumsy, awkward body becomes agile and expert: the child who tumbles down to-day will not tumble down next week; he runs more fleetly, dodges with more agility, plays more expertly in every way, showing thereby a neuro-muscular development.

Social development: The social development through games is fully as important and as pronounced. Many children, whether because of lonely conditions at home, or through some personal peculiarity, do not possess the power readily and pleasantly to cooperate with others. Many of their elders lack this facility also, and there is scarcely anything that can place one at a greater disadvantage in business or society, or in any of the relations of life. The author has known case after case of peculiar, unsocial, even disliked children, who have come into a new power of cooperation and have become popular with their playmates through the influence of games. The timid, shrinking child learns to take his turn with others; the bold, selfish child learns that he may not monopolize opportunities; the unappreciated child gains self-respect and the respect of others through some particular skill that makes him a desired partner or a respected opponent. He learns to take defeat without discouragement and to win without undue elation. In these and in many other ways are the dormant powers for social cooperation developed, reaching the highest point at last in the team games where self is subordinated to the interests of the team, and cooperation is the very life of the game.

Will training: Most important of all, however, in the training that comes through games, is the development of will. The volitional aspect of the will and its power of endurance are plainly seen to grow in power of initiative; in courage to give "dares" and to take risks; in determination to capture an opponent, to make a goal, or to win the game. But probably the most valuable training of all is that of inhibition—that power for restraint and self-control which is the highest aspect of the will and the latest to develop. The little child entering the primary school has very little of this power of inhibition. To see a thing he would like is to try to get it; to want to do a thing is to do it; he acts impulsively; he does not possess the power to restrain movement and to deliberate. A large part of the difficulty of the training of children at home and at school lies in the fact that this power of the will for restraint and self-control is undeveloped. So-called "willfulness" is a will in which the volitional power has not yet been balanced with this inhibitive power. One realizes in this way the force of Matthew Arnold's definition of character as "a completely fashioned will."

There is no agency that can so effectively and naturally develop power of inhibition as games. In those of very little children there are very few, if any, restrictions; but as players grow older, more and more rules and regulations appear, requiring greater and greater self-control—such as not playing out of one's turn; not starting over the line in a race until the proper signal; aiming deliberately with the ball instead of throwing wildly or at haphazard; until again, at the adolescent age, the highly organized team games and contests are reached, with their prescribed modes of play and elaborate restrictions and fouls. There could not be in the experience of either boy or girl a more live opportunity than in these advanced games for acquiring the power of inhibitory control, or a more real experience in which to exercise it. To be able, in the emotional excitement of an intense game or a close contest, to observe rules and regulations; to choose under such circumstances between fair or unfair means and to act on the choice, is to have more than a mere knowledge of right and wrong. It is to have the trained power and habit of acting on such knowledge—a power and habit that are immeasurably important for character. It is for the need of such balanced power that contests in the business world reach the point of winning at any cost, by fair means or foul. It is for the need of such trained and balanced power of will that our highways of finance are strewn with the wrecks of able men. If the love of fair play, a sense of true moral values, and above all, the power and habit of will to act on these can be developed in our boys and girls, it will mean immeasurably for the uplift of the community.

Evolution of play interests: The natural interests of a normal child lead him to care for different types of games at different periods of his development. In other words, his own powers, in their natural evolution, seek instinctively the elements in play that will contribute to their own growth. When games are studied from this viewpoint of the child's interests, they are found to fall into groups having pronounced characteristics at different age periods.

Games for various ages: Thus, the little child of six years enjoys particularly games in which there is much repetition, as in most of the singing games; games involving impersonation, appealing to his imagination and dramatic sense, as where he becomes a mouse, a fox, a sheepfold, a farmer, etc.; or games of simple chase (one chaser for one runner) as distinguished from the group-chasing of a few years later. His games are of short duration, reaching their climax quickly and making but slight demand on powers of attention and physical endurance; they require but little skill and have very few, if any, rules, besides the mere question of "taking turns." In short, they are the games suited to undeveloped powers in almost every particular but that of imagination.

Two or three years later these games are apt to seem "babyish" to a child and to lose interest for him. His games then work through a longer evolution before reaching their climax, as where an entire group of players instead of one has to be caught before the game is won, as in Red Lion, Pom Pom Pullaway, etc. He can watch more points of interest at once than formerly, and choose between several different possible modes of play, as in Prisoners' Base. He gives "dares," runs risks of being caught, and exercises his courage in many ways. He uses individual initiative instead of merely playing in his turn. This is the age of "nominies," in which the individual player hurls defiance at his opponents with set formulas, usually in rhyme. Players at this time band together in many of their games in opposing groups, "choosing sides"—the first simple beginning of team play. Neuro-muscular skill increases, as shown in ball play and in agile dodging. Endurance for running is greater.

When a child is about eleven or twelve years of age, some of these characteristics decline and others equally pronounced take their place. "Nominies" disappear and games of simple chase (tag games) decline in interest. Races and other competitive forms of running become more strenuous, indicating a laudable instinct to increase thereby the muscular power of the heart, at a time when its growth is much greater proportionately than that of the arteries, and the blood pressure is consequently greater. A very marked feature from now on is the closer organization of groups into what is called team play. Team play bears to the simpler group play which precedes it an analogous relation in some respects to that between modern and primitive warfare. In primitive warfare the action of the participants was homogeneous; that is, each combatant performed the same kind of service as did every other combatant and largely on individual initiative. The "clash of battle and the clang of arms" meant an individual contest for every man engaged. In contrast to this there is, in modern warfare, a distribution of functions, some combatants performing one kind of duty and others another, all working together to the common end. In the higher team organizations of Basket Ball, Baseball, Football, there is such a distribution of functions, some players being forward, some throwers, some guards, etc., though these parts are often taken in rotation by the different players. The strongest characteristic of team play is the cooperation whereby, for instance, a ball is passed to the best thrower, or the player having the most advantageous position for making a goal. A player who would gain glory for himself by making a sensational play at the risk of losing for his team does not possess the team spirit. The traits of character required and cultivated by good team work are invaluable in business and social life. They are among the best possible traits of character. This class of games makes maximal demands upon perceptive powers and ability to react quickly and accurately upon rapidly shifting conditions, requiring quick reasoning and judgment. Organization play of this sort begins to acquire a decided interest at about eleven or twelve years of age, reaches a strong development in the high schools, and continues through college and adult life.

Relation between development and play: Such are the main characteristics of the games which interest a child and aid his development at different periods. They are all based upon a natural evolution of

Viewpoints on Play and Sport	
PLAY	**TEAM SPORT**
Created for children by children, or for children by adults	Created for adults by adults
Focuses on the needs and preferences of children	All-star teams, medals, playoffs, trophies etc.
Anything can happen	Anything can happen, but only within framework of hard and fast boundaries & rules
Anyone can play	Team members must be "good enough" and will be selected or excluded in order of skill level
Winning is very fleeting; or, everybody wins	Winning is the point; in order for one side to win, someone else must lose
Losing (i.e. becoming "It" in tag) may be desirable or is soon redeemed by a feature of the game	Losing is undesirable and must be accompanied by self criticism
Pictorial imaginative processes govern	Linear strategic processes govern
Rules are pliable and can be transformed by and for players	Rules are written, fixed and non-negotiable
Rule violations are viewed subjectively	Rule violations are viewed objectively
The player cannot yet distinguish between himself/herself and the rules	The athlete sees him/herself as separate from the rules
Movements are created by the players and are spontaneous, free	Movements are dictated by the sport, repetitively practiced, carefully refined
Language and vocabulary are created by the players	Language and jargon are dictated by the sport
Developmentally appropriate for ages 2 to 12. This is the primary window of time in the human lifespan in which true play occurs.	Developmentally appropriate for older-preteens and adolescents at the onset of puberty, at which time the openness to imaginative play fades or closes

Note that there is a bridge stage between play and sport: playing at sport, i.e., imagining oneself as Brett Favre or Serena Williams while playing the sport.

physical and psychological powers that can be only hinted at in so brief a sketch. Any one charged with the education or training of a child should know the results of modern study in these particulars.

The fullest and most practical correlation of our knowledge of the child's evolution to the particular subject of play that has yet been presented is that of Mr. George E. Johnson, Superintendent of Playgrounds in Pittsburgh, and formerly Superintendent of Schools in Andover, Mass., in *Education by Plays and Games*. The wonderful studies in the psychology of play by Karl Groos (*The Play of Animals* and *The Play of Man*), and the chapter by Professor William James on Instinct, show how play activities are expressions of great basic instincts that are among the strongest threads in the warp and woof of character— instincts that should have opportunity to grow and strengthen by exercise, as in play and games. We have come to realize that play, in games and other forms, is nature's own way of developing and training power. As Groos impressively says, "We do not play because we are young; we have a period of youth so that we may play."

The entire psychology of play bears directly on the subject of games. Indeed, although the study of games in their various aspects is comparatively recent, the bibliography bearing on the subject, historic, scientific, psychologic, and educational, is enormous and demands its own distinct scholarship.

Age classification: It is highly desirable that a teacher knows the significance of certain manifestations in a child's play interests. And if they do not appear in due time, they should be encouraged, just as attention is given to the hygiene of a child who is under weight for his age. But it should not be inferred that any hard and fast age limits may be set for the use of different plays and games. To assign such limits would be a wholly artificial procedure, and yet is one toward which there is sometimes too strong a tendency. A certain game cannot be prescribed for a certain age as one would diagnose and prescribe for a malady. Nothing in the life of either child or adult is more elastic than his play interests. Play would not be play were this otherwise. The caprice of mood and circumstance is of the very soul of play in any of its forms.

Games become sports — organically

As an example of how traditional childhood games can provide a seamless progression from free play in toddlerhood to athletics in adolescence, let's take the sport of wrestling. I suggest that a good place to start the learning process is with games like London Bridge in first grade. London Bridge teaches two key wrestling principles: someone will grab and jostle you, and that can be okay; and sooner or later you'll lose, and that can be okay too.

Wrestling as a sport skill can be built up, small step by small step, through tumbling and partner gymnastics, through the classic rough-and-tumble challenges like the little wresting matches in the Zoorobics chapter, and then on to Stork Wrestling, King of the Mountain, Leg Wrestling, and scores of other games. In this way, by sixth grade an introduction to the goals, rules and techniques of Collegiate Wrestling— for boys and for girls — is a natural rules and skill progression, and the proper sportsmanship culture of this intense form of one-on-one interpersonal competition has been well established.

Sports are not games

Television, movies and videos, rock music, computers, and team sports like soccer have all come to be regarded as normal for elementary age children. While there might be a few positives to these "new normals," there are many, many games (and tasks) childhood can be filled with that offer more fun and more developmental benefits.

Every child is different, and every family has its own circumstances and life situation. Organized sports could be one part of a healthy childhood development. But before you sign up your child, I strongly recommend reading the book *Just Let the Kids Play: How to Stop Other Adults from Ruining Your Child's Fun and Success in Youth Sports*, which was written by former NBA player Bob Bigelow.[69]

Early participation in team sports is often motivated by parental concern that children will not be ready for high school sports if they don't build specific skills long before the teenage years. While there is no perfect answer to the "when to begin" question, there are quite a few successful professional athletes who started late. Tim Duncan switched from swimming to basketball in high school; other late-starting NBA standouts include Hakeem Olajuwon and Dikembe Mutombo. Alex Morgan didn't take up soccer until she was 13 years old, very late by soccer standards, but rose to become one of the best female strikers in the world. Early participation in organized sports can lead not only to overuse and growth-plate injuries, but also to early burnout and lowered participation in athletics in high school; i.e., during the years when daily exercise is vital as a balance to the lengthier sedentary stretches of academic classes and homework.

"Is my child ready for team sports?" "Will my child be left behind if he or she doesn't get going on a team?" If you're asking questions like this, or know someone who is, here are five aspects to consider.

Developmental/physical readines. Children are not usually ready to fluidly cross the vertical midline for things like batting or tennis until about age eight and a half, after which such sports will indeed provide a developmental boost. Other aspects to think about: is the activity primarily in the "upper triangle" of head, chest and arms, or in the "lower triangle" that relates to puberty? Is the activity one that places a value on physically stressful repetitive motions? Year-round single-sport training is not physiologically healthy for children or adults, but especially at the age when growth plates have not yet closed.

Emotional readines. Is the child ready for the degree of self-consciousness and self-criticism that the activity will entail? Will the child be pushed to specialize, and thereby limit his or her self-definition, closing off openness to many other possible activities. A play-values based program will allow each child to feel he or she made an important contribution to the fun, and to not "practice" focusing on personal limitations.

What parts of childhood might be sacrificed to make time. Is so much time required by the team that there will be substantially less time for riding bikes, playing in the yard, etc.?

Parents' time. Certainly, there are all kinds of trade-offs in daily life, but regularly having dinner and evenings together, sharing family stories, making time to just check in with each other are at some level at least as important parts of growing up as learning to dribble a basketball or perfect a back handspring.

Social aspects. For many elementary age students, organized team sports can be a very positive avenue to making and keeping friends outside of school, and to start friendships for the day when he or she enters a local high school. The other side of the coin: most team sports, and perhaps especially soccer, bring out critical thinking; and children who play a lot of soccer are often ready to speak critically.

Summary

Historically—and right up through most of the twentieth century—children acquired the ability to play team sports by playing imaginative and age-related games that evolved as they grew. The traditional non-sport imaginative games made up by children provide gross and fine motor building blocks that lead up to the ability for organized sports in due time. The play-builds-capacities method is more productive and more fun in the long run.

Thousands of such games are available, and have been played happily throughout the centuries. Almost any games or physical education book published before 1959 is full of them. On the other hand, for children past the age of 12, rules, measured and coached achievement, and exact scores are indeed elements that will help the adolescent in many positive ways.

Movement Standards for Third Grade

In first grade, many students will still lack fine motor control of eye movement, may still exhibit some ambidexterity and other early-childhood movement patterns, and should still be quite satisfied with imaginative free play.

In first and second grades, we can observe the child reshaping, slowly working to change his or her kindergarten presence to a form more fitting for life ahead. The softness and head-to-trunk proportions we see in the toddler are almost but not yet completely outgrown.

Third grade (9 years old) should mark the change to a new, more individualized presence and a new readiness for academic challenge.

The following movements will help to promote and consolidate this important shift in development.

Definites

1. All forms of individual jumping rope: frontward, backward, cross-rope. Double-dutch with partners (jumping and turning).
2. Seven-up/ballie on the wallie progression: a) two hands; b) right hand; c) other hand; d) crossie; e) under leggie; f) spinnie ... then all of the above with a clap, nose touch, etc.
3. Copper rods: passing with a partner while counting out times tables; pencil, palmar and crocodile grip; twirling; "pepper and salt" dexterity exercise. Optional: rod twirl while tossing/catching one ball with other hand.
4. Cross skipping (skipping while slapping the opposite knee).
5. Balance on one foot with eyes closed and counting backward from 12.
6. Pencil grip with thumb and pointer opposed, ideally, three other fingers behind.
7. Correct posture while seated, for all work.
8. Movement independence between arms, e.g. able to raise both arms overhead, then continuously swing one arm clockwise and the other counterclockwise; or to toss a ball with one hand and snap the other fingers.
9. Able to write out the alphabet while speaking.

Pointers from *The Extra Lesson*

1. Above-below ball tosses (with one ball; with two balls) – maintaining direction.
2. Left-right ball tossing; able to switch direction.
3. Cross-step ball bounce.
4. Cubes between fingers; marbles between toes.
5. Ball twirling –able to maintain movement with all 3 balls while speaking.
6. Moving straight line and lemniscate drawing.
7. Mirror form drawings.
8. See "Waking up to Learning with the Copper Rod Exercises".
9. Body geography: able to complete a sequence with three crossing or varying-side instructions, e.g. touch left knee with right hand, then head with left hand, then right ear with left pinkie.
10. Legible writing with feet: a block or stick crayon held between toes, with a large sheet of paper taped to the floor.

Pointers from *Take Time*

1. Timing and Rhythm: able to march and clap, keep up in rhythm during group circle activities
2. Direction and Goal: able to complete a sequence of steps with sides given. See #8 above also.
3. Spatial Orientation: observe in games, and ask the eurythmy teacher.
4. Sequencing: an 8 year old should know the seasons and the months of the year in order; and be able to count by twos backward from 24 while jumping rope.

5. Fine motor control: carefully observe speech, writing and reading (for reading, if child tires easily or seems to strain).
6. Laterality: earlier-stage ambidexterity, if any, has been resolved; reversals no longer frequent.

Movement Program Organization

The following aspects of movement program organization are summarized from the approach developed and provided by the author during his career at Aurora Waldorf School. In this program, all students in grades 1 to 8 have at least three 45-minute periods a week of games/gym/tumbling (in addition to their eurythmy classes and outdoor recess).

Model mission statement

Through a movement program in harmony with human development, bringing appropriate activities and exercises for each stage. The main goals are:

To prepare the student for kind deeds — developing the ability to work and play with (and as) a group.

To prepare the student for brave deeds — developing a sense of growing strength, flexibility and stamina.

To prepare the student for responsible deeds — fostering the ability to listen to and follow instructions.

To prepare the student for graceful and joyful deeds, balance in movement and life, through gymnastics and Bothmer gymnastics.

To develop an understanding and a healthy approach to movement and exercise, as well as specific skills in relationship to sport and games.

To prepare each graduate with the four foundations for high-school level team sports:

Interest – Ability – Attitude – Effort

Components of the program

Games/Gym focuses primarily on skill-building imaginative games, pre-sports that provide good exercise and social activity, and the learning of teamwork skills. For instance, the sequence of games from "Clean Up Your Room" to "Curtain Ball" to "Newcombe" provides the progression that leads up to volleyball in sixth grade. Each class from 1st though 5th has two periods of gym per week.

Tumbling and gymnastics includes recreational, basic and intermediate tumbling, gymnastics, apparatus, acrobatics, juggling, wrestling and balancing activities that are effective vehicles for completion of "physical" development. Every class has one period of tumbling and gymnastics/week. The tumbling program culminates each year in the popular AWS Circus.

Enrichment, a once-weekly class for grades 1, 2 and 3, is an added period for strengthening developmental progress and improving skills via a whole-class approach to movement, drawing and painting based on *The Extra Lesson* and similar foundational modalities.

Middle School students have gym every day. On Monday, Tuesday and Friday they have a half-hour gym class that replaces the half-hour lunchtime recess provided for lower grades. On Wednesdays they have a two-period life sports class, and on Thursdays a two-period team sports class.

Description of goals in the primary grades

Grade 1: Completion of imitation; form group. Ability to work in "team learning" environment; imitation and anticipation — the capacity to carefully observe before acting; mastering space in above/below and front/back spatial planes; body geography/proprioception; balance; completion of early childhood movement patterns; learning right from left, and strengthening laterality. A gentle introduction to games with competition in a story context.

Grade 2: Complete development of first 7 years. Solidifying the goals of grade 1, i.e. ability to work in "team learning" environment, capacity to carefully observe before acting, mastering space in above/below and front/back spatial planes, completion of early childhood movement patterns. New grade 2 goals include increased eye-hand coordination, aiming/precision, moving out of the circle game setting, games with a "danger" story element, Preparation for grade 3 includes beginning to work in the left/right spatial plane, midline crossing.

Grade 3: Come into symmetry plane, independence. Leaving young childhood behind, waking up to individuality, aiming, precision and judging. Mastering the left/right spatial plane and midline crossings (foundations for the later development of critical thinking and reasoning). Beginning of games that students will understand to be precursors to sports, i.e. kickball as a skill builder for baseball, fireball as a workup for volleyball. Greater formality in gymnastics exercises.

Grade 4: Individual accountability. Continuation of goals begun in third grade, that is, aiming, precision, judging of individual achievement. Introduction to the foundations of team sports through skill-building games and activities (but not through sports themselves). Sports that we begin working toward in fourth grade (through related games) include volleyball, tennis, baseball, track & field, basketball, and football.

Grade 5: Year of balance, introduction to competition. Introduction of formal judgment of the individual, by objective standards, and in the context of specialization. The Pentathlon is the first time where some will be singled out for special honors, and all participants are held to account for preparation; there is still "play value" in this preparation but it is nearing a more "athletic" mood. This is the last year in which the majority of activities will have a story basis (i.e., the Ancient Greek Olympics). Also, basketball rules are introduced.

AWS middle school Gym curriculum

Overview: Introduction to sports; "waking up to muscle and strength." All middle school students participate in our three sports teams, with intermural competition in soccer, basketball, and track & field. AWS students in 6th, 7th and 8th Grade have 30 minutes of "phys ed" three days a week, and 90 minutes of sports/athletics two days a week. Our primary goals are to enhance current fitness, to inspire a lifelong love of movement, and to prepare every graduate to have the background needed to choose a high school team sport if desired.

Lunchtime Fitness/Games: a 30-minute class. A mixture of coed, non-coed, single class or combined class (i.e., 7th and 8th grades together) periods.

Life Sports: a double-period (90-minute) class includes a wide variety of athletics and life-sports with a goal of enhancing the fitness of every student, and providing a baseline minimum of daily physical activity. Sample activities are: archery, tennis, badminton, ultimate volleyball, ballroom, hip hop and African dance, swimming, and cross-country skiing.

Team Sports: a double period (90 minute) class. All AWS middle school students participate in and play on the soccer, basketball and track teams that compete against area independent schools.

8th Grade graduation requirements: students are given a year-long assignment to accumulate proficiency points in a set of required core skills plus skills of their choosing in any of the above AWS sports offerings. Final letter grade is based on steady work to accumulate points in the various skill areas. Required items include juggling, running two miles, doing a set number of pushups and sit-ups, holding a handstand for at least a second, double dutch jump rope, swimming 300 yards, and cross country skiing for two miles.

Safety rules — providing structure in gym class

It is important to take time during the first gym class of the year, and occasionally during the year, to read and explain a written "code of conduct" to each grade. For grades 1, 2 and 3, children seem to like to know that they're going to have "manners class" incorporated into gym. For older grades, the wording can be simplified but the same rules need repeating — usually several times a year.

1. Every class begins with a quiet opening. This is not just a manners rule, but also a safety rule: Athletes who cannot quietly prepare, or quietly stop and rest, are not ready to be safe athletes.
2. There is never any free play in the gym. You are either waiting for the class activity, watching, or doing the class activity. If you don't know what the class activity is, go to the teacher or sit down.
3. You must stop an activity the moment a teacher calls for stopping.
4. We keep our hands and feet to ourselves except as part of an activity.
5. No shrieking.
6. Never touch any equipment in the gym, until the teacher begins a supervised activity with it. For example, if there is a ball in a corner and the teacher hasn't started a ball game, you don't start playing with the ball.
7. Safe clothing and hair. No jewelry or watches.
8. Gymnastics/tumbling: no head-first forward dives or slides any time, including relays and the jump mat. Never do gymnastics or equipment work without a spotter, unless with specific permission.
9. After class, walk quietly out of the gym, and stay in line all the way down the hall to your class. The rules, including no free play, hands and feet to yourself, etc., still apply in the hallway.

Children who fail to observe these rules may, at the discretion of the teacher, be excluded from gym activities for a period of time.

On teasing and competition

Learning to not take oneself too seriously is a key trait needed for the acquisition of good sportsmanship; not taking oneself too seriously requires a certain sense of humor and appreciation of our universally imperfect human nature. This capacity for acceptance is greatly strengthened through traditional childhood games and will serve students well in all future phases and walks of life. Dr. König notes the following about laughter and weeping:

> Among the most striking characteristics of man are his emotional outbursts of weeping and laughing. They are common to almost every human being; they belong to all races and are the ever-present companions of humanity." After noting that fairy tales often include giants and dwarfs, he continues: "Our unconscious is the giant in us. He is imprisoned like the genie in the flask who continually tries to escape. Laughter is set as his guardian and helps to keep him at bay. Our mind is the dwarf in us; small and witty, clever and cruel, as he appears in the fairy tale.…When the giant of our unconscious is not only tamed but transformed and moulded, then grace begins to appear. When the dwarf of the mind grows up, matures and becomes human, dignity unfolds.[70]

A Taxonomy of Games and a Sampler

Lesson ingredients and rhythm

In many ways, because of changes in the culture over the past few decades, class teachers are having to become games teachers. That is, to teach, through curriculum design, attitude and example, how to play, how to have child-like fun in active movement — to just be a kid for a few years and get along with others without the precocious self-awareness that modern screen time and team sports tend to engender. This involves, in part, keeping everything moving and developing the magical teaching art of ending each activity precisely two minutes before (!) the class becomes a little out of tune with it.

Successful games class lessons almost always demand cycling between active/strenuous out-breath activities and quieter/more individual in-breath activities. While it is generally best to start at the narrow end of the funnel and work outward, which mood comes first in a given lesson is really a matter of reading the children, of meeting them where they are.

The number of cyclings between active and quiet in a period depends largely on the students' age: children in grade one will usually need several transitions from quiet to active to quiet within even a 45 minute period. A class on a good day for grades one or two might include four or five different activities between the opening and closing circles. By middle school, students are physiologically ready to have a few brief moments of quiet at the beginning and end of the period, and to go all out for the majority of a period. Because of this, games teachers for the lower grades need to have enough material at the ready in their back pockets to keep things moving and harmonious. To this end, here is one way of classifying and organizing games and activities, together with a few illustrations of each type. There are no new games, just new children!

In addition to all of the whole-class developmental activities in Section 3, games and pastimes like the following are strongly recommended as part of a school's program for the lower grades.

Active Games and Skills

Within the general category of very active games and activities, three families can be identified. These games should always end with no child having an abiding feeling having won or lost.

Danger/Pursuit: includes all games with a chasing, running, tagging element. Classic games of tag can have enough thematic and story variations (freeze tag, turtle tag, steal the bacon, etc.) to be fresh and exciting forever throughout childhood. Adding complexity by bringing in balls, obstacles or other objects, or partnership aspects, will create an endless supply of imaginative fun, as well as avenues for building running skills and spatial awareness. An important feature of all such games is that over time every student is tagged or becomes It.

Relays: All sorts of skills — not only running, but also ball skills, jump rope skills, gymnastics skills, and more — can be introduced through relay races. And with enough variety of challenges, the basic relay format can hold all student interest day after day.

Throwing & Catching: Games that involve a primary element of throwing and catching (in addition to whatever running around is called for) help build foundations for all sorts of team sports in middle school and beyond.

General Active/Exercise: There are tons of games that more or less fit all of the above descriptions. On the following pages are some of my favorites.

Danger/Pursuit Games

Tiger Hunt

Source: Traditional
Outdoor
Supplies: One "spear" made from a tree branch for each student, with tip only slightly sharpened; two old basketballs or similar

Students stand side by side in a line, holding their spears in upright position, just as they will in 5th Grade for the pentathlon. Teacher (or teachers) forcefully roll an old basketball in front of the line — about 15 feet away — and students attempt to "spear the tiger" as it rolls along. The game works more expeditiously if you happen to have a helper so balls can go in both directions at the same time. It's good to rotate the student throwing line from ends toward the middle every so often so that students get a turn to throw from different points (the ball slows down as it rolls to the far side).

Lily Pad Hoops

Source: Traditional
Outdoor
Supplies: Two dozen or more hula hoops

Set up several rows of about 6 or 7 hula hoops, starting the first row with about a foot between hoops, then succeeding rows progressively farther apart. Tell students the first row is the "kindergarten lily pad row," the next is "first grade," etc. Students are to jump with feet together along a row without getting a "hot foot" in the space between. If a student misses a jump, she goes "back to kindergarten." When the activity has reached the time when students have had enough turns hopping with two feet together, additional challenge can be added by re-starting hopping on one foot only. For older grades, the same setup can be used for running stride jumps with one foot landing per hoop.

Catch of Fish

Source: Bancroft (with variation)
Indoor/outdoor
Supplies: cones or other field markers

Mild version: mark off a wide circle as the Fish Pond, and choose three of the students to begin the play as the Fish Net. These take hands and, without letting go of their grasp, run together to catch Fish, who if caught join the Net. Either have the net continue to grow until all Fish are caught, or make a rule that when a Net grows to six students, it will break into two nets of three.

Rougher version for grade 3 and up: Start with two teams, each at a goal line. One side is "the Fish Net," clasping hands in a line; the other are Fish. Sides advance toward other ends, fish trying to swim down river, elude the net and reach ocean. When the net has caught some fish, they encircle them, and these get one try to break out of the net; those who cannot escape the net without breaking clasps go to "the cat food factory."

Curtain Ball

Source: Bancroft (variation) Indoor/Outdoor
Supplies: a large curtain, volleyball stands or similar, about a dozen gator-skin foam balls

This game is always a student favorite, and provides an excellent first step in the acquisition of volleyball skills. A curtain is strung between two volleyball stands, height such that it is not possible for students to see over the curtain. The class is divided onto two sides to begin, and they start throwing balls back and forth over the curtain. A player who catches a ball in the air can go to the outside of the curtain, take 3 more steps, and dodgeball anyone on the opposing team (below the shoulders). A successful throw results in the player hit going back with the thrower to join the other team; a throw that is caught results in the thrower joining the team on that side.

Streets and Alleys

Source: Traditional
Indoor/outdoor
Supplies: none, (requires at least 27 students)

All players but two, who will be a Chaser and a Chased, stand to make even rows and columns, (e.g., with 27 players the setup would be 5 x 5) spaced so that they can just touch hands with adjoining players either way (i.e. north-south or east-west). The Chaser starts outside of one corner of the form and the Chased at the diagonally opposite one. The teacher calls out "streets" or "alleys" from time to time, being the signals to change the direction in which the hands make lanes for the pursuit. Neither runner may break through a lane, but must immediately change direction when the teacher calls the change of lane direction. For a new race, the Chaser and Chased change places with two others.

Rooster Tails Tag

Source: Traditional
Indoor/outdoor
Supplies: One "rooster tail" for each student; a strip of fabric about 15 inches long, with a knot tied at one end so that when tucked into the back of student's pants it will not readily fall out.

Each player has shirt tucked in all around, and only the knot tucked in so that the full length of the "tail" is hanging out in back (no shirts untucked). On go signal, players chase each other within a marked space, and attempt to pull out others's tails without themselves being so caught (no fair holding your tail). Those who lose their tail pick it up and go to a "chicken coop" waiting area.

Animal Chase

Source: Bancroft
Indoor/outdoor
Supplies: cones to mark a playing area

All children except the Hunter are given forest animal names, such as bear, lion, etc., and stand at one end of the play area (there are two finish lines, or walls, or safe areas). There should be 3 or 4 of each kind. Hunter stands in the field wherever she wants but not too near the animals, and calls out an animal name (not knowing who will spring for the other side). This is similar to Red Rover or Uncle Sam.

Chick-ur-mur

Source: Traditional
Indoor/outdoor
Supplies: cones or rope to make a safe line

Begin with students holding hands in a side-by-side line, at the safe line. One student is chosen as the Witch, who crouches and stirs over an imaginary cauldron about 15 or 20 yards away. Children march forward holding hands in line. As they approach the Witch's den, the ends of the line join to close the circle around the Witch. Then the students slowly circle the Witch and chant "Chick-ur-mur, chick-ur-mur, cravy crow, I went to the well to wash my toe. When I came back, the witch I found, how many chickies has she ground?" The Witch answers with any number she wants, but when the number is "six" all students drop their grasp and run for safety as the Witch gives chase. Those who are caught in the chase, or who prematurely release their grasp before "six" is shouted out, join the Witch as pursuers in the next round. The line, now reduced in numbers, returns to the beginning. After a few turns, when several have been caught, start a new game with a new selected Witch..

Grizzly Bear

Source: Traditional
Outdoor
Supplies: a basket or pail with several dozen tennis balls; cones or rope to make safe line; a thick rope about 6 to 10 feet long to be the "bear's tail"

Children wait at the safety line with an empty pail, and the Grizzly Bear (the teacher) stands about 15 yards away with the pile of honey (tennis balls) on the ground, swaying his 'tail'. On calling 'Go' children run out to try to steal the honey, and the Bear tries to tag them (carefully) with his tail. When the teacher calls "run home," the stealing must cease. Those tagged join in holding the rope and helping bear defend. When the number of children also holding the rope after several rounds reaches about six, call a "jail break"; continue until the children have won by taking back to the pail all the old Bear's honey.

Foxes, Squirrels and Trees

Source: Traditional
Indoor/outdoor
Supplies: Boundary cones or lines

Teacher chooses a few to be Foxes (chasers/taggers) and a few to start as Trees. All the rest are Squirrels at the beginning. A Tree consists of two students who stand facing each other about 2 feet apart, but joined by their hands above head level. Foxes begin to pursue Squirrels. Any squirrel who wants to get to safety ducks into the middle of any tree and gently pushes one of the partners of that tree out; that child becomes a squirrel and may not directly return to the same tree for safety. Any Squirrel caught raises his hands and looks for another who has been caught to form a new Tree, i.e. as the game progresses there will be more and more Trees until all, or almost all, are caught. Repeat.

Giant's Cave

Source: Gilb File
Supplies: marking for a starting/safe line

One child is chosen as the Giant and is put at a distance from the safe line, crouching in a sleeping position with eyes covered by arms. The children also pretend to sleep until the teacher says "wake up children." The children say, "Mother (or Father) may we go out to play?" The teacher answers, "Yes but don't go too near the Giant's Cave." When the children are skipping and running near enough to the sleeping Giant to give a reasonable chance of tagging a few, the teacher shouts "Look out! the giant!" and the children run for home. Children who are caught become Giant's Helpers in the next round.

Relays — Samples

Jump Rope Relay

Supplies: one jump rope for each relay team; cones or lines for start.

Straightforward race with jump ropes: one at a time from each line runs out to the jump rope area, jumps rope a given number of times and/or performs a given trick or tricks, leaves the rope in its spot, runs back and tags up for the next runner/jumper.

Club or Ball Switch Relay

Supplies: two or three hoops set at a distance for each line, with one cone or bowling pin in each. (Used bowling pins may be available as discards from a local bowling lanes. Substitute cones if needed.)

Runner must move pins from one hoop to the other, i.e. pick up pin 1 and put it in hoop 2, pick up pin 2 and put it in hoop 3, pick up pin 3 and run back to put it in hoop 1, and then run back to tag up the next runner. The main point of the race is the agility of moving the pins. Can also be a basketball dribbling drill in later grades.

Exercise Relay

The first in line runs out to the exercise line, performs a given exercise (e.g. 3 pushups, 6 jumping jacks, etc) then runs back and tags the next in line.

Clean Up Your Room

Source: Traditional
Indoor/outdoor
Supplies: at least two dozen tennis balls

Two teams facing each other across a line; boys vs. girls works well if the numbers are fair. Teacher tells this story: "Once there was a family with many, many children, and only two bedrooms for them all. The children were a little naughty and often didn't put their toys away. One day when the parents were going out for a walk, they got very strict with the children and said the rooms had to be completely cleaned up before they got back, or there would be trouble. But when the parents left, the boys just picked up all their toys and rolled them across the hall into the girls's room. The girls kept picking up all the mess in their room and rolling it into the boys' room." Then scatter a more or less even number of balls on each side of the playing area and shout "clean up your room!" Teams compete to have the fewest number of balls on their side when you occasionally call a halt to check their rooms. Emphasize that the game is only rolling, and that students need to remain standing.

Bowling Bombardment

Source: Gilb File
Indoor/outdoor
Supplies: bowling pins or cones; to be played on gym floor, or smooth outdoor surface

Set up a line of bowling pins or cones on each side of the playing area. The object is to knock down pins on other side. No score is kept; knocked-over pins must be set back up asap. It's just the fun of knocking things down. Ball rollers must stay on their half of the court. Emphasize that balls are only to be rolled.

Throwing and Catching Skills Development

Pages 76 to 78 provide a number of activities for eye-hand coordination and the build-up of throwing and catching skills. Those games, and others like them, are equally appropriate as classroom and recess breaks, and as parts of a comprehensive games/gym program for the early grades.

Quieter Activities

A general principle of Waldorf education is that "the job of the Class Teacher is to form the class in first grade," meaning to strive, from the beginning to establish a culture of students getting along with each other and learning together. Games of this quieter type — in the classroom, the schoolyard or the Games class — can help in reaching this objective.

Little Skills: On any given day, a class might become out of sorts and not really able to get along with each other in doing the lesson you planned. Signs of this include a rise in arguing about fairness, or a series of slight "boo-boo"-level injuries reported as a need to sit out. Being prepared with quieter things to be done individually or with a chosen partner will serve not only the basic need to maintain a breathing rhythm in any lesson, but also the occasional need that children will have to be given time and space to refocus. A lesson that's not going well sometimes could be social things going on in the class that have nothing to do with the teacher's work.

Circle/Musical/Clapping: The form of a circle has an innate healing quality, and the added advantage of the teacher being easily able to see each child's movements.

Party/Quiet/Blindfold: "Phys ed" books from the mid-twentieth century almost always include chapters on games with a little movement and a lot of fun, or humorous challenges.

Don't Do That!

Source: Gilb File
Indoor/outdoor
Supplies: none

Children in a circle, or in rows facing the teacher. Teacher leads a rapid succession of movements saying either "Do this!" or "Do that!" as he shows them. Players are caught if they move when "Do that" is called. For grade 3, you might let a student be the Leader.

Bear – Zoo Escape

Source: Traditional
Indoor/outdoor
Supplies: a basketball or similar

Children make a circle, standing with legs wide, feet astride, hands on hips. "It" is in the middle with a basketball (the bear) and attempts to roll the ball "out of the zoo gate" between legs. Players are not allowed to block the ball with knees or feet, only to bend at the waist and block with palms once the ball is released. Those through whom the "bear escapes" or who move to block too soon are turned to stone (crouch down in their spot on the circle), and are saved when a player succeeds in stopping the escape.

Fire on the Mountain (Moto - Kimbiza)

Source: Traditional
Indoor/outdoor
Supplies: none

An African circle game similar to musical chairs: Half plus one or two are "Village Children" who skip around the mountain; the others are the "Parents" who form a circle and squat with backs to skippers. There is a call and response: parents rhythmically chant "Moto, moto" (we see a fire); children reply as they keep vigorously skipping around the distant outer circle: "Kilimanjaro, kilimanjaro" (we're playing on the mountain). Then the "Chief" cries out "Kimbiza! kimbiza!" (run, run for home).

Each child then rushes to place hands on the back of an available parent. The one(s) left out go to the middle. Then switch, the parents become the next round of children, plus add one or two to that group; there should always be one or a few more Children than Parents.

Right Shoulder, Left Shoulder

Source: Variation on traditional "A Tisket, A Tasket"
Indoor/outdoor
Supplies: none

Students stand in a circle with arms at sides. If "It" who is skipping around the outside of the circle, taps one's right shoulder, chase is given once around back to the starting spot; but if the left shoulder is tapped, then the student must not move at all. "It" keeps going with the object, through feints and speed, of getting the whole class "turned to stone" (crouching). If a player holds still with a left shoulder tap, or can catch It after a right shoulder tap, all the poor stones are saved and a new round can begin.

Quarter and Stone

Source: Variation on traditional "A Tisket, A Tasket"
Indoor/outdoor
Supplies: a quarter, and a river stone or similar

Same basic game as above, but with students standing in the circle with hands making a shelf behind back, ready to receive an object. Tell the following story: a tricky Squirrel comes by one day and asks to borrow a quarter. He promises to give it back the next time he comes to town. Now, if he gives you the quarter, that's what he promised and you must not try to chase him (or flinch or move in any way). But if he tries to give you this worthless stone, you chase him. Then the teacher or a chosen student skips around the perimeter, and every so often puts one or the other object in a student's hand. If it's the quarter, and the student moves in any way; or if it's the stone, and the student can't catch the It during one run around the circle, the student is turned to stone. A player who succeeds by either holding still for the quarter or catching It is said to "save all the poor stones" and then may have a turn to be It.

All Birds Fly

Source: Traditional
Indoors
Supplies: none

Students sit at their desks, or crouch. Leader, standing in front, calls out "All robins fly!" and flaps arms; or "All ducks fly" and flaps (etc.). Each time, students are to immediately rise up to standing, also flap their arms, and say: "Yes, Chief, all (blanks) fly!" Occasionally, the leader tries to catch them out by saying a nonsensical thing like "All porcupines fly."

Blind Shepherd and Goat

Source: Traditional
Indoors if possible
Supplies: Blindfold, gator-skin foam ball (for safety in seeking Goat), cowbell

The class stands, arms at sides and about 3 feet apart to form a protective circle, "the pasture posts." The blindfolded Shepherd in the circle is spun around a few times. The teacher tells the Goat to take a certain number and type of steps, and to then ring the bell: "the Goat may take 4 steps and then ring the bell." Then teacher tells the Shepherd a number and type of steps to take: "the Shepherd may take 6 giant steps." A variety may be given, e.g., tiptoes, marching, run twice around the pasture (for the Goat). To include more children, have the Goat be two students with back holding front's shoulders from behind.

Find the Leader

Source: Traditional
Indoor/outdoor
Supplies: none

Group in a circle, all doing some simple movement like tapping knees. "It" chosen by teacher hides eyes until the teacher has chosen one student to be the "Chief'" who will initiate changes of movements (e.g., clapping waving, wiggling. "It" stands in the middle of the circle and tries to guess who the "Chief" is; the "Chief" changes the movement when "It" is not looking. "It" gets three guesses.

Giant's Treasure

Source: Traditional
Indoor/outdoor
Supplies: A wallop (an adult calf-length sock with another old sock or two rolled up inside. A supply of these is useful to have for many games, and can be safer than tagging by hand) and a small basket of stones or large beads placed about 8 inches off the floor atop a pillow or similar.

The blindfolded Giant sits cross-legged behind the basket of treasures, guarding it with the giant's club (a wallop). The rest of the class sits in two rows to form a lane down which the Robber (a student chosen by the teacher) will attempt to tiptoe, approach the treasure basket, and either (a) by stealth make a quick grab of some treasure without being struck by the wallop; or (b) by feints and patience induce the Giant to use up his three allotted swings with the club without being struck, in which case the Robber is said to have won all the treasure.

Jackstones

Source: Traditional
Indoors or on a smooth surface
Supplies: river stones, five or six per player

Jackstones is a traditional Korean game, similar to the game Jacks. Students can play individually or pair up for competition. Players use only one hand to play the game. The player picks up one stone and throws it upward; before the stone falls onto the ground, he tries to pick up another stone from the ground and then catch the one that was thrown. The picked-up stone is set to the side. This is repeated until there are no stones on the ground. If a stone is dropped in the process, the rule can be simply that it is still to be picked up, or that another stone which has already been set aside goes back into the playing area. The game can then advance to attempting to pick up two stones at a time, three, etc. For a pairs or group competition, there can be a shared pile of stones, and rules like: the player is out if she doesn't catch the stone in the air; or catches must be made on the back of the hand.

Jackstones Shooting Game

Source: Traditional, similar to marbles
Indoors or on a smooth surface
Supplies: river stones, six or seven per player

Players sit or squat facing each other at a distance of about 3 feet; each drops his stones from about 8 inches above the floor so that they scatter a bit. Players take turns with a chosen "shooting stone" that they slide toward their opponent's stones. Any stones that are hit get added to the shooter's pile; whether any are hit or not, the shooter gets back the stone that was slid, which is to be placed back in the playing area for the opponent's turn. A new game begins when one of the players has all the stones.

Polished river stones are available from garden centers and can be used for many developmental activities, including the in The Extra Lesson.

It's My Birthday!

Source: Traditional
Indoor/outdoor
Supplies: coins or gems, and a few wallops. A cone to mark the distance around which It must run while being chased and walloped

Students stand shoulder to shoulder in a line, with hands behind their backs. It (the birthday boy or girl) turns his/her back to the line and steps away a few paces. The teacher walks behind the line and distributes three to five coins, and two or three wallops. The teacher calls on the It to approach the line, hold out palms and proclaim to a player of his choice, "It's my birthday." The goal of the It is to collect a given number of coins before calling on a wallop-holder. Responses depending on the individual are:

a) "Bless you" — shows hands to be empty or perhaps places hand to heart.

b) "Happy birthday" — places coin in hand.

c) "You lie!" — and gives chase while shouting "it's NOT your birthday."

The Chaser must complete the verbal response before taking the first swing.

Thus, the It might be punished for lying and greed.

Poor Kitty

Source: Gilb File
Mostly indoor
Supplies: none

Children sit cross-legged in a circle, and teacher chooses one to begin, who turns to the student at her right and attempts to cause him to break into a smile or laugh, using any form of narrative humor or teasing. This could include stroking the Poor Kitty's head, picking at mangy fur, references to smelly food or things that might disappoint a feline. Ruled out are tickling or any disrespectful words or gestures. Biting one's lips or looking away are not allowed. If the Kitty can avoid smiling for around 30 seconds, then the Kitty wins. Then the Kitty continues to the next player on the right in the circle. This game will hold interest only once or twice in third or fourth grade; setting the circle up so there is an alternation of boys and girls can add some zest at this age.

Shorebirds

Source: Traditional
Indoors, or out if the surface is suitable
Supplies: a basket of polished river stones; two or three empty trays or shallow baskets; smooth floor or surface suitable for hopping barefoot

Each student takes ten stones (or amount of your choosing). Divide the class into two or three teams depending on class size (boys vs. girls works well for this game). Have each team pool their stones in a pile at their starting line; set a tray or low basket (the Nest) for each team at finish line. (Because of the setup, the number of students on each team does not have to be equal.) On "go," all children in each team race to pick up one stone at a time with their toes and hop "across the river" on one foot like shorebirds. Use of hands is not allowed, even if the basket is knocked over. The team that carries home all their stones first wins. Students need to hop on the carrying lap, but they can run back to get the next stone

Roughhousing Games

Roughhousing is play that flows with joy; it's the most common form of play in the animal kingdom. According to the authors of *The Art of Roughhousing* (and many other sources) rough and tumble play releases chemicals in the brain that promote neuron growth in the cortex and hippocampus, both of which are vital to higher learning and memory. You can tell that healthy rough and tumble play is going on if it's playful. You'll hear laughter, see fierce but happy eye contact, and observe that there's a balance between competitors so that winning and losing are equally distributed.

Little Wrestling Matches

The playful wrestling activities described at the end of the Zoorobics chapter are essentials in building a culture of playful, safe roughhousing (see p. 73).

Bull in the Ring

Source: Bancroft (variation)
Indoors on mats/outdoors on soft ground
Supplies: none

A Bull is in the pit formed by all others firmly holding hands in a circle, wide enough that their arms are mostly but not fully extended. He is given 30 seconds to try to get out of the pit by running and breaking holds. The circle are not allowed to use their arms to trip (block too low) nor clothesline (block too high) — blocking must be at more or less chest level.

Catch and Pull Tug of War

Source: Bancroft
Indoors on mats, or outdoors if surface okay
Supplies: dividing line rope

A line, with two teams, each to its side. They try to pull over opponents, who become their team members. The side wins with the most players at the end.

Chicken Market

Source: Bancroft (variation)
Indoors, or out if surface okay
Supplies: none

Children crouch down in a wide circle and firmly hold fists in armpits, with elbows out wide. A "Buyer" and "Seller" go around inspecting the "Young Chickens" for ones that are "ready to go to market." They test their weight by standing one at each side and attempting to lift the Chicken by the elbows, making comments all the while. Every so often they say "this one feels ready," pick him up and carry off to "the market". If the arms are wobbly, they pass by for a time.

Royal Body Guards

Source: Bancroft
Outdoors, grass or softer ground
Supplies: cones for boundaries, pinnies for team identification

Two goal lines are marked off, a King or Queen plus four or five Royal Guards are chosen for each team; the remainder are Invaders against the other team. The object is for one of the Royals to reach the other goal line without being tagged by an Invader. To begin, the Guards hold hands in a circle around their monarch and try to protect him or her from being tagged as they advance down the field. Any Invaders that are tagged by the Guards go to the dungeon. (Invaders do not tag Invaders.) A team wins if either they are first to tag the opponent's monarch, or if their Royal reaches the other goal line.

Ruler of the Sea

Source: Maureen Curran
Indoors on mats, or carpet with defined playing area
Supplies: none

The playing area is "the sea" and students squat just off the edge. The teacher proclaims "I am the ruler of the sea, and you are all seals. When I say the sea is stormy, you try to seal crawl across the sea to the other side without getting caught.... 'and the sea is stormy!'" As students cross the sea, the teacher tags a few, who become her "Subjects." For each round, the Ruler announces what her Subjects are and do, such as sharks who slither and snap their arms as jaws, seaweed that kneels in place waving their arms to tag; sea boulders who just create obstacles; etc. Those who are still in the game crossing the sea are also given roles, such as crab walks, eels, walruses, etc. When there are more Subjects than children who are crossing, start another round.

Slugs

Source: Maureen Curran
Indoors on mats or carpet
Supplies: none

Children begin doing roly polys (p. 69) without stopping. The teacher or teachers are the Hungry Giants, who tromp around the playing area chanting: "Hungry giants looking for slugs, lying so lazy on the rugs. If you falter, if you stop, we will drag you to the pot!" Or, "Hungry giants, making a stew, finding poor slugs just like.... you! Fee fie foe fum, hungry giants here we come. I found a flat slug to throw in the pot, I like to keep looking 'til I've captured a lot!" Any children who stop doing more or less vigorous roly polys get dragged to a "pot" area where they are lined up and put together side by side like sardines, and must remain where they are placed, limp, until the end of the game.

Sandwich

Source: Traditional
Indoors on mats or carpet
Supplies: a heavy mat, or two layers of tumbling mats to place on students

Half of class lies face up on carpet or mats, pushed tight together like sardines, and with all shoulders lined up and all arms strictly by sides. Then the heavy mat or layers of mats are placed over them, covering from shoulders to feet, so they are is sandwiched under. The other half of the class lines up at one end of the sandwich and log rolls across one by one — no diving on at the start, or hopping up and down; just rolling. When this half of the class has had two or three turns to roll, switch.

Games and Movement Resources

There are many very fine Waldorf-related books about games and movement, and I'll list them below. The following suggestion about "the best books" is not meant to diminish the wealth of activities and insights they contain. For one thing, a well-balanced program in a Waldorf school should include Bothmer/Spacial Dynamics elements, at least at the beginning and end of most classes.

The Five Best Books

If you are a beginning Games/Movement teacher in a Waldorf school, or relatively new in that career, I strongly recommend you find copies of the following five books, immerse yourself in them, use them as a "starter kit," work on making them your own, and then build your program from there. Admittedly, this advice reflects a personal bias: it worked for me! As of this writing, each is still available, for surprisingly little money, through online used book sellers.

Stunts and Tumbling for Girls
An invaluable resource for an elementary and middle-school tumbling program ... for girls AND boys! Virginia Lee Horne, The Ronald Press Co., NY, 1943

The Gilb Card File of Games
A treasure-trove of time-honored games. One of the many aspects I love about games books from before the modern era is that the activities are often described as suitable for groups of 50, 60, even 100 students. Stella S. Gilb, Hurst Printing, Lexington KY, 1962

Games for the Playground, Home, School & Gymnasium
More than 400 pages of active and quiet games for students of all ages. Jessie H. Bancroft, The MacMillan Co., NY, 1927

Games and Sport the World Around
A compendium of games from every continent. Sarah Etheridge Hunt, Ronald Press Co., NY, 1964

The Art of Roughhousing
This wonderful book shows how rough-and-tumble play can nurture close connections, solve behavior problems, boost confidence, and more. Anthony DeBenedet and Lawrence Cohen, Quirk Books, Philadelphia PA, 2011

Additional Waldorf-related games resources

Looking Forward
Games, rhymes and exercises to help younger children develop their learning abilities. Molly von Heider, Hawthorn Press, Gloucestershire UK, 1995

Games Children Play
How games and sport help children develop hundreds of creative games and movement ideas, with clear background support. Kim Brooking-Payne. Hawthorne Press, Gloucestershire UK, 1996

Child's Play 1 & 2
> Wil van Haren and Rudolf Kischnick. Hawthorne Press, Gloucestershire UK, 1996

Additional foundations for a program of developmental tumbling and gymnastics

Circus Techniques: Juggling, Equilibristics, and Vaulting
> Covers juggling, balance and vaulting circus activities that have elements of theatricality. Hovey Burgess. Drama Book Specialists, 1976.

Balancing and Sport Acrobatics
> The art of balancing and sport acrobatics for the beginner as well as the more advanced participant, with clear and helpful pictorial pointers. Stan Buchholtz. Arco Publishing, NY, 1978

Basic Circus Skills
> Introduces Juggling, Balancing, Tumbling, Vaulting, Hand Balancing, Pyramiding, Stunts with Chairs, Trampolining, Ladders, Bicycling, Unicycling, Trapeze, Tightwire, and Clowning. Jack Wiley, Stackpole Books, Mechanicsburg, 1974.

5 Building a Schoolwide Culture

Sharing the Work

Adopting a whole-class model of enriched developmental movement, drawing and painting can start and live anywhere and can grow from even the modest efforts of one teacher who will try things, observe the results, and spread the word.

Everything in teaching is a research project!

- In the Games class, or even on the playground.
- In Early Childhood programs that begin with crawling and tussling games.
- In the morning main lesson or extra mains, with a teacher who's inspired to read the exercise instructions, find a few things that seem to fit class circumstances, and become a "first responder" as noted in Section 1.
- In subject classes, with teachers looking to have a supply of a few extra (and meaningful) breaks from chair-centered learning.
- By the Extra Lesson teacher who feels moved to offer classroom inservices and/or push-in breaks, or to provide trainings as part of faculty meetings. Making this a part of one's Extra Lesson job description will lead to more children receiving the benefit of his or her training… and, ultimately, fewer students needing time away from the class for individual Extra Lesson pullouts or other Academic Intervention Services.
- By sharing the preparation around — one class teacher teaches herself copper rods, another teaches himself the clay ball progression, and they switch classes for 10 minutes a day.

Templates for the inservice model and for possible block rotations follow, as well as a talk I have given to teachers on centering oneself for the challenges of championing new approaches.

A Model for Inservices and Classroom Blocks

One approach to widening the circle of teachers who are ready, willing and able to provide whole-class developmental activities is for the school's Extra Lesson teacher and/or Spacial Dynamics teacher to provide inservice trainings to interested Class Teachers (or others). Here is a template for getting the ball rolling — a listing of developmental/remedial activities recommended for regular inclusion in morning Main Lesson work. There are three possible modes for inservicing these repertoire additions:

1. Teach a teacher or teachers outside of class;
2. Lead the activity with the class, and let the teacher observe/assist as she learns it for future inclusion in her morning rhythm; and/or
3. Assist/observe teacher's work with her class, help with set-up, etc.

Again, the goals are to support a schoolwide culture in which all teachers know the reasons for and practicalities of these whole-class developmental/remedial activities, and to help teachers make them their own. In my experience, starting by helping even one class teacher with a few basics, giving an opportunity for that teacher and others to observe the effects on students and on the harmony of the class, can create the springboard for many wider discussions, as well as a broader understanding and appreciation for the work of an Extra Lesson teacher.

Movement Exercises	When/How Often
Ball and Balance activities (Gr. 2 and up). Similar to "Bal-A-Vis-X". For development of movement sense, midline crossing, focus. Promotes focus, teamwork.	At least one block a year
Bothmer Walks and Exercises, Gr. 2 and up. For development of movement sense, midline crossing, focus.	Get up and move" breaks any time in Gr. 2 and up.
Bean Bags and/or ball passing and tossing from *"Take Time"* or *"Games Children Play"* (Gr. 1); also the Above/Below & Left/Right Integration activities from the Extra Lesson (Grades 2 or 3). Strengthen rhythm and development of midline crossing.	At least one block a year.
Chime Balls (Gr. 2 and up). Promotes spatial and interpersonal intelligences; anticipation, rhythm and breathing.	At least one block a year in Gr. 3 to 6.
Clay Ball Progression (Gr. 1 and up). A progression of 10 to 15 minute exercises with clay, to develop harmonious breathing, touch sense; also an exercise for the temperaments.	At least one 6x block a year in Gr. 1 to 4.
Copper Rod Exercises (Gr. 1 and up). Strengthens/supports: posture, fine motor control, rhythm/breathing, engaging the will, fine motor control for handwriting.	Once a week for 12 weeks, or in a 6 week block rotation
Cross Step Ball Bounce (Gr. 2 and 3). For midline, eye-hand, integration. Goal is mastery while speaking alphabet or times table.	One or more blocks.
Juggling (Gr. 3 and up. Strengthens/supports: Eye-hand coordination, spatial organization, movement patterns.	As occasional "get up and move" breaks in Gr. 3 and up, or one block a year.
Jumping Rope (Gr.1 and up). Strengthens/supports: Readiness for desk work - enhancing focus and attention. Sets the stage for harmonious receptivity to new material. Bodily/kinesthetic and spatial integration. Strengthening the will. Rhythm and duration: All children need to progress through the steps to mastery. Certain students can also benefit from jumping rope when they need a time out.	Once a week for at least half a year - great for Mondays to help class settle down to work.
Lifting One's Weight (Gr. 1 and up); Whole Body Exercise (Gr. 4 and up); and other posture and balance activities. General posture/standing and stretching exercises – a progression of two-minute movement to bring awakeness.	As regular part of morning activities or anytime a 'wakeup call' is needed.
String Games; Hand Clapping Games (Gr. 1, 2 & 3). Inservice for age-appropriate games, finding supplies	Any time a little movement break is needed.

Drawing Exercises	When/How Often
Moving Straight Line and Lemniscate ("1 & 8 Drawing" – Gr. 2 through 4). One of the most important exercises from the Extra Lesson, supports midline development, harmonious rhythm. A very dynamic 'assessment' picture. Can be introduced during an Enrichment class or extra main.	Once a week for 6 weeks.
Shaded Drawing (second half of Gr. 1, and up). Shaded drawing engages and strengthens the will, and helps to wake up thinking capacities. Once good ability has been developed, it can be brought into occasional Main Lesson Book pages for illustrations.	To mastery over the years. Introductory lessons in a 6-week block; then as regular part of Main Lesson Book.

Painting Exercises	When/How Often
Painting Exercises with a Left-to-Right Component (Gr. 1 and up). Strengthens/supports: Spatial orientation for reading and writing, development of radius and ulna, the "bones of reading and writing". The Extra Lesson describes a number of painting exercises which consist mainly of or include careful left-to-right strokes filling the entire paper. Harmonious integration of this movement pattern is critical to the development of stress-free reading and writing.	Very helpful that each class do at least one 6-week block of these per year. (Ideally, two a year.)
Extra Lesson painting exercises with a lemniscate or spiral theme, and that work with Steiner's description of the currents of the earth (Gr. 2 – 8).	Once a week for 6 weeks.

Rhythm/Breathing Exercises	When/How Often
Ball Twirling Exercise (Gr. 3 and up). A calming/integrating exercise that takes about 4 minutes; helps with focus, rhythm, development of reading and writing.	As part of morning routine for 12 days in a row.
Cubes Between Fingers, Marbles Between Toes (Gr. 1 & 2). Activities to bring awakeness and Touch sense.	As part of morning routine for 12 days in a row.
Drawing Circles with the Feet (Gr. 1 and up). Strengthens/supports: Spatial orientation, bodily/kinesthetic integration, balance, rhythm and breathing, engaging the will. The end result desired is a good size red circle on the right, half overlapped by a similar size blue circle on the left.	Once a week for 6 weeks, for one or two 6-week blocks a year. Can be combined with foot writing.
Threefold Spiral (Gr. 1 to 5). Strengthens/supports: Bodily-kinesthetic integration, spatial orientation, laterality, readiness for learning. Rhythm and duration: Once a week for 12 weeks, or in a 6 week block rotation. A calming, quieting activity that will help the entire class, and will be especially helpful for nervous, fidgety students; and for children who experience sleep problems.	Ideally, rhythm of 12: once a week for 12 weeks, or 12 days in a row.
Tracing and Coloring Hands – a calming activity that helps with laterality confirmation.	Once in a while in Gr. 1; could repeat once or twice in Gr. 2.
Wool Winding (Gr. 1 and 2) – development of radius & ulna; rhythmic calming & integrating; laterality.	To mastery, in Gr. 1. Could be repeated in early Gr. 2.

Sample suggested block system for morning support exercises

The following charts for Grades 1 through 4 are given as one possible example of how exercises for the whole class can be integrated into a regular lesson plan, optimally at the beginning of the school day, and worked at with a beneficial rhythm over the course of a block schedule during a school year. When I've discussed this particular approach during professional-development workshops at other

First Grade - *exercises appropriate for ages 6 and up*

BLOCK	MONDAY	TUESDAY	WEDNESDAY	THURSDAY	FRIDAY
1	Jumping Rope	Copper Rods	Take Time Beanbags	Left-to-Right Painting	Zoo Exercises
2	Clay Ball	Threefold Spiral	Writing with the Feet	Wool Winding	Introduce Shaded Drawing
3	Jumping Rope	Copper Rods	Take Time Beanbags	Left-to-Right Painting	Zoo Exercises
4	Clay Ball	Threefold Spiral	Writing with the Feet	Wool Winding	Introduce Painting Handwriting (basic shapes)
5	Jumping Rope	Copper Rods	Take Time Beanbags	Eye-Hand Painting	Foot Circles and Writing

Second Grade - *exercises appropriate for ages 8 and up*

BLOCK	MONDAY	TUESDAY	WEDNESDAY	THURSDAY	FRIDAY
1	Jumping Rope	Copper Rods	Take Time Beanbags	Eye-Hand Painting	Zoo Exercises
2	Moving Straight Line & Lemniscate (1&8)	Threefold Spiral	Writing with the Feet	Painting Handwriting	Wool Winding
3	Jumping Rope	Copper Rods	Take Time Beanbags	Blue and Red Spiral Painting	Drawing Circles with the Feet
4	Moving Straight Line & Lemniscate (1&8)	Threefold Spiral	Writing with the Feet	Painted Lemniscate	Shaded Drawing practice (alphabet booklet)
5	Jumping Rope	Copper Rods	Cross-Step Ball Bounce; Ball Twirling	Blue and Red Spiral Painting	Clay Ball

schools, some have responded that a block system requiring a daily rotation of activities like the one shown would create a logistical headache because it requires constantly passing materials like clay or copper rods around. An alternative model that has worked well at these schools is to instead create their own schedule in which a given class does Activity A (e.g. Threefold Spirals) each day or almost every day for two or three weeks, and then passes the set-ups along to another teacher.

Third Grade - *exercises appropriate for ages 9 and up*

BLOCK	MONDAY	TUESDAY	WEDNESDAY	THURSDAY	FRIDAY
1	Jumping Rope	Copper Rods	Take Time Beanbags	Blue and Red Spiral Painting	Cross-Step Ball Bounce; Ball Twirling
2	Clay Ball	Threefold Spiral	Writing with the Feet	Painting Handwriting exercises	Drawing Circles with the Feet
3	Jumping Rope	Copper Rods	Take Time Beanbags	Secondary Color Exercise (painting)	Cross-Step Ball Bounce; Ball Twirling
4	Moving Straight Line & Lemniscate (1&8)	Shaded Drawing practice	Writing with the Feet	Painted Lemniscate	String Games (cat's cradle)
5	Jumping Rope	Copper Rods or Chime Balls	Juggling introduction	Secondary Color Exercise (painting)	Clay Ball

Fourth Grade - *exercises appropriate for ages 10 and up.*
If class has had all or most of the rotation of exercises as given in the previous tables for Grades 1, 2 and 3, the teacher will need to gauge which exercises are still most needed before the class rounds the bend toward middle school. In any

BLOCK	MONDAY	TUESDAY	WEDNESDAY	THURSDAY	FRIDAY
1	Jumping Rope	Moving Straight Line & Lemniscate (1&8)	Juggling practice; Ball Twirling	Secondary Color Exercise (painting)	Drawing Circles with the Feet
2	Copper Rods	Writing with the Feet	Clay Ball	Painting Handwriting	Shaded Drawing
3	Jumping Rope	Spatial Lemniscates form drawing	Juggling practice; Ball Twirling	Magenta and Viridian Painting	Teacher Choice
4	Copper Rods	Writing with the Feet	Threefold Spiral	Painting Handwriting	Teacher Choice
5	Jumping Rope	Balancing Lemniscates form drawing	Chime Balls	Magenta and Viridian Painting	Teacher Choice

The Fourfold Process for Success

The following is a written version of a talk I've given to teacher groups during the past few years as a companion to the lecture on hope, love and faith in Section 1. This one also relies on an audience that's familiar with Steiner's pedagogical indications, particularly his description of the fourfold structure of the human being and of the "Pedagogical Law." During this lecture, I'd progressively build up some diagramming on the chalkboard, corresponding to our progression with the subject.

In December 1916 and January 1917, Rudolf Steiner delivered a series of thirty lectures in which he spoke about the karmic or suprasensible causes of the tragic conflagration then raging in Europe and beyond. It was at this time that Steiner began to speak out more directly about politics and to place himself more squarely in the public eye, advocating that Germany adopt a new threefold cultural/political/social organization as a way of rebuilding when peace returned. In twenty-nine of these lectures, Steiner gradually lead his audience to an understanding of personalities such as Wilson, Clemenceau, and Lloyd George; of the new era that would arise from the ashes; and of a new social structure that could arise after the Great War and prevent its repeat. For those interested in a study of the true struggles hidden behind the veil of world history, this very lengthy series has much to offer. However, in the middle of this courageous lecture cycle, Steiner seemed (at first) to be diverging from his discussion of the world leaders and events of that time. In lecture 19, he delineated—in one concise lecture—a comprehensive basis for a modern psychology; an analysis, as he put it, of the three realms of soul sickness that beset all human beings.[71]

This lecture contains essential reading for all Waldorf teachers who seek to work on how to stand—physically, emotionally and spiritually—in front of students, colleagues and the wider community. But my purpose at the moment is to suggest that lecture 19 — combined with Steiner's "Hope, Love and Faith" lecture of December 2, 1911 — can also be of tremendous help to the inner workings of your Waldorf school, and to any organization of individuals, each with human desires, strengths and occasional shortcomings. I hope to show how these two lectures can provide the framework for greater success with all sorts of issues that require group effort, and can also give us a sort of magnifying glass for detecting why things might all too often go less well.

Let's say, for instance, that after attending this course [or reading this book] you've become inspired to propose or champion changes to your school's movement or remedial program — or to bring anything new into the working of your school. These two lectures map out the best way forward and highlight specific types of obstacles you may encounter along the path. Now, in most aspects, you're probably already following this fourfold model in your individual teaching. In other words, you kind of already know this! So let's start with a look at the typical teaching year. Then I'll relate these two lectures to the teacher's year, and go from that point to a better way to approach initiatives at your school.

The fourfold rhythm of the teaching year

Here [following] is a sketch of an annual rhythm, but the general idea could just as easily apply to a lesson block or a weekly rhythm. A sketch of a twelve-month cycle will help us start to talk about what really has to happen for you to try to change something at your school. Here we have what occurs in the summer. I mean, some parents picture that this is from June 15 to September 3, or something like that, but really our summer break is when we're done with the previous year and we maybe have time to not think about the following year for a little bit. How long is that? Let's just say it's [teacher in audience calls out "30 seconds"]. Yeah, I agree. Well, it's sometime in late June or early July, right? Where ideally you can relax a bit; it's not that you have nothing to do but at least it's maybe fewer hours a day or whatever. So we have a pause in late June/early July; and then certainly by the latter part of July and into August, class teachers are collecting and organizing all the materials for a new year, planning out what is to be. And then we have this really long sweep from September all the way through May and June where you're teaching almost nonstop; you're in the thick of it and hopefully the plans that you made here [summer] are working out. At the end of the cycle when school is out we have our year-end work days and the Review phase. Review feeds into the early summer pause for reflection and new inspiration, and around we go again.

So that's a pretty condensed way of looking at a cycle of the year, or a block, or any period of teaching time. You'll notice I didn't draw a closed circle, and the reason for that we'll come to in a couple of minutes. [Adding labels to diagram.] But let's just name this part of the year "HAVE" which is figuring out what we need to have, whether it's as simple in my case is I need to have six more basketballs or in a class teacher's case you need to have stacks of books two feet high all over your dining room table. This is the planning and organizing phase. Then we get to a "DO" phase, when we enthusiastically move ahead all the way through the school year with whatever we had planned…of course with review and planning updates during breaks. And then, usually in June, we have faculty work days, and so at this point there needs to be a "REVIEW" phase—self-evaluation, what you did individually and as a teaching team, professional assessment of pluses and minuses during the year—before you get to thinking about next year and how you want that to be.

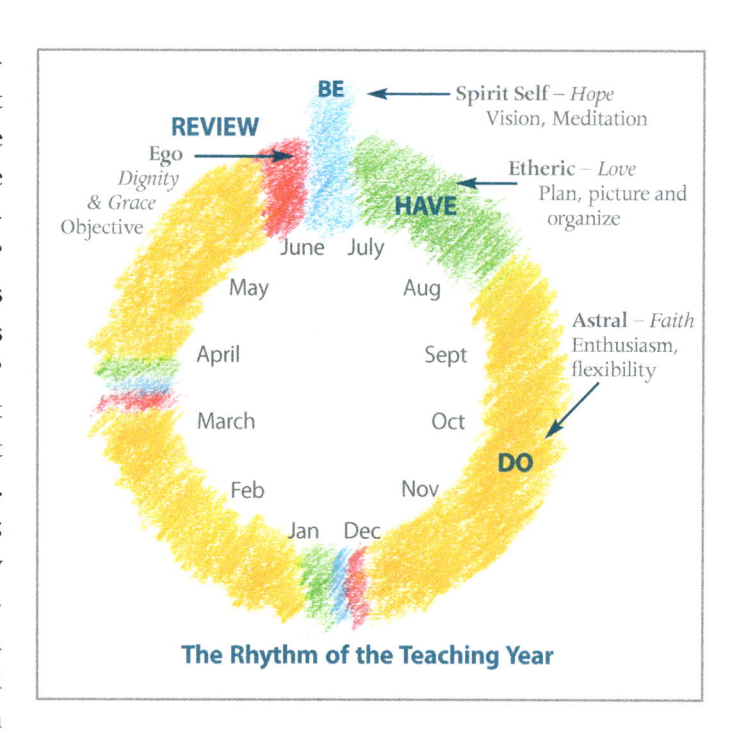

Let's see what else we could map onto these phases. First of all, I left a little gap here at the top of the circle because we need to take our review into a sort of sleep life, and enter a time when, as Steiner suggested, we try to think away the physical picture from the past year and contemplate what the children will be striving for in the year ahead. To try to picture the coming physical, physiologic and emotional reality of the children, but also including in our picturing the review that we need as a guide for our visioning. This interlude is when we need to call on the help of the Spirit Self. We're seeking higher wisdom in envisioning what is meant to be. The "BE" phase.

Next, as we sketch out what resources and preparation we need to have for this new vision, we need to infuse ourselves with true love of what a rising nine year old or a fourteen year old will want and need to learn. So to a certain degree when we're planning, we're doing picture thinking; and not that one can parse it out totally, but there's an interior, etheric quality to this phase. And then here with Doing, we're in movement, we're carrying out our plan, we're enthusiastically moving ahead with whatever it is we thought we'd do … so there's an astral quality to what's happening here [points]. We're in motion; we made a plan, now we're executing it.

Maintaining balance

For a team of teachers, the Review phase can be the most difficult, a time when the meetings must have well-anchored egos if real communication is to find a space and teachers can talk openly with colleagues about positives, but also bring in some constructive analysis or broach ideas about possibly better approaches to students or lessons. That sort of thing. To enable forthright conversation in a way that strengthens professional teamwork. A proper review at the end of the year is truly an ego exercise: we need to discipline ourselves to firmly monitor our postural control, individually and as a group.

Any teacher with enough self-reflection to be able to make a career at teaching already knows and follows this cycle, even if not familiar with the fourfold anthroposophic terminology I mapped onto it. But the terminology can be a helpful pointer to lapses. When a lesson or a block goes off the mark, maybe there was a missing piece at the "etheric" step, a lack of lovingly picturing it out and collecting resources. The sticking point might have fallen at the "astral" step of forging ahead: you brought either too much or too little enthusiasm. Not enough objective review after the fact: taking the time for an ego-anchored review and writing it down is essential for turning the corner to the future. Or, perhaps most undermining of all, not making real time to meditate and to be open to help from the world of our and our students' higher selves; preparing to bring a new experience into the physical world is an incarnation moment. Maintaining one's balance in teaching requires health in each of these four phases.

Starting something new

The same fourfold pattern applies to any effort to change things in an organization. The cycle that works for one teacher with his or her teaching year is truly the only approach that will lead to lasting change in a school; the only difference is that with a new initiative, there is a definite and necessary starting point, and that is the REVIEW step, the step for egos to work together in a professional and objective way. This can proceed in the same manner as a Child Study. First, observable facts: what is so. Then (and only then) soul aspects: wishes, desires. Also at this step, it can be productive to consciously bring to the surface any feelings of shame, anger or fear around the issue; remember that from our readings in *The Human Soul* by Karl König we know that these three emotions can be our helpful guides to matters that need addressing.

A good review will lead over into step two, BE. That is, with regard to the issue at hand, what do we want to be as a school? What is "the Being of the School" or the Spirit Self calling for? What is our striving as a teaching community, how does it relate to our stated mission and vision? Only when this has been identified, named and well articulated is it time to move to the HAVE or planning phase, for a teacher or group to consider a way that resources could be applied to the envisioned new direction. (Or even better, a choice of alternative ways for group consideration.)

Subconscious impulses

And this, my friends, brings us to why so many good impulses can hit a wall. Because if the first two steps are rushed or skipped, the problem-solution spin cycle mentioned yesterday will be flipped to the full-on position. Starting any group conversation with phrases or intentions like "We need to have…" or "We need to do…" will almost always lead to suboptimal results because of the three types of subconscious impulses that can enter the picture. And this is where lecture 19 comes in.

Steiner began it by noting how complicated the nature of the human being is; that true self knowledge is very difficult to obtain because the things we become conscious of are like waves washing up on the shore, rising from distant depths we can't see. "Today," he says, "we shall look a little into this nature of man in order to gain an idea of how the subconscious soul-impulses in the human being really work."

He states that the ego-nature of man is the most supersensible part we've so far acquired, but that it works through the physical. "In the intellectual sense, it works in our physical being mainly through the nervous system, through the ganglia radiating from the solar plexus; this is the actual point of contact for real ego-activity. This does not contradict the fact that when we begin to see ourselves spiritually, we have to seek the center of the ego in the head. Since the ego-component is supersensible, the point at which we experience our ego is not the same as the point at which it mainly works in us. We must be quite clear what we mean when we say: The ego works through the point of contact of the solar plexus…. The real ego intervenes as a formative force in the whole human organism through the solar plexus."

Steiner then goes into careful detail about three forms of soul sickness. The first of these will occur when the ego is not well anchored in the system of ganglia radiating from the solar plexus, often because of an illness or disturbance in the area of the organs of the abdomen. The human ego, given to man during the course of earthly evolution as a gift from the Spirits of Form, he says, has been subjected to the temptation of Lucifer. "The ego, as it now exists in man, and because it has been infected by Luciferic forces, would be a bearer of evil forces. The truth of this fact must certainly be recognized. The ego is not a bearer of evil because of its own nature. but because it has become infected through temptation by Lucifer. It is in fact the bearer of truly evil forces which… tend to distort the thought life of the ego towards evil…. If there had been no Luciferic temptation, man would think only good thoughts about everything."

Because of this temptation, Steiner told his audience, the ego can become egotistical, malicious, spiteful, cunning, lying and dastardly — thinking only of putting itself in a favorable light and consigning everything and everyone else to the shadows. In order to resist this temptation and to behave itself, the ego must remain chained in its "home" in the region of the solar plexus, the region of the organs of the abdomen. "Assume now that these abdominal organs are unhealthy in some way, or not in a normal state…. The ego can be somewhat freer in its activity if the abdominal organs are not quite healthy."

Here is a summary of the second form of soul sickness: "Just as the ego has its point of contact in the area of the solar plexus, so does the astral body have its point of contact in all the processes that are linked with the nervous system of the spinal cord. Naturally, the nerves run through the whole body; but in the nervous system of the spinal cord we have a second point of contact." If the astral body is not bound to everything connected

A fourfold approach to change

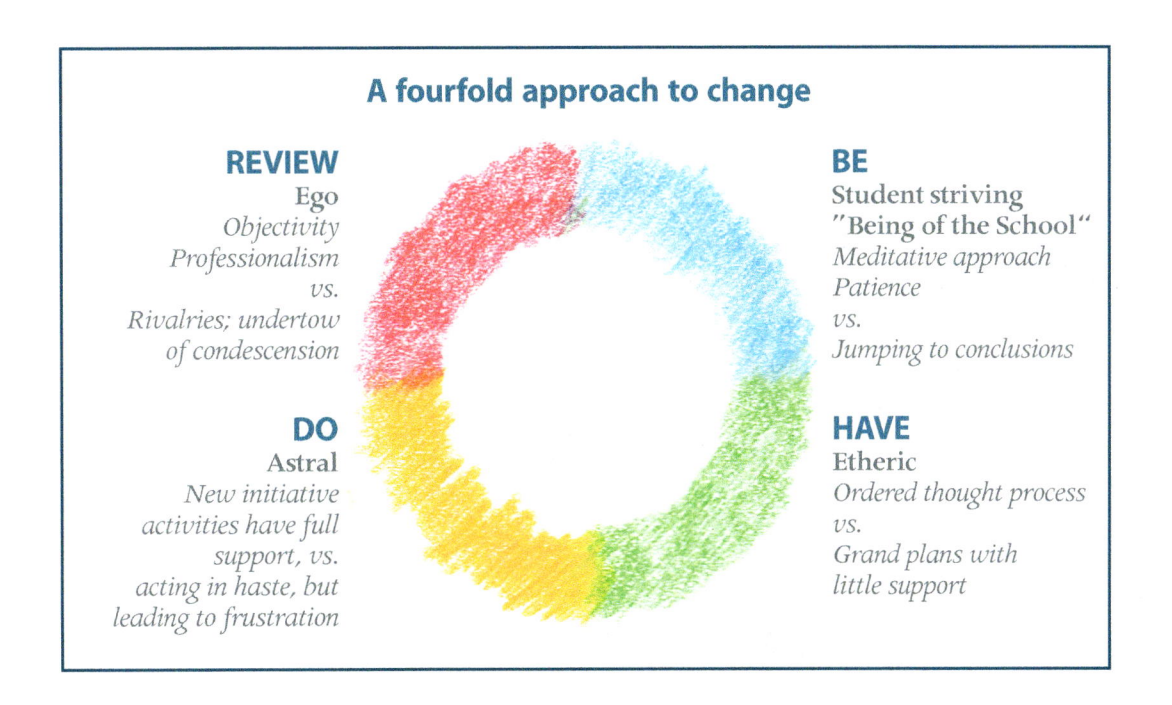

REVIEW
Ego
Objectivity
Professionalism
vs.
Rivalries; undertow
of condescension

BE
Student striving
"Being of the School"
Meditative approach
Patience
vs.
Jumping to conclusions

DO
Astral
New initiative
activities have full
support, vs.
acting in haste, but
leading to frustration

HAVE
Etheric
Ordered thought process
vs.
Grand plans with
little support

with this spinal system in the chest region and becomes free—for instance, from illness—it can become subject to Luciferic and Ahrimanic influences, leading to volatility of ideas and lack of cohesive thought; and to either manic states or withdrawal, depression, and hypochondria. "Just as the ego can be freed, causing signs of madness, so too can the astral body be released, which again leads to signs of madness."

The third form of soul sickness described in this lecture relates to the etheric body. This, Steiner states, has its "prison" in the region of the head and must remain anchored or chained there. Madness or hypnotic conditions can result if the physical body is unwell and the etheric body is let loose. The etheric body, subject to Ahrimanic influences, has the tendency to reproduce itself, spill over into the world, carry its life into other things, go on its own adventures. When the etheric is freed, envy, jealousy, avarice and similar states will be pathologically exaggerated. The thought life, he said, will tend to become disordered and muddled. I think we've all experienced someone who seemed to be on an "ego trip." Because of these various temptations, Steiner noted that humans have many bad dispositions and moods of soul life that are the result of meeting with the demon in us. The appearance of the demonic element comes about because "what is bound can become unbound."

Problems in group process

This may be just my interpretation, but I believe that these same three forms of soul problems can infect the inner workings of a Waldorf school and, really, any group of people who are striving to work together.

When something new may be called for and there's an impulse to breeze past a careful review of the biography of the issue, that can start a loosening of the group ego, with results not unlike those that Steiner describes for individual conditions. For example, during June work days someone wants to discuss something and it's truly well intentioned … you know, "I have an inspiration that we really should have" (or do) a certain thing, and then others chime in with alternative ideas or issues, and pretty soon my idea becomes something we vaguely remember we talked about four years ago. Or sometimes the words start flying because someone else says something along the lines of "well you know that didn't work three years ago," and topics get all mixed up. Do you experience this? It's understandable because quite frankly who loves work days at the end of June when the school year is over you just want fly out the building, I would imagine.

For group process, when the review phase—the ego phase — is not well anchored, what can we see? Steiner talked about "putting oneself on a pedestal, and others in the shade." Well, a faculty-meeting version of that might feature an undertow of departmental rivalries.

When a planning phase is begun without a good anchoring by a proper Review and Be phase, it's similar to what Steiner describes for the freeing of the etheric body. The planning group is free to go on their own adventures, write up all kinds of things that will probably never happen, or go well if they do happen. Then they'll end up like the tailor in many a fairy tale, figuratively crying when their clever plans didn't work out.

And finally, starting the Do phase without the preceding anchors may, in ways similar to what Steiner talks about here, lead to a sort of manic beginning and a depressed or frustrated result.

So I think it is very important for us as aspiring Waldorf educators to keep in mind, in general, Rudolf Steiner's indications for how we are to conduct our business together. Attempting to push things through or skip steps in the fourfold process that I believe we are called upon to strive for—out of respect for Rudolf Steiner, to say nothing of respect for each other — can be a recipe for many missed opportunities. Yes, it is harder to take the time to be sure each step is complete and to make the time for listening to each other. But there's a great saying: "The hard way is the best way — not because it's the best way, but because it is the hard way."

Posture Work in Faculty Meetings

The ideal of harmonizing body and spirit seems almost universal. Personal development movement practices for adults as diverse as yoga, Alexander Method, tai chi, and Bothmer gymnastics all seek, in varying ways, to improve posture and mind/body integration. They include an element—explicitly or not—of working with what might be labeled with words like chakras or centers.

As a teacher, you know it matters if you're able to maintain a balanced physical and emotional posture; the students notice and it affects their experience. All kinds of mainstream research shows that if you change your movement habits, you'll change your mood and even shift your outlook on the same experience or person.

I think a form of personal development suggested by lecture 19 is to mindfully note, from time to time throughout the day, the physical areas where the ego, astral body and etheric bodies are to be anchored; that working on one's posture or stance with this lecture in mind can produce quite a benefit. And it seems to me that Bothmer gymnastics and Spacial Dynamics are practices that generally work in this way. So if your school is fortunate enough to have a Spacial Dynamics graduate or Bothmer gymnast, posture work in the faculty meeting — perhaps accompanied by shared study of these two lectures — will definitely be worthwhile in countless ways, both for teachers as individuals and for how your group is poised to move ahead with flexibility and grace.

6 Building Bridges with Parents

Parent-Teacher Meetings

Rudolf Steiner's Pedagogical Law can also be of great help in thinking through how to prepare for and conduct a parent-teacher conference with the parents of an individual student, as well as a meeting with the parents of a class or grade. Let's look at this topic first from a somewhat mainstream perspective, drawing on the work of psychologist Abraham Maslow.[72]

The hierarchy of needs

Maslow's theory is that there is a classifiable hierarchy of universal human needs; this parallels many other theories in modern developmental psychology, some of which focus on describing the stages of growth in humans. He posited that each level of need must be satisfied within the individual in order for motivation to occur at the next higher level.

1. **Physiological:** satisfaction of the primary physical requirements for survival.

2. **Safety:** once a person's physiological needs are relatively satisfied, physical, emotional and/or economic safety needs then take precedence and dominate behavior.

3. **Social belonging:** at the third level, needs are seen to be interpersonal: feelings of belonging to and being loved in family and in a circle of friendships. This need is especially strong in childhood and adolescence, and can override the need for safety.

4. **Self-esteem:** humans have a need for stable self-respect and self-esteem. Maslow described a lower tier of esteem as the need for respect from others—status, recognition, fame, prestige, and attention. The higher tier manifests as the need for self-respect, which may be gained via developed success in strength, competence, mastery, independence, etc. This higher version means that esteem and the subsequent levels are not strictly separated; rather, this and the succeeding levels are closely related.

5. **Self-actualization:** refers to the realization of one's full potential; the desire to accomplish everything that one can, to become the most that one can be. Aspects of this level include career success, mate acquisition, pursuing goals, seeking happiness.

6. **Transcendence:** in his later years, Maslow added altruism, i.e., giving of oneself to something higher for fellow humans, nature or the wider world.

While this psychological terminology is not well-aligned with an anthroposophic approach, it does provide an analytical lens for what things might need to be on your unwritten agenda for a parent meeting, and/or what issues might be on the parents' minds, and where to begin your discussions. That is, if a child is not coming to school rested, happy, etc. there may need to be a focus on support from home. If the parents are expressing a concern about their child's self-esteem, you might need to focus on helping the child build social connections through play dates or other friendship activities.

Maslow's hierarchy and the twelve senses

As a lens on childhood development, Steiner's exposition of the four lower senses of touch, life, movement and balance directly relates to the three base levels in Maslow's theory. The life sense equates, one might say, to the sum of physiological and safety needs. Health in the realms of touch, life, movement and balance can affect the growing child's capacity to build friendships and to begin to gain respect from others. Nurturing the four middle senses, surrounding the child with wholesome or beautiful smells, tastes, sights and a feeling of physical and emotional warmth — these are keys to sustaining feelings of safety, of being loved and valued. And the four higher senses as presented by Steiner — hearing, language, concept and ego — correspond to development of self-respect, self-actualization and transcendence. In my experience, the vocabulary offered by Steiner's model of the twelve senses can be a more holistic and accessible avenue for parent-teacher discussions, perhaps because the same issues can be addressed, but in a manner that is less judgment-laden than the terms from modern psychology.

Shame, anger and fear in parent meetings

Being told that one's child has a learning challenge can be emotionally upsetting; sometimes parents are stunned by such news during the first PT conference in which a problem is broached. According to Maslow (and modern psychology in general) the teacher communicating the news of a learning problem may encounter a parent going through the "stages of grieving" that include surprise, denial, anger, sadness, negotiation or resignation before reaching "acceptance" and a readiness to move forward with positivity. Research has shown that, at least initially, some parents can't distinguish between the unconscious wish for an idealized normal child and the unexpected reality of one who is not. Whether this theory may be precisely true, it's certainly the case that discussing learning challenges can be stressful for the teacher as well as the parents.

The pedagogical law—and Steiner's paradigm for an approach to human problems as presented in lecture 19 of *The Karma of Untruthfulness*—again provide a vocabulary and approach that are more useful, healing and holistic.

For any meeting with parents be prepared for some level of shame, anger, or fear to be in the room with you. Practice watching out and identifying them in the same way that a birder might be looking for the arrival of the first robin in the spring; remember that Karl König referred to them as helpful companions. Here are some prominent features that may help you be on the lookout and ready to respond in a balanced way.

Shame — the learning challenge a child has might be one that one or both parents also dealt with in their own childhood. This is perhaps why some parents will react as if the problem does not concern them, and might say "I had that issue when I was growing up," implying a sort of unconcern inconsistent with the teacher's desire to address the need. Medical doctors know that patients often at first react to an unexpected diagnosis with deflecting humorous remarks. In any event, just as a student may go into "shutdown" mode in a classroom, parents beginning to deal with a learning challenge can be embarrassed, and just need time (and help) to process the new information.

Anger. Parents sometimes start here, displacing the source of the problem to the teacher, the school, the child or even the spouse (or ex-spouse!). Expression of anger or disappointment with the child, even in a mild form, should be especially noted.

Fear. Some parents may exhibit overwhelm, i.e., cry or appear distressed, launch into a discussion of a wide range of alternative therapies, etc.

Keep in mind, too, that in lecture 19, Steiner provided other pointers to what may be going on at deeper levels than what is seen on the surface;

that volatility of ideas and lack of cohesive thought, for instance, point to a weakening in the middle region.

The pedagogical law is our best lens on how to navigate all dealings with parents, but especially when the waters ahead are not smooth.

Hope. Set a hope-filled tone, in the physical setting and in your demeanor. Use etheric powers to help with any possibility of shame.

Love. Be sure to be demonstrative about your caring for the student(s). Use optimism and unwavering love for the student (and his or her areas of strength) to help move anger away from the door and keep the focus on the child.

Faith. Have an objective and professional plan for student support, one that has worked well in similar circumstances that you can speak about from experience. Review for yourself in every case the Hierarchy of Readiness for Learning given in Section 1, so that you are as clear as one can be which tier or tiers need to be considered and addressed. Your steady and enthusiastic ego presence can be very healing to parents who might become, for a moment, un-anchored in some form.

Education for Balance and Resilience

The following article first appeared on my website. It's included here as a possible aid to teachers and others who work to introduce the values of Waldorf education to the wider community.[73]

Why do Waldorf Schools devote so much time (and salary lines!) to specialty subjects like eurythmy, languages, handwork, woodwork, gardening, form drawing, painting, music and games? On top of that, why is the first twenty minutes or so of the daily main lesson devoted to movement and singing activities that seem sort of non-academic… and then why does the noontime usually include up to an hour for lunch and outdoor play? Let's put a pencil to this question: a typical school week will comprise 32 to 35 hours in school; then subtract a typical 12 hours for specialty classes and 5 hours for lunch/recess. Answer: about half the school week is spent on other than the "Common Core" of math, science and English language skills (although the foreign language classes must be counted in the "Academics" column).

I believe that in looking at almost any such question, our Waldorf movement can be strengthened when we read and re-read Rudolf Steiner's foundational lectures, and at the same time assiduously look to more modern research and writings to find parallels or further verification. Keeping "up to date" with newer approaches will give us a vocabulary that can help us speak with our wider communities in accessible terminology, and also to avoid the pitfalls of unexamined adherence to Steiner's lectures from a century ago. So, let's look at those time allocation questions from both ends — the past and the present.

On balancing academics

Rudolf Steiner indicated that our primary task as educators is to "teach the children to breathe." I'm quite sure he wasn't recommending yoga or the like in our classrooms. So perhaps for our modern times this might be better translated as "help the children learn to self-regulate, to be able to find balance in daily life." In the series of lectures collected as *Education for Adolescence*, Steiner had this to say:

> Essentially our lessons consist of two interacting parts. We instruct, we exhort the children to participate, to use their skills, to be physically active. Be it in eurythmy, music, physical education, even writing or the mechanical processes in arithmetic — we try to engender activity. The other part of our lessons is concerned with contemplation. Here we ask the children to think about, to consider the things we tell them. Although these two aspects always interact, they are fundamentally different. It is not generally appreciated how much the teacher of a contemplative subject, such as history, owes to a colleague who is more concerned with skills and aptitudes. Concentrating merely on contemplation leads the children to a stunted, prosaic adult life, with a tendency to boredom. They will have a superficial view of life, will not feel inclined to observe accurately, will not pay attention to events around them.... We really owe a great deal, as teachers of contemplative subjects, to the teachers of handwork, music, and eurythmy. We can go so far as to say that the history teacher actually lives off the music or singing teacher and that, vice versa, the singing and music teachers live off the contemplative elements in history, and so forth.
>
> — Rudolf Steiner, *Education for Adolescence*

Secondly, Waldorf schools are supposed to provide — month after month and year after year — a progression of academic content for which the students are, or almost are, emotionally and physiologically ready, and at the same time helps them take the next step. (I would underscore the "almost are" because some struggle and even frustration is a necessary part of learning.) Thus, a cycling between active and contemplative moods throughout the day has been a bedrock principle since the beginnings of Waldorf education. The active subjects help prepare receptivity to synthesis; the contemplative subjects help create readiness for experience, observation and analysis. In the early grades, the rhythm of quiet to active and back again may be several times within an hour; by the upper grades, students have built up enough balance and resilience to be ready for lengthened cycles.

Have you ever known a math wiz who can't jump rope? Or maybe you know the world's most competent linguist who is musically tone deaf or cannot balance his checkbook. Our daily experiences demonstrate that "smart" is not defined by a single measure. Howard Gardner, American developmental psychologist and Hobbs Professor of Cognition and Education at the Harvard Graduate School of Education, developed the theory of multiple intelligences that has revolutionized the way educators think about learning.

Gardner's research and writings on this topic began as a response to the incomplete picture of students provided by SAT and IQ tests. Thanks to Gardner, who first published his theory of multiple intelligences in 1983, the idea of one "general" intelligence ruling human abilities has become an outdated notion. He continued with a series of best-selling and academically acclaimed books which followed a well-researched and documented scientific approach, defining "an Intelligence" as: (a) A set of skills for the solving of genuine problems; (b) Able to create an effective product; (c) Having the potential to find or pose problems; (d) Important/valued in a cultural setting; and (e) The presence of geniuses, and/or loss of skill caused by trauma (i.e., a stroke diminishing language ability).

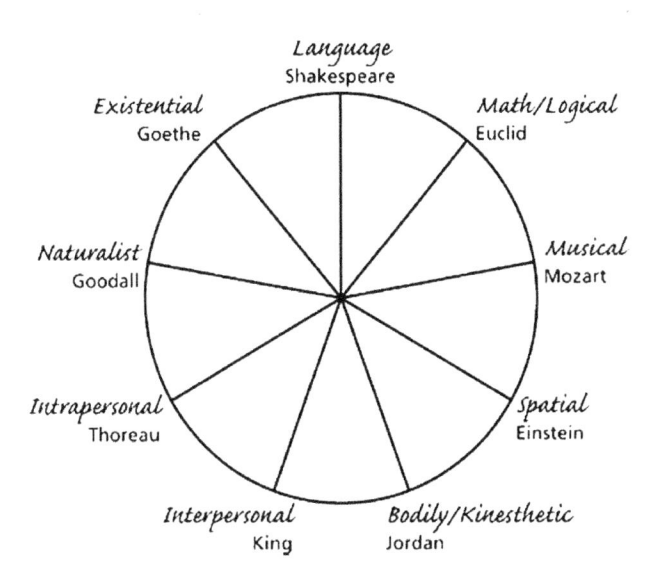

As depicted in the graphic above, Howard Gardner redefined intelligence to include nine facets of human capacity. This list suggests some fields in which particular intelligences will be useful:

1. Language - poets, playwrights, lawyers
2. Math/logical - mathematicians, engineers, philosophers
3. Musical - musicians
4. Spatial - architects, navigators, fine artists
5. Bodily/kinesthetic - athletes, actors, dancers
6. Interpersonal - teachers, politicians, sales people
7. Intrapersonal - poets, philosophers
8. Naturalist - scientists, gardeners, farmers
9. Existential/spiritual

Waldorf educators can feel a strong kinship with Gardner, who said: "I want my children to understand the world, but not just because the world is fascinating and the human mind is curious. I want them to understand it so that they will be positioned to make it a better place. Knowledge is not the same as morality, but we need to understand if we are to avoid past mistakes and move in productive directions. An important part of that understanding is knowing who we are and what we can do. Ultimately, we must synthesize our understandings for ourselves." [74]

The values of the subject classes

As a now long-time Waldorf teacher, I can share that one of the more frustrating aspects of being part of the Waldorf movement is hearing the impression that many outsiders have that our school is "artistic" or that core academics seem to be less valued. I believe, rather, that the wide variety of daily activities provided by the class teachers and the specialty subject teachers proves that we value academic standards, if anything, even more, because we go to greater lengths to be sure the foundations are laid for emotional and physiological readiness for a classic academic curriculum and to provide learning paths for the full spectrum of human capacities.

Balance and resilience

Waldorf educators, following the impulses of Austrian scientist and philosopher Rudolf Steiner, have been focusing on the education of the whole child since 1919. Balance and resilience are inseparable qualities. The possibility of a balanced life can only be enhanced by an education that helps each student in the learning community come to find his or her areas of strength and enjoyment, while at the same time providing a setting for widened exploration, and even unexpected achievements won by overcoming antipathy or adversity. Finally, a key to meeting life's challenges in a resilient way is knowing when to take a deep breath and think things through, and when to act.

How the Waldorf grade school subject classes help develop all of the nine intelligences

Intelligence	EURYTHMY	FOREIGN LANGUAGE	GAMES/GYM & GYMNASTICS	HANDWORK	MUSIC	PRACTICAL ARTS, GARDENING	WOODWORK
Visual/ Spatial	♦♦♦ Large-group choreographic forms; angles of movement	♦ Recognition and identification of pictures; movement & gestures	♦♦♦ All movement is space/time related	♦♦♦ Design, patterns, beauty; ability to move between 2 dimensions and 3	♦♦♦ Musical notation, instrument fingering patterns, awareness of surrounding musicians	♦♦ Form and detail	♦♦♦ Balance of form, function and beauty
Math/ Logical	♦♦ Dance elements support math*	♦ Grammar/logic connections; counting and applying 4 operations	♦♦♦ Lower senses as foundations for math*; sequencing, rules	♦♦♦ Success in math requires neat and orderly processes	♦♦♦ Notation requires knowledge of basic math; internal counting in all music	♦♦ Measurement, ratio, project steps, garden grid	♦♦ Measuring, leveling, calculating; geometry of parts; steps sequence
Language	♦♦♦ Language made visible; stories, poetry, rhythmical and picture language	♦♦♦ Enhancing vocabulary abilities through constant stimulation	♦♦ Links between movement development and speech articulation	♦ Learning technical vocabulary; asking process questions	♦♦ Lyrics, prose, poetry & music from different lands builds literacy	♦ Terminology for tools and processes	♦ New vocabulary for technical aspects
Intra-personal	♦♦♦ Whole being becomes vehicle of personal expression	♦ Sense of accomplishment in mastery of foreign language	♦♦ Opportunities for self-evaluation and actualization; life sense	♦♦ Meeting oneself in the work and adjusting for personal abilities	♦♦ Listening to oneself; bringing inner to outer	♦♦ Awareness of personal capacities; overcoming obstacles; patience	♦♦ Awareness of capacities; reaching beyond expectations; patience
Inter-personal	♦♦♦ Coordinated and cooperative group movement	♦♦ Learning to communicate with new conventions of thought	♦♦♦ Cooperative, coordinated movement; gaze and teasing; sportsmanship	♦♦ Helping or being helped; appreciation for others' abilities	♦♦ Being "in harmony"; give and take with other voices; staying in unison	♦♦♦ Collaboration, taking turns, helping others, service to community	♦♦ Projects usually require group effort; or can be compared
Bodily/ Kinesthetic	♦♦♦ Very demanding — lightness, agility, awareness of own and group motion	♦ Classes include games to help students who are movement-style learners	♦♦♦ Widest variety of movement	♦♦♦ Eye-hand coordination, eye tracking, fine and gross motor, posture	♦♦ Postural control; fine & gross motor for vision, speech, and playing instruments	♦♦♦ Fine and gross motor skills; stamina	♦♦♦ Fine and gross motor; tools as extensions of hand and eye
Nature	♦ Many forms (stars, spirals, etc.) drawn from nature	♦ Interaction outdoors Cycle of nature through poetry, prose and music	♦♦ Outdoor classes	♦♦ Use of natural materials	♦ Songs to celebrate seasons, life, growth and humanity	♦♦♦ Outdoor work, natural materials (wood, seeds, beeswax, clay, etc.)	♦ Finding beauty "hidden" in a block of wood and other materials
Musical	♦♦♦ Melody, beat, different voice tones	♦♦ Rhythmic movement to sounds, singing in rounds and in harmony	♦ Circle games, folk dance, games with sequencing and rhythm elements	♦♦ Rhythm in movement of stitching "creates music in the soul"	♦♦♦ Music promotes whole-brain learning	♦ Rhythmic movements in many tasks; sequencing; singing at work	♦ Rhythmic movements in many tasks; sequencing
Meta-physical	♦♦♦ Language and movement become soul experiences; the universe in movement	♦♦ Furthering understanding of the world and others	♦ Experiencing the beauty of human movement	♦♦ Projects that help awaken the intellect	♦♦ Experiencing the beauty of the tone world	♦♦ All work is good for the soul; service to the earth and mankind	♦♦ Morality of finished projects

KEY: ♦ = Somewhat ♦♦ = Quite a bit! ♦♦♦ = Tons FOR EXTRA CREDIT: add a column for lunch and outdoor recess and see how many diamonds you can add!

Appendix and Resources

Observation, Documentation and Support

I believe every Waldorf class can and should include a few students with learning challenges.

Can: For many types of learning difficulty, a Waldorf school program may be the best possible academic and social environment. For instance, students who in other settings would be given an ADHD label are well served by a pedagogy with lots of kinesthetic learning and the consistent empathy and ego presence of the same class teacher year after year; and primary students who by nature are on the slower end of readiness for reading are very well served by a whole-language curriculum that emphasizes vocabulary, listening and speaking before writing, and then writing as a path to reading.

Should: Students with learning challenges can contribute important social diversity to a class, and are especially valuable because they help keep us teachers on our toes. Jaimen McMillan once told my Spacial Dynamics class the following tenet: "If you want to know what you're teaching, look at the bottom third of your class." That's quite a nugget! Realistically, the top third of a class pretty much teach themselves — if you lead them to water, they will drink it right up. The middle third learn not only from the teacher, but also from the top third. Thus it is the bottom third that provide us with muscle-building opportunities for our craft. A classroom with nothing but easy-to-teach kids would probably get boring for the teacher (at some imagined distant time). All students in a class benefit by the teaching strengths drawn forth by the ones who need a variety of approaches to thrive.

A few: In a class with an experienced teacher and around 20 students, there should be room for about two students with a formal Learning Disability label, and another three or four with needs that can be met by Extra Lesson, therapeutic eurythmy, tutoring, or other regular support at an Academic Intervention Services (AIS) level. A first-cycle teacher might consider taking on a little less at the beginning.

But: Looking at the issue of class constellation through the lens of the four questions mentioned in the chapter on Practical and Ethical Considerations, a student who is weak in the ability to do the academic work (question 1) must (2) have the will to do the work, (3) have parents who support the Waldorf approach, and (4) be a social plus. Also, since there is always a duty to educate, a Waldorf classroom is probably not an appropriate learning environment for a student whose general intelligence is below the "normal" range.

So, how to responsibly identify and support the ones who need evaluation and services?

On promoting objectivity

Part of the reason I have developed the structured, step-by-step paper trail protocols in this section is that as a member of my school's Educational Support Team I sometimes felt like the whole collaborative process of identifying which students needed pullout resources was taking me into the land of Goldilocks and the Four Bears. Some teachers, perhaps of either a more phlegmatic or more choleric bent, tend to under-identify student needs or under-ask for help ... respectively, out of placidity or because they are not well motivated to share with others what progress is (or is not) being made. And, there are other teachers, perhaps of a more melancholic or more sanguine bent, who tend to over-identify or over-ask… either out of sympathy and caution, or else a cheerful readiness to voice requests. Since you, dear reader, are not like any of those, nor wish to enable those who may be, this section offers ways to help you and your colleagues maintain support processes that are "just right"!

Rudolf Steiner on student observation

The forms on the pages that follow are given as aids to careful observation of facets of student development, and as one way to approach the difficult task of tracking the basics of what has been seen and said over the months and years of a young student's career. However, I hasten to state that these "data points" are meant only as a supplement to—and not a replacement for—the depth of meditative, holistic observation that Steiner called on teachers to acquire and apply. The following is from *The Essentials of Education*:

> The primary focus of a teacher's training should be the very heart of human nature itself. When this is the situation, every experience of a teacher's development will be more than lifeless pedagogical rules; they will not need to ponder the application of one rule or another to a child standing in front of them, which would be fundamentally wrong. An intense impression of the child as a whole being must arise within the whole human nature of the teacher, and what is perceived in the child must awaken joy and vitality. This same joyful and enlivening spirit in the teacher must be able to grow and develop until it becomes direct inspiration in answer to the question: What must I do with this child? We must progress from reading human nature in general to reading an individual human being. Everywhere education must learn to manipulate (pardon this rather materialistic expression) what is needed by the human being. When we read, what we have learned about the relationships between the letters is applied. A similar relationship must exist between teacher and pupils. Teachers will not place too much nor too little value on the material development of the bodily nature; they will adopt the appropriate attitude toward bodily nature and then learn to apply what physiology and experimental psychology have to say about children. Most of all, they will be able to rise from a perception of details to a complete understanding of the developing human being.

A warm-up exercise for whole-class observation

Making use of the Class Pencil Grip and Posture Inventory form (p. 141) can be a good way to begin a practice of writing up concrete observations that will help you to discover unexpected nuances here and there.

Pencil Grip: As noted in the chapter on strengthening the pencil grip (p. 81), a relaxed, coordinated, mature pencil grip has the ends of the thumb and index finger facing each other. This grip allows for fine and gross motor movements to be in balance. In order to more easily record a class-full of pencil grips, the accompanying pictures provide a numbered system. Grip #1 is the desired grip as described by McAllen. Grip #2 is close to this goal, but the middle finger also wraps over. Grip #3 is also close to the desired grip, but the thumb wraps too far over. Grip #4 can be recorded for any version of multiple fingers over. Grip #5 can be coded for a "claw grip" similar to the one in the photo, or for any other clumsy grip.

Hand Position for Writing: The position of the student's hand may be a pointer to whether the

Appendix and Resources   **139**

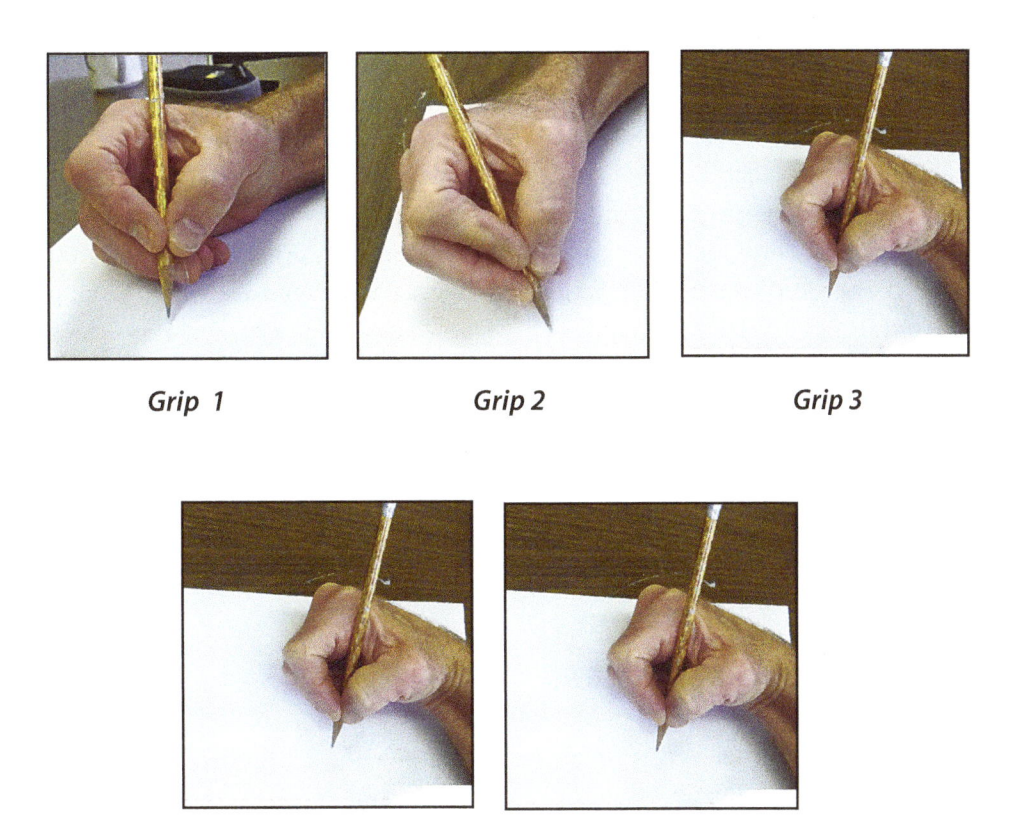

Grip 1   *Grip 2*   *Grip 3*

Grip 4   *Grip 5*

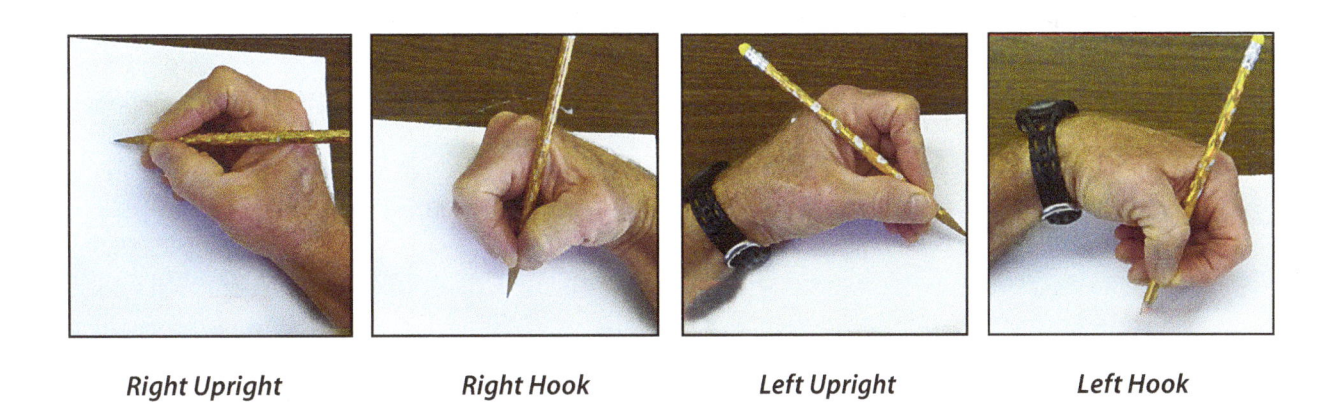

Right Upright   *Right Hook*   *Left Upright*   *Left Hook*

child tends to be predominantly a detail-oriented or big-picture learner. According to the research cited below, right-handed writing with the hand in the (most-common) upright position indicates that language processing is centered on the opposite side of the brain, i.e., this "Right Upright" position indicates language processing taking place predominantly in the left brain; a Right Hook indicates that language processing is predominantly on the same (right) side. In an article titled "Variations in Cerebral Organization as a Function of Handedness, Hand Posture in Writing, and Sex," authors Levy and Reid state:

> During the past century, it has become increasingly apparent that there is a great deal of variation in the direction and degree of cerebral lateralization, a plurality of people having language and related functions strongly specialized to the left hemisphere and visuospatial functions strongly specialized to the right, with substantial minorities manifesting various deviations from this pattern. In particular, in 35%-50% of sinistrals and 1%-10% of dextrals, the right hemisphere is specialized for linguistic skills, and in some unknown fraction of the two handedness groups, verbal and/or spatial abilities are, to varying extents, bilateralized. Levy (1973) suggested that the hand posture adopted during writing might be an index of the lateral relationship between the dominant writing hand and the language hemisphere, a normal posture indicating contralateral language specialization, and an inverted posture indicating ipsilateral language specialization. In the present investigation, two tachistoscopic tests of cerebral lateralization, one measuring spatial functions and one measuring verbal function, were administered to 73 subjects classified by handedness, hand posture during writing, and sex.
> Among both dextral and sinistral subjects with a normal writing posture, language and spatial functions were specialized to the contralateral and ipsilateral hemispheres, respectively, and lateral differentiation of the brain was strong. The reverse was seen in subjects having an inverted writing posture. In all groups, females were less laterally differentiated than males. In 70 out of 73 subjects, the direction of cerebral lateralization was accurately predicted by handedness and hand posture. The 3 subjects (2 females and 1 male) who failed to manifest the predicted relations were all left-handers having an inverted hand posture. In this group, lateral differentiation was so weak that the reliability of the tachistoscopic tests was reduced, and we attribute these three predictive failures to this cause. Thus, almost all of the variation in the lateral organization of the brain was accounted for by handedness, hand posture, and sex.[75]

For more detail on this topic, see *Sex Differences in Cognitive Ability* by Diane F. Halpern.[76]

Desk Size and Sitting Posture: Spaces are also provided on the form for noting whether the student's desk is too tall or too short for ease of working; and for a few words about posture (e.g., slumps, wraps legs around chair, leans down to write, etc.).

Hair Whorls: Limited scientific research supports a theory that hair whorls on humans point to laterality, possible learning challenges, and other personality traits. Even though the research with humans is far from conclusive, it is interesting to note that very many horse owners believe that whorl placement and rotation direction provide an excellent predictor of a horse's temperament and trainability. In one study, for instance, Irish researchers identified a unique link between equine motor laterality, or "handedness," and specific

CLASS PENCIL GRIP & POSTURE INVENTORY

GRADE _____ DATE OBSERVED _____ OBSERVER _____

STUDENT	PENCIL GRIP #	HAND POS'N	DESK SIZE	WHORL DIR.	POSTURE/NOTES

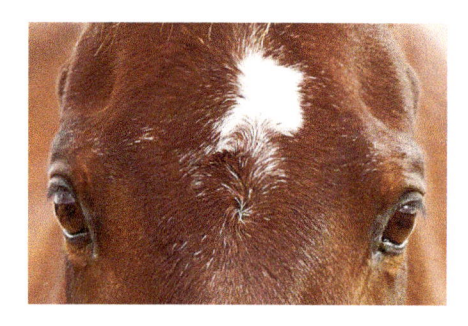

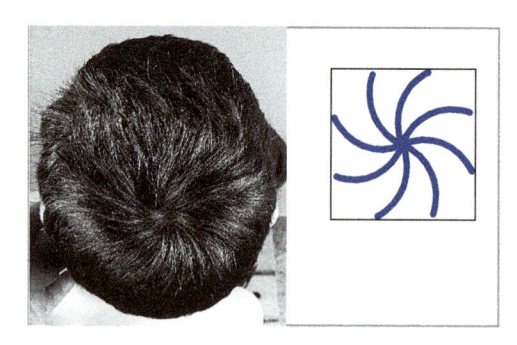

characteristics of facial hair whorls: horses that step forth with the right front leg had significantly more clockwise whorls, whereas whorls were more likely to flow in a counter-clockwise direction in "left-handed" horses.

The majority of humans have a single, clockwise whorl at the crown of the head. My suggestion is only that you might want to observe this feature over time as a research project.

A Paper Trail Protocol

In considering whether a student might need classroom adaptations and/or an individualized developmental support program for a child, the broader, deeper and more objective that observations can be, the better. Carefully observing every child in a class—not just the ones "we know" need remedial attention—never fails to reveal new understanding.

On the following pages is a sequence of forms I've used over the years to supplement the First Grade Readiness Screenings and the Second Grade Extra Lesson Developmental Assessments that are standard at my school. These can be filled out by the class teacher and/or remedial teacher. A team effort is always the best!

Maintaining a clear trail of parent and teacher communication and coordination at every step is vital to the success of an Educational Support Team (EST). The forms offered on the following pages can be implemented in a variety of sequences, depending on the situation in individual cases.

Step 1 might be used first, when a parent or teacher other than the class teacher requests that EST "take a look" at a student. In this instance, EST would want the class teacher to fill out

Step 2 before doing the assessment, so that more background is available.

If a class teacher is initiating the request, it would probably be best for him to fill out Step 1 and Step 2 at the same time.

In **Step 3** the form will help class teachers distill the thousands of impressions that build up for each child, and assign an objective value to defined aspects of capacity for learning. This form can be highly useful even as a whole-class evaluation modality, i.e., not just as part of the paper trail for selected students who may need help. One way to approach this observation project is for the class teacher to complete a form for one student a day.

Step 4 provides information from the parent side that can be useful in how the student's challenges can be helped, and also provides an avenue for parent "buy-in" to the work of the EST.

Step 5 documents what support services, class modifications or exemptions have been recommended, and the parents' acceptance (or not) of the school's recommendations.

―――――――――――

Note: You are welcome to photocopy the forms in this book and adapt them for use in your school.

Step 1 of 5: Request for Assessment, Page 1 of 1

Student _____ Completed by _____ Date _____

Teacher(s) or parent(s) requesting assessment: _____

Reason for request (i.e., developmental insight needed, or areas where student is having difficulty):

_____
_____
_____
_____
_____

What have you already tried in the classroom to address this?
_____
_____

Assessment(s) requested – check all that apply:

___ Developmental/Extra Lesson   ___ Reading & Writing   ___ Math   ___ Therapeutic Eurythmy

___ Other: _____

(note: most assessments are done during class time)

Class Teacher approval:_____ Date:_____

PARENTS APPROVE	PARENTS DECLINE
I/we have been informed of the aims and methods of the Educational Support Team and give permission for the above assessment(s).	I/we have been informed of the aims and methods of the Educational Support Team and decline permission for the above assessment(s).
Parent signature(s)	Parent signature(s)
_____	_____
_____	_____
Date:_____	Date:_____

Step 2 of 5: Inventory of Readiness for Classroom Tasks, Page 1 of 2

Student _____ Completed by _____ Date _____

(1 = no problem, 5 = significant difficulty) 1 2 3 4 5

Constitutional observations

Unusual diet, e.g. a lot of soft foods, or refusal of an entire category of foods; strong aversion to some common textures, tastes or smells	○ ○ ○ ○ ○
Mouth breathing	○ ○ ○ ○ ○
Allergies, asthma	○ ○ ○ ○ ○
Appears physically immature	○ ○ ○ ○ ○
Seems over- or under- stimulated (circle one)	○ ○ ○ ○ ○
Lost on a cloud, or over-aware of environment (circle one)	○ ○ ○ ○ ○
Tired, sickly, stubborn, nervous (circle as applicable)	○ ○ ○ ○ ○
Other	

Behavior observations

Quick to feel attacked/bothered, e.g. when in line	○ ○ ○ ○ ○
Avoids eye contact	○ ○ ○ ○ ○
Seeks excessive physical contact; or avoids physical contact (circle one)	○ ○ ○ ○ ○
Hesitation or refusal to participate in group activities	○ ○ ○ ○ ○
Slow with tasks or work; reluctant to move to next activity; fixates	○ ○ ○ ○ ○
Rushes ahead with tasks or work; difficulty with transitions	○ ○ ○ ○ ○
Trouble with spoken directions, multi-step directions	○ ○ ○ ○ ○
Trouble with written, drawn or moved directions	○ ○ ○ ○ ○
Other	

Movement observations

Falls off chair	○ ○ ○ ○ ○
Tucks feet under legs or twists around chair	○ ○ ○ ○ ○
Twirls body	○ ○ ○ ○ ○
Makes noises or twitches	○ ○ ○ ○ ○
Fidgets, plays with objects	○ ○ ○ ○ ○
Clumsy	○ ○ ○ ○ ○
Difficulty or avoidance of personal care items like shoe tieing	○ ○ ○ ○ ○
Itching, picking	○ ○ ○ ○ ○
Soft speech or baby talk	○ ○ ○ ○ ○
Messiness - work or clothes, desk, etc.	○ ○ ○ ○ ○
Uncertain laterality; switches hand use	○ ○ ○ ○ ○
Tries to shake hands with left hand	○ ○ ○ ○ ○
Movements appear immature, i.e. toddler-like movements	○ ○ ○ ○ ○
Mirrors movements (3rd Gr. & up) i.e. uses left hand when you hold up right	○ ○ ○ ○ ○
Can't stay in rhythm or tone with marching, clapping, singing	○ ○ ○ ○ ○
Other	

Step 3 of 5: Request for Support Services, Page 1 of 2

Student _____ Completed by _____ Date _____

Teacher(s) and/or parents requesting:

_____

SECTION 1
Teacher or parent to describe goals/challenges to be addressed:

_____
_____
_____
_____
_____

Program request – check all that may apply:

___ Developmental - Extra Lesson

___ Therapeutic Eurythmy

___ Reading/Writing Support

___ Math Support

___ Exemption from Standard Curriculum Requirements (see Step 5, page 2)

Do you feel this student's challenges are primarily (check one or number in order):

___ Organic/medical/constitutional

___ Emotional/psychological

___ Developmental

___ Needs more repetition for skills

Has this student been evaluated by an outside source, e.g. psychologist or district?
___ Yes ___ No

If Yes, attach copy of all reports

SECTION 2
To be completed by Class Teacher. Indicate your observations of challenges. 1 = no problem, 5 = significant difficulty

	1 2 3 4 5
Reading	○ ○ ○ ○ ○
Writing	○ ○ ○ ○ ○
Spelling	○ ○ ○ ○ ○
Math	○ ○ ○ ○ ○
Hearing	○ ○ ○ ○ ○
Speech	○ ○ ○ ○ ○
Form drawing	○ ○ ○ ○ ○
Memory	○ ○ ○ ○ ○
Will forces - i.e. easily discouraged	○ ○ ○ ○ ○
Reverses letters/numbers	○ ○ ○ ○ ○
Moves paper or torso to side	○ ○ ○ ○ ○
Writes bottom-up	○ ○ ○ ○ ○
Sequencing & Rhythm	○ ○ ○ ○ ○
Other classroom:	○ ○ ○ ○ ○
Physical Limitations or Handicap	○ ○ ○ ○ ○
Fine Motor/Eye-Hand	○ ○ ○ ○ ○
Laterality - i.e. switches hand use	○ ○ ○ ○ ○
Touch Sense - e.g. collisions or avoidance	○ ○ ○ ○ ○
Life Sense - e.g. often tired or can't hold thoughts	○ ○ ○ ○ ○
Movement Sense/Gross Motor - e.g. clumsiness	○ ○ ○ ○ ○
Balance Sense - e.g. trouble sitting still	○ ○ ○ ○ ○
Disruptive Behavior, Anxious or Nervous	○ ○ ○ ○ ○
Socialization	○ ○ ○ ○ ○
Body Awareness/Geography	○ ○ ○ ○ ○
Orientation in Time	○ ○ ○ ○ ○
Orientation in Space	○ ○ ○ ○ ○
Other:	○ ○ ○ ○ ○

Step 4 of 5: Developmental/sensorimotor and learning needs history, Page 1 of 3

Student _____ Completed by _____ Date _____

Current Grade: _____ Date of Birth: _____

The following optional information can help the Educational Support Team develop a more complete picture of your child from early infancy to his/her present developmental stage. This form will <u>not</u> be added to your student's main file; it will be kept in his or her working file by the EST and shredded after your child departs AWS. Please complete information that you feel is important and that you're comfortable sharing.

PREGNANCY AND INFANCY

_____
_____
_____

CURRENT HEALTH and HOME SETTING

Please describe any current home or health conditions which may affect learning; if child is on routine medication; any history of learning disabilities (student or family); social problems, etc.

_____
_____
_____
_____
_____
_____
_____
_____
_____
_____
_____
_____

Childhood

Please think of the various stages of your child's development, considering behavior that comes to mind as you answer these questions. Which behavior do you think of as being different from other children you know? Were there times when your child's behavior was difficult to cope with in the family unit? Circle the choice which applies: – Y (Yes), N (No), U (Used to), or D (Doesn't apply because child is not yet old enough, or for another reason).

Tactile (touch) – Did/does your child:

Dislike to be touched, held or cuddled??	Y N U D
Seem easily irritated or threatened when touched by siblings or playmates?	Y N U D
Have a strong need to touch people & objects?	Y N U D
Pinch, bite or otherwise hurt self or others?	Y N U D
Dislike the feeling of certain clothing?	Y N U D
Over or under dress for the temperature?	Y N U D
Other touch/sensory issues	

Vestibular (movement) – Did/does your child:

Enjoy being rocked, tossed in air, etc.	Y N U D
Like fast rides?	Y N U D
Like to swing?	Y N U D
Spin or whirl more than other children?	Y N U D
Get carsick easily?	Y N U D
Get nauseous and/or vomit from other kinds of movement?	Y N U D
Have fear in space (stairs, heights)?	Y N U D
Lose balance easily?	Y N U D
Walk on toes (not whole foot)?	Y N U D

Visual – Does your child:

Have a visual problem?	Y N U D
Seem very sensitive to light?	Y N U D
Have trouble using eyes?	Y N U D
Avoid eye contact?	Y N U D
Get distracted by visual stimuli?	Y N U D
Make reversals when writing, copying or reading?	Y N U D
Have trouble with shapes, colors and/or size?	Y N U D
Squint often?	Y N U D

Taste and Smell – Does your child:

Explore with taste?	Y N U D
Chew on non-food items?	Y N U D
Have any feeding problems?	Y N U D
Have trouble changing food textures?	Y N U D
Seem hypersensitive to smells?	Y N U D

Auditory & speech (sound) – Does/is your child:

Have a hearing loss?	Y N U D
Have PE tubes?	Y N U D
Have a lot of ear infections?	Y N U D
Hypersensitive to sounds?	Y N U D
Fear unexpected noises or unusual sounds?	Y N U D
Distracted by sound?	Y N U D
Miss sounds or words?	Y N U D
Have trouble listening?	Y N U D
Hum or make odd noises?	Y N U D
Have trouble imitating rhythmic sounds?	Y N U D
Have trouble understanding or following directions?	Y N U D
Talk or make noises excessively?	Y N U D
Talking interferes with listening?	Y N U D
Have delayed speech development?	Y N U D

Muscle Tone – Does your child:

Feel heavier than he/she looks?	Y N U D
Have good endurance?	Y N U D
Have muscle problems?	Y N U D
Have flat feet?	Y N U D
Slump when sitting?	Y N U D
Get tired easily?	Y N U D
Seem weak?	Y N U D

Coordination – Did/does your child:

Sit, stand or walk late?	Y N U D
Sit, stand or walk early?	Y N U D
Have a short creeping or crawling phase (or none at all)?	Y N U D
Have a very long creeping or crawling phase?	Y N U D
Creep on tummy or bottom?	Y N U D
Have slow, plodding, deliberate movements?	Y N U D
Play with toys appropriately for his/her age?	Y N U D
Have trouble dressing, buttoning, zipping and/or tying shoes?	Y N U D
Have trouble holding a pencil correctly?	Y N U D
Trip or fall a lot? Seem awkward?	Y N U D
Which hand is dominant?	R L
Have poor handwriting?	Y N U D
Handle small things easily?	Y N U D
Eat neatly for his/her age?	Y N U D
Have rigid movements?	Y N U D
Grimace or use tongue when performing fine motor tasks?	Y N U D
Like sports, PE, etc.?	Y N U D

Step 4 of 5: Developmental/sensorimotor History, Page 3 of 3

Behavior/Temperament – Is/was your child:

An irritable baby?	Y N U D
Quiet, calm, patient?	Y N U D
Active, outgoing?	Y N U D
Intense, anxious?	Y N U D
Explosive, aggressive?	Y N U D
Easy going, predictable?	Y N U D
Clingy?	Y N U D
Rigid, set in ways?	Y N U D
Adaptable/flexible?	Y N U D
Distractible?	Y N U D
Moody?	Y N U D
Frustrated frequently?	Y N U D
Difficult to get to sleep?	Y N U D
Destructive with toys?	Y N U D

Did/does your child:

Have a high activity level?	Y N U D
Have a low activity level?	Y N U D
Have erratic sleep patterns?	Y N U D
Wet the bed? How often:	Y N U D
Wake frequently?	Y N U D
Have night terrors and/or nightmares?	Y N U D
Play well alone?	Y N U D
Have a short attention span?	Y N U D
Find it hard to make choices?	Y N U D
Dislike schedule changes or surprises?	Y N U D
Demonstrate self-stimulation behaviors?	Y N U D
Anger easily or have frequent tantrums?	Y N U D
Have difficulty with change?	Y N U D
Act out?	Y N U D
Make friends easily?	Y N U D
Prefer older children?	Y N U D
Prefer adults?	Y N U D
Prefer being alone?	Y N U D
Have low self-esteem?	Y N U D
Seem discouraged or depressed?	Y N U D

Learning Styles – Does your child:

Recognize own errors?	Y N U D
Learn from mistakes?	Y N U D
Acquire materials for tasks independently?	Y N U D
Set up his/her own workspace?	Y N U D
Maintain his/her workspace?	Y N U D
Work independently?	Y N U D
Generalize known skills to new ones?	Y N U D
Have age-appropriate memory?	Y N U D
Ask for help when necessary?	Y N U D
Plan ahead?	Y N U D
Create new ideas and/or new ways of doing things?	Y N U D
Use age-appropriate content in written language?	Y N U D
Get work done on time?	Y N U D
Perform at or above an average reading level?	Y N U D
Perform at or above an average math level?	Y N U D

School history

Has your child ever received any screening or evaluation for learning support needs, been given a 504 Plan or an IEP, or needed regular tutoring to move ahead in school? If so, please provide dates and details.   Y N

_____

_____

_____

_____

_____

_____

Please add anything else that will help us better educate your child

_____

_____

_____

_____

_____

_____

_____

_____

An Educational Support Team Model

Following is an excerpt from the handbook of the Educational Support Team at Aurora Waldorf School (AWS) near Buffalo, NY. It is offered here as one way to organize and provide information about an Educational Support Team in an independent Waldorf school environment.

The Aurora Waldorf School program is one in which all the students are provided with an education rich in literacy and numeracy foundations, developmental movement, music and art, and health-strengthening rhythm. Thus, the regular day at AWS is, in a way, a whole-school "remedial program" that helps every child. For those students who need more support, this chapter describes the AWS protocols and procedures for an intermediate level of intervention, provided by the AWS teachers who directly provide extra academic or developmental support to students. These specialists, the members of the Educational Support Team (EST), study and work with the remedial aspects of Waldorf education.

Our EST goals are:

1. Provide individualized or small-group support by a team of trained teachers who are consistent in their approach and can work together on a student's challenges over a number of years;
2. Strengthen right practices in the classroom;
3. Create better learning environments for children with learning style differences;
4. Assist teachers in a team-based approach for observation and intervention;
5. Develop and deliver a repertoire of screenings, interview procedures and assessments;
6. Guide faculty studies of individual children, learning styles and classroom accommodations;
7. Build bridges in the AWS community and with outside service providers. This includes maintaining a clear paperwork flow.

Supporting student progress

The Educational Support program at AWS emphasizes pedagogical methods and interventions based in our understanding of the Waldorf curriculum and of the universal progression of child development. By improving our abilities to perceive and respond to each individual whom we wish to further engage in the process of education, we can help students who meet challenges as they move up the grades.

Class teachers and members of the EST work together to observe every child in the school, and to identify candidates for a program of extra support. However, we also want parents to let us know of any concerns about academic or developmental progress, so that we can decide whether and how to intervene; please contact any member of the EST, or your student's class teacher.

Standard Assessments provided by the EST

In addition to the many daily observations and assessments made by teachers throughout the school, it is a standard part of our program for students to receive the following types of assessments provided separately by an EST teacher.

Evaluation Lessons: When a class teacher believes that a student might need more support than he or she can provide via added in-class adjustments and attention, the EST may provide a limited schedule of interim pullout evaluation lessons, and will report observations to the class teacher and parents.

Developmental Readiness: An evaluation of developmental progress is provided by one of our Extra Lesson teachers before First Grade entry; during the Second Grade year; and when a student is applying to enter the lower grades at other points.

Please note that children will not experience this assessment as "testing," but rather as an interesting hour or so of mostly movement and drawing activities, plus a few academic basics. There's nothing to prepare the students for, except a special time for individual attention and interesting things to do!

Fourth Grade Reading/Writing and Math Assessments: Every Fourth Grader receives standardized reading/writing and math evaluations. These provide another avenue to support class teachers as they continue to observe and assess each student's unfolding abilities. Results are reported to parents in the year-end report cards.

Educational Support provided by AWS

Four modes of one-on-one or small group support are provided by AWS as integral parts of the curriculum.

Reading and Writing Support; Math Support: Academic intervention services consistent with our Waldorf approaches to literacy and numeracy are provided by AWS specialists. All lessons are in one-on-one or small group settings, and run 20 to 45 minutes on a regular schedule. Reading/Writing Support assists students with difficulties in the areas of reading, writing, spelling, and auditory processing, among other educational issues. Math Support classes work on basic math skills, grade-appropriate math abilities, and support students who need additional practice to succeed.

Extra Lesson: derives its name from work begun in the 1970s in England by Audrey McAllen. Taking up Rudolf Steiner's many lectures about the developing child, she was inspired to develop a curriculum of assessment techniques and movement, speech, drawing and painting exercises. Development during the first seven years of life normally produces the capacities needed for classroom learning, including: spatial orientation, movement coordination, the ability to change sight perception instantaneously between three-dimensional and two-dimensional space, good body geography and confirmed laterality. Without such faculties, no curriculum—even a Waldorf curriculum—fully works. The goal of our Extra Lesson program is to help the child awaken to and reach a new level of developmental readiness for learning.

Therapeutic eurythmy: Eurythmy, which means "harmonious rhythm," was developed by Dr. Rudolf Steiner as a renewal of the movement arts. Therapeutic eurythmy is a holistic therapy which addresses issues of imbalance on a physical, constitutional level as well as in the emotional and spiritual realms. Through the active participation of the individual, a new balance can be achieved.

Lesson scheduling: Lessons take place during the normal school day; for the most part, students are pulled out of a Subject class. (Some Extra Lesson sessions take place during the individual book work portion of Main Lesson.) In any event, the EST and the student's class teacher will work together to devise the least disruptive schedule possible.

Parent involvement

Written parent permission is required for any ongoing schedule of the above services. Homework is very often a component of the support programs provided by AWS. EST members and the Faculty work together to best allocate the resources for these services. Parents who wish their student to receive a higher level of help may elect to engage AWS teachers or other tutoring providers outside of the school day setting.

Description of intervention levels at AWS

- Level 1: Student has been identified with mild difficulty with progress; extra help is provided in classroom setting, and a homework support program may be added.

- Level 2: After a period of extra in-classroom assistance, student continues to have moderate difficulty with academic progress. Level 2 will include one or more of the following: (a) Guided homework program created by class teacher and/or EST teacher(s); (b) After-school tutoring by an appropriate AWS teacher; (c) One six-week block of once-a-week pullout support during the school day, in a small EST group and/or by an AWS teacher.
- Level 3: After the above, if student progress still is not as hoped for, the pullout program may provide once-a-week, one-on-one lessons; plan may include partial modification of regular academic goals and/or program.

If we conclude that a student's needs are beyond the capacity of our EST intervention services, we will meet with parents to discuss the possible options for them to provide their child. These may include:

- Third-party Educational/Psychological evaluation;
- Outside tutoring;
- An individualized academic program at AWS, with modified academic goals; and/or
- Learning Disability Classification for an Individualized Educational Plan (IEP), and possible services from East Aurora Union Free School District under NYS law. Please note that the available program of academic interventions at AWS may not, in some cases, conform to the amount of AIS level services usually required by the district prior to their provision of evaluation or services; therefore, AWS parents who wish to have their child evaluated or classified for a learning disability may need to secure outside services for a period of time prior to district intervention.

Other services that support the Waldorf educational approach

For needs that may go beyond the scope of our AWS resources, such as the need for a medical or an Educational/Psychiatric evaluation, the EST maintains a list of providers for parents to investigate. These include the following resources consistent with our understanding of child development.

- Screening by an Occupational Therapist who specializes in Sensory Integration.
- Anthroposophic Medicine; this may include a recommendation for homeopathy
- Biodynamic Cranial Sacral Therapy
- Social Coaching
- Speech

To assist parents and teachers with any of the above, the EST Coordinator can answer questions or provide liaison with outside providers.

Process for New Student Placement

We consider it an important duty to maintain a picture of whether our school is a good (or, the best) placement for each individual; we use a framework of interrelated assessment tools to help us with this responsibility. If a prospective student has been in another school setting, our process is as follows.

Our application form helps us identify points for further conversation with the family before admission. For instance, a family seeking to place a student with support needs when the family lists school-age siblings who don't have support needs and will continue in their existing school, may in some cases perceive Waldorf as a remedial school, or an artistic school, or a school with an unstructured approach.

One or more days "shadowing": attending a full day, or two days, of Main Lesson, recess, lunch, and subject classes. All teachers who see the student fill out a form addressing strengths and concerns. The shadowing day will give us a a general impression about will to work, social harmony, contribution to the class constellation, and how our curriculum seems to resonate with the student. During the day, the student is given an Educational Evaluation that will include, as age appropriate, elements of the Second Grade Assessment, reading and math screenings, etc.

We require all records from previous schooling and evaluations prior to the shadowing day. Our application form includes specific questions about whether the student has in the past received any support services or Ed Psych evals, has had an IEP, etc.

In cases where there is some doubt whether our school (or sometimes, just the grade placement requested) is appropriate, we convene an Admissions task group that includes the Grade teacher(s), EST, and subject teachers.

After we've completed the above steps, we may have a meeting with the parents that includes the class teacher, the EST staff who have participated in our evaluations, and others as needed. This is often a good time to discuss topics that may still remain from either side, to discuss media and other home support aspects, and in many ways to get things started as a team. If the decision is to not admit the student, the meeting can have the purpose of providing the parents with the EST's opinions of other schooling or support avenues for them to pursue.

Afterword

> *"Movement is the foundation of stillness"*
> – Lao Tzu

I completed the manuscript for the foregoing in August. Then, as the new school year began at Aurora Waldorf, it came about that we were visited by several experienced teachers from both Waldorf and public school settings, all of whom remarked on the general feeling of calm in the building, and on the notable degree to which students were harmoniously able to take up academic work.

Helene Gross, a very experienced and well-traveled teacher from Toronto Waldorf School, was kind enough to put her observations in writing:

> *I recently had the pleasure of visiting the Aurora Waldorf School and I was deeply impressed by the quality of the movement program at the school and how engaged all the students were in their movement lessons. I observed that there was a general feeling of calm in the building and that the students were able to settle into their academic work harmoniously. I attributed this mood directly to the fact that they are engaged in healthy movement activities throughout the day. In conversation with a retired local high school principal I heard that students graduating from AWS consistently display a high level of athletic preparation for their high school years.*

I also received, just this September, a nicely encouraging letter from Jennifer Snyder, whom I have known professionally for about three years. A highly experienced class teacher in a public Waldorf school, Jennifer is also a member of the Pedagogical Section Council of North America. She offered the following in support of my effort to finish pushing the book draft into publication:

> *I had stumbled across Jeff's articles and useful schematics on child development through a newsletter from the Association for a Healing Education. I sought out opportunities for many years to learn from him in person, but he was a teacher at the Aurora Waldorf School outside of Buffalo, New York, across the country from my home in California.*
>
> *Then, in January of 2017, I did meet him in person at a weekend workshop during an Alliance for Public Waldorf Education Conference held in Sacramento. I was transfixed by his presence and presentation of a comprehensive movement program for children through all of the grades. His presentation almost seemed as if it had been tailored for me, a class teacher. Most of the workshop participants were public Waldorf school class teachers, and Jeff was nimbly able to describe what lives behind commonly used behavioral labels. Jeff could weave Waldorf terminology into a mainstream perspective and interspersed all group discussions with movement and artistic activity. I was from then on enthralled with the body of his work, and have subsequently attended three of his intensives. This book represents a full workshop of projects developed over many years, on offer for those teachers who will choose to go beyond reading the words, and who can commit to trying the practices that Jeff has perfected in his profession over his long career. His ideas are immediate and practical for the work of resource specialists, and movement and class teachers alike. This accessible book is having a mentor's words and practical guidance resting together in a comprehensive book that you will revisit again and again. Jeff has dedicated himself to passing on his collection of resources to interested people everywhere.*

I've always thought the above was true—in theory, anyhow—because right from the early days of Aurora Waldorf, creating and maintaining a program of movement excellence has been one of our highest priorities. By "movement", we include not only what happens in the Gym, but daily classroom activities, Eurythmy, Handwork, Woodwork, Music, Drama, practical tasks and recess. Even the visual arts fall under the umbrella of movement: painting and drawing, for instance, can be called "movement brought to rest."

Looking back over this book today, and in light of these recent affirmations, I'd like to re-emphasize one point in closing: allocating more Main Lesson and other school-day periods for a consistent program of developmental movement, drawing and painting is not a subtraction from academics, but rather can be a plus … or even a multiplier.

Bibliographic Notes

1. Steiner, Rudolf, *The Spiritual Ground of Education*, SteinerBooks, Hudson, NY, 2004
2. Vienna, February 8, 1912. Lecture 16 in *Esoteric Christianity and the Mission of Christian Rosenkreutz* (CW 130), Rudolf Steiner Press, East Sussex, UK 2001. Also in *Anthroposophy in Everyday Life*. Four Lectures by Rudolf Steiner, Anthroposophic Press/SteinerBooks, 1995
3. McAllen, Audrey, *The Extra Lesson*, RSCP, 2013
4. McAllen, *The Extra Lesson*; Ellis, Monica (trans.), *Second Grade Development Observation and Assessment* (typescript booklet), Advisory Service of the Waldorf Schools of Holland
5. Kipnis, Jonathan, "The Seventh Sense," *Scientific American*, Volume 319, Issue 2, August 2018
6. König, Karl, *The Human Soul*, Floris Books, Edinburgh UK, 2006; and *A Living Physiology*, Camphill Books, UK, 1999
7. Soesman, Albert, *Our Twelve Senses*, Hawthorn Press, Stroud, UK, 2000
8. Childs, Gilbert, *5 + 7= 12 Senses: Rudolf Steiner's Contribution to the Psychology of Perception*, Fire Tree Press, Stroud, UK, 1996
9. Steiner, Rudolf, public lecture, Dec. 30, 1917. Typescript copy may be available from Rudolf Steiner Library
10. König, Karl, *A Living Physiology*, Camphill Books, UK, 1999
11. König, Karl, *Conferences and Seminars on Arithmetic, with Zoological Considerations*, http://www.waldorfresearchinstitute.org/pdf/Arithmetic.pdf, 2009
12. Steiner, Rudolf, *The Boundaries of Natural Science*, SteinerBooks, 1987
13. König, Karl, *The Human Soul*, Floris Books, Edinburgh, Scotland, 2006
14. Steiner, Rudolf, *The Foundations of Human Experience*, SteinerBooks, 1996; *Balance in Teaching*, SteinerBooks, 2007
15. Holtzapfel, Walter, *Children with a Difference*, Lanthorn Press, UK, 2008
16. König, Karl, *The Human Soul; Conferences and Seminars on Arithmetic*
17. Steiner, Rudolf, *Education for Special Needs*, Rudolf Steiner Press, East Sussex, UK, 2015
18. Holtzapfel, Walter, *Children with a Difference*
19. Steiner, Rudolf, "Faith, Love, and Hope: The Third Revelation," lecture on Dec. 2, 1911. In *Love and Its Meaning in the World*, SteinerBooks, 1998
20. Steiner, Rudolf, *The Karma of Untruthfulness*, Rudolf Steiner Press, East Sussex, UK, 2005
21. Bobby Matherne (1940-2019), writer and publisher, *DIGESTWORLD*, online monthly newsletter, and Good Mountain Press, Metairie, LA
22. The second Mystery Play. In *Four Mystery Dramas* (CW 14), SteinerBooks, 2015
23. von Heider, Molly, *Looking Forward*, Hawthorn Press, Stroud, UK, 1996
24. December 5, 1909, lecture by Rudolf Steiner, "The Mission of Anger." In *Transforming the Soul, Vol. 1* (CW 58), Rudolf Steiner Press, East Sussex, UK, 2005
25. December 17, 1912, lecture by Rudolf Steiner. In *Love and Its Meaning in the World*, SteinerBooks, 1998
26. Steiner, Rudolf, *The Spiritual Ground of Education*
27. Holtzapfel, Walter, *Children with a Difference*
28. Steiner, Rudolf, *The Spiritual Ground of Education*
29. Steiner, Rudolf, *The Karma of Untruthfulness*, lect. 19
30. Ellison, Katherine (December 2015) *Being Honest about the Pygmalion Effect*, Discover, CV1215
31. Redford, Robert and Brannaman, Buck, *Buck* (movie) Directed by Cindy Meehl, 2011
32. Hunt, Ray, *Think Harmony with Horses*, American West Books, Sanger, CA, 1991
33. Hunt, Jean and Nash-Wortham, Mary, *Take Time*, Robinswood Press, Gloucester, UK, 2008
34. Ibid
35. Goddard Blythe, Sally, *Attention, Balance and Coordination: The A.B.C. of Learning Success*, Wiley-Blackwell, Hoboken, NJ, 2017
36. Steiner, Rudolf, *The Essentials of Education*, SteinerBooks, 2006
37. Steiner, Rudolf, *The Child's Changing Consciousness*, SteinerBooks, 1996
38. Ibid
39. Glöckler, Michaela, M.D., "Non-Verbal Education: A Necessity on the Developmental Stages,"

originally published in *Steiner Education*, Vol. 34, No. 2; available at https://www.waldorflibrary.org/journals/24-waldorf-journal-project/942-waldorf-journal-project-2-non-verbal-education-a-necessity-on-the-developmental-stages

40. Stephens-Davidowitz, Seth, *Google, Tell Me. Is My Son a Genius?* Available at https://www.nytimes.com/2014/01/19/opinion/sunday/google-tell-me-is-my-son-a-genius.html

41. See https://nces.ed.gov/fastfacts/display.asp?id=72

42. See March 28, 2010, *New York Times* opinion page

43. Verma, Ragini et al., *Sex Differences in the Structural Connectome of the Human Brain.* Proceedings of National Academy of Sciences, 2013

44. Steiner, Rudolf, *Education for Adolescents*, SteinerBooks, 1996

45. Ibid

46. DeBenedet, Anthony T., *The Art of Roughhousing: Good Old-Fashioned Horseplay and Why Every Kid Needs It*, Quirk Books, 2011

47. Ibid

48. Hughes, Fergus, *Children, Play and Development*, SAGE Publications, Thousand Oaks CA, 2009

49. König, Karl, *Conferences and Seminars on Arithmetic*

50. Madaule, Paul, "The Dyslexified World," in *About the Tomatis Method*, The Listening Centre Press, Toronto, 1989

51. Mullan, M. R., "Children's play and play therapy," in *Motor Development and Children's Play*, T. D. Yawkey & A. D. Pellegrini, eds., Technomic Publishing, Lancaster PA, 1984

52. McAllen, *The Extra Lesson*

53. Eikenboom, Joep, *Foundations of the Extra Lesson. Beyond What Is Seen in the Exercises*, Rudolf Steiner College Press, Fair Oaks, CA, 2007

54. Whicher, Olive, "Gravity and Levity in Human Movement," in *The Golden Blade*, 1960

55. Many versions are available on youtube

56. Gold, Svea, *If Kids Just Came with Instruction Sheets*, Fern Ridge Press, Eugene, OR, 2000

57. Horne, Virginia Lee, *Stunts and tumbling for girls*, A.S. Barnes & Co., 1943

58. Blanning, Nancy, and Clark, Laurie, *Movement Journeys and Circle Adventures*, self-published, available through WECAN

59. Belgau, Eric, *A Life in Balance: Discovery of a Learning Breakthrough*, Outskirts Press, 2010

60. McAllen, Audrey, *The Extra Lesson*

61. König, Karl, *Conferences and Seminars on Arithmetic*

62. Steiner, Rudolf, *Education for Adolescents*

63. Whicher, Olive, *Sunspace: Science At a Threshold of Spiritual Understanding*, Rudolf Steiner Press, 1989

64. Lecture given by Rudolf Steiner on September 9, 1922. In *Philosophy, Cosmology and Religion*, Anthroposophic Press, 1984

65. https://www.ncbi.nlm.nih.gov/pmc/articles/PMC3756513/

66. Ganley, Colleen, and Lubienski, Sarah, "Current Research on Gender Differences in Math", posted May 2016 at https://www.nctm.org/Publications/Teaching-Children-Mathematics/Blog/Current-Research-on-Gender-Differences-in-Math/

67. Shumway, Jessica, *Number Sense Routines: Building Numerical Literacy Every Day in Grades K-3*, Stenhouse Publishers, Portsmouth, NH, 2011

68. Bancroft, Jessica, *Games for the Playground, Home, School and Gymnasium*, Sagwan Press, 2018

69. Bigelow, Bob, *Just Let the Kids Play*, Hcibooks, 2001

70. König, Karl, *The Human Soul*

71. Steiner, Rudolf, *The Karma of Untruthfulness*

72. Maslow, Abraham H., *Toward a Psychology of Being*, Sublime Books, 2014

73. movement for childhood.com, 2015

74. Howard Gardner (1983), "Multiple approaches to understanding," in: Charles M. Reigeluth (ed.) Instructional-design Theories and Models: A new paradigm of..., Volume 2. p. 69-90

75. Levy, J., and Reid, M., *Variations in cerebral organization as a function of handedness, hand posture in writing, and sex,* on the website of the National Center for Biotechnology Information, www.ncbi.nlm.nih.gov/pubmed/670905

76. Halpern, Diane F., *Sex Differences in Cognitive Ability*, Routledge, 2011

Index of Exercises

Active Games and Skills 108-112
   Danger/Pursuit Games 109-111
      Animal Chase 110
      Catch of Fish 109
      Chick-ur-mur 110
      Curtain Ball 109
      Foxes, Squirrels and Trees 111
      Giant's Cave 111
      Grizzly Bear 111
      Lily Pad Hoops 109
      Rooster Tails Tag 110
      Streets and Alleys 110
      Tiger Hunt 109
   Relays — Samples 111-112
      Bowling Bombardment 112
      Clean Up Your Room 112
      Club or Ball Switch Relay 111
      Exercise Relay 112
      Jump Rope Relay 111
   Throwing and Catching Skills Development 112, see also 76-78
      Circle/Musical/Clapping 112
      Little skills 112
      Parts/Quiet/Blindfold 112

"Baby Crawling" Activities 68
   Block Building 68
   Forward, Backward, and Sideward Relays 68
   Mail Delivery 69
   Potato Race 68
   Puppies and Wolves Tag 68
   Race for Objects 68
   Red Light, Green Light Race 68
   Tent Making 68
   Treasure Hunt 68
Balance, Ball, and Beanbag Activities 75-78
   Above/Below and left/Right exercises 77-78
      Bal-a-vis-x or similar 77
      Bouncing Balls Exercise 77
      Chimes Balls Circle 78
      Cross-Step Ball Bounce 78
      Partner Bouncing 77
      Partner Juggling 77
      Trigon 78
   Complementary modalities 75-76
      Belgau Balance Board and Balametrics 76
      Bal-a-vis-x 76
      Dalcroze Eurhythmics 76
   Throwing and catching — step by step 76-78
      "Teacher" 76-77
      Ballie on the Wallie (Seven-up) 77
   Waldorf related 75

Clay Activities 79
Copper Rod Exercises 63-66
   Additional Balance Games 66
      Circle Pass 66
      Drawing a Circle 66
      Rod Vertical Balance 66
   Arm and hand exercises 64-66
   Beginning — for every age 64
   Foot and floor exercises 66
   Collecting the Rods 66
      Circle Trace 66
      Reverse the Beginning 67
Crawlasthenics and Zoorobics 67-75
   Baby crawling activities 68
   Games on the Mats 74-75
   Little Wrestling Matches 73-74
   Trip to the Zoo, Parts 1 and 2 69-74

Foot Circles 80
Foundations for Arithmetic 87-96
Foundations for Developmental Movement 60-80
Foundations for Writing and Reading 81-86

Games and Movement Resources 118-119
Games on the Mats 74-75
   The Cat in the Attic 75
   Doggies and Wolves 75
   Ruler of the Sea 74
   Slugs 74-75
   Sandwich 75

Jumping Rope 60-63

Mat Games 74-75
   Cat in the Attic 74
   Doggies and Wolves Tag 74
   Ruler of the Sea 75
   Sandwich 74
   Slugs 75

Pencil Grip Exercises 81-82
   Finger Finder Partner Game 82
   Crab Walk across the Desk 82
   Thumb Twirling Exercise 82
Painting Handwriting 83-84

Quieter Activities 112-116
    Little Skills 112
    Circle/Musical/Clapping 112
    Parts/Quiet/Blindfold 112
        All Birds Fly 114
        Bear-Zoo Escape 113
        Blind Shepherd and Goat
        Don't Do That! 113
        Find the Leader 115
        Fir on the Mountain 113
        Giant's Treasure 114
        It's My Birthday 115
        Jackstones Shooting Game 116
        Poor Kitty 115
        Quarter and Stone 114
        Right Shoulder, Left Shoulder 113
        Shorebirds 115

Roughhousing Games 116-118
        Bull in the Ring 116
        Catch and Pull Tug of War 116
        Chicken Market 117
        Little Wrestling Matches 116
        Royal Body Guards 117
        Ruler of the Sea 117
        Sandwich 118
        Slugs 117

Shaded Drawing 85-86
Strengthening the Pencil Grip 81-82

Throwing and catching 76-78, *see also* 112
Trip to the Zoo, Part 1, 69-70
        Beautiful Butterfly 69
        Books Open, Books Closed 69
        Frozen Frog 69
        Funny Fish 69
        Potato Bug 69, 72
        Roly-poly Hedgehog 69
        Soaring Eagle 69
        Squash! 69
        Speedy Frog 70
        Tadpole 70
        Tadpole Turning into Frog 70
Trip to the Zoo Part 2, 70-73
        Baby Frog Hop 70, 71
        Baby Race 70
        Backward Inchworm 70
        Big Frog Hop 70
        Bear and Frog Dances 70, 72
        Cat Walk 70, 71
        Crab Walk 70, 71, 75, 117
        Circus Seal 70
        Creepy-Crawley Caterpillar 70
        Cricket Walk 71
        Dog Walk 70, 71
        Duck Walk 70, 71
        Egg Roll 70-71, 72
        Egg Sit 72
        Elephant Walk 71
        Kangaroo Hop 71, 72
        Knee Walk 71, 72
        Log Roll 71, 72
        Motorboat 71
        Pony Race 71
        Pop-up Squirrel 71, 72
        Rabbit Jump 72
        Ring-tailed Lemur/3-Legged Race 72
        Sack of Potatoes 73
        Seal Slap 72
        Sled Dog 73
        Sniffing Dog 73
        Sword Fish 73
        Tunnel Race 73
        Walrus and Seal Walks 72, 73
        Wheelbarrow 73

Wrestling Matches, Little 73-74
        Ankle Escape 73
        Back to Back 73
        Back to Back Teams 73
        Balance Beam Bridge 73
        Bear Wrestling 74
        Bear Tug of War 74
        Dinosaur Wrestling 74
        Mousetrap 74
        Pancake Escape 74
        Stubborn Cows 74

Zoorobics 67-75